PUT POWER
IN YOUR PERSONALITY!

Florence Littauer

Other Books by Florence and Fred Littauer

Personality Plus (also available in French, German, Spanish, Polish, Dutch, and Indonesian)
Personality Puzzle with Marita Littauer (also in Indonesian)
Beat the Blahs (also in Afrikaans)
Blow Away the Black Clouds
After Every Wedding Comes a Marriage
It Takes So Little to Be Above Average
How to Get Along with Difficult People
Out of the Cabbage Patch
Freeing Your Mind from Memories That Bind (also in Spanish)
The Promise of Healing
Get a Life without the Strife
I've Found My Keys, Now Where's My Car?
Silver Boxes (also in Spanish)
Dare to Dream (also in Spanish, French)
Raising Christians Not Just Children
Your Personality Tree (also video album)
Hope for Hurting Women
Looking for God in All the Right Places
Wake Up, Women
Wake Up, Men
The Gift of Encouragement

CLASS BOOKS
Christian Leaders, Authors, and Speakers Seminar (tape, album, and manual)
The Best of Florence Littauer

For information on seminars and workshops conducted by Fred, Florence, and Marita Littauer, please call 1-800-433-6633.

PUT POWER
IN YOUR PERSONALITY!

Match Your Potential
with America's Leaders

FLORENCE LITTAUER

Fleming H. Revell
A Division of Baker Book House Co
Grand Rapids, Michigan 49516

© 1995 by Florence Littauer

Published by Fleming H. Revell
a division of Baker Book House Company
P.O. Box 6287, Grand Rapids, MI 49516-6287

Originally published as *Personalities in Power* by Huntington House, Inc.

Printed in the United States of America

Library of Congress Cataloging-in-Publication Data

Littauer, Florence, 1928–
    [Personalities in power]
    Put power in your personality! : match your potential with America's leaders / Florence Littauer.
        p.   cm.
    Originally published : Personalities in power. Lafayette, La. : Huntington House, 1910.
    Includes bibliographical references (p.)
    ISBN 0-8007-5563-4 (paper)
    1. Politicians—Psychology. 2. Politicians—Psychology—Case studies. I. Title.
JA74.5.L565   1995
155.2'6'088329—dc20   95-6912

CONTENTS

PART 4: APPLYING WHAT WE'VE LEARNED

Part I

THE POWER
OF PERSONALITY

1

THE PRESIDENTIAL HANDSHAKE: A FULL-BODY EXPERIENCE

In July 1994 when the National Speakers Association held its annual convention in Washington, D.C., the top speakers, recipients of the Council of Peers Award of Excellence, were invited to a private briefing in the Indian Treaty Room in the Old Executive Office Building. The White House staff member selected to address us was Mark Gearan, director of communications, a logical choice for a group of professional communicators.

Gearan, a graduate of Harvard University and Georgetown University Law School, had been chosen to replace George Stephanopoulos, whose boyish image had kept the press corps from taking him seriously. As a White House deputy chief of staff, Gearan had been happy in his background position. He had even tried to help Stephanopoulos with his young, upstart appearance by telling him, "Half your battle is your body language. Take it, smile, and stand up straight!"

Despite Stephanopoulos's best efforts, Clinton needed a change—someone who was sharp and articulate and who could take the heat without wilting. Gearan was surprised when Clinton chose him to move into the more visible job and Stephanopoulos was shuttled off to the sidelines as "adviser on policy and strategy." The president's advice to Gearan as he took this new position was, "You have got to be older and boring."

9

When Gearan walked into the Indian Treaty Room and placed his portfolio on the lectern, he looked very young to us veteran speakers, and he was anything but boring. Showing obvious command of his material and exuding confidence in his position, Gearan told us about the difficulties of dealing with the press. All of us had lived through our own press distortions, and we could imagine the magnitude of his job and the huge margin of error that would be possible in reporting news from a president who changed his mind so frequently that even those standing beside him were unsure of his position on various issues.

Gearan explained the current urge of the press to "rush to judgment" before the facts were laid on the table. To sell papers or get higher ratings, reporters are required to give opinions, presumptions, and rationalizations, he said, and to create scenarios that haven't yet occurred.

As a whole, we had sympathy for what Gearan was striving to do and for the enormous responsibilities his position put upon someone who looked so young to us. He spilled no family secrets and stayed generally nonpartisan in his report. When he invited questions, Zig Ziglar asked about the moral standards of the country, and Carl Mays asked why the press made no mention of the sixty thousand Christian men who had met as a group called Promise Keepers. Gearan fielded each question calmly and wisely.

When it seemed to be my turn, I asked about the accuracy of Bob Woodward's book detailing the chaos of the White House staff. "I've just finished reading *The Agenda*," I said. "Could you comment on whether you and the staff see this portrayal of confusion as relatively accurate?"

"I haven't read it," he replied.

I was surprised by this, since he was referred to in the book in twelve different situations, and in most cases political people can hardly stay away from press reports about themselves. In fact, Gearan was quoted in *The Agenda* on the exact point I was questioning, saying he felt the White House problems were "organization and discipline. The staff was too often like a soccer league of ten-year-olds. No one stuck to his part of the field during a game. The ball—any ball—would come on the field, and everyone would go chasing it down field."[1]

"I have read reviews of it," Gearan added. Then with a puzzled look, he asked me, "Why do you want to know?"

"Because I'm writing a book on the personalities in the White House."

He took a deep breath and then smiled at me like the artful dodger. "I really like your outfit," he said.

For a young man, he knew the old ploy: To avoid answering sticky questions, give the questioner a compliment. This usually makes the individual so happy he or she will be diverted from the original question, and then you can move on.

"Anyone else have a question?"

At the conclusion of our session, Gearan picked up his papers, smiled with the confidence of a job well done, and humbly accepted our standing ovation. Had he known our group, he might not have been so impressed since we speakers give each other standing ovations for everything—sometimes even the blessing!

The "Sexy Handshake"

Following the briefing, our group was led through some back passageways, past the dumpsters, to emerge on the south lawn of the White House. President Clinton was about to depart in a helicopter to fly to New Jersey and promote his healthcare plan, and we would be allowed to watch his ascension. Our group was the first to arrive, and we had the front position against the ropes of wrought-iron links. We held our ground for more than an hour, validating the complaint that Clinton always runs late.

By this time, there was a crowd behind us and Secret Service agents were appearing. An aide of some sort came down the line to give us instructions: "Don't ask for autographs, and don't detain him. He'll shake hands with as many as he can and respond to simple questions." In other words: Be nice. He's had a rough day.

As we waited, we talked about how author Judith Krantz had described Clinton's "sexy handshake" as being a "full-body experience." We discussed that we didn't know what a sexy handshake was. My friends dared me to ask the president for one of these special handshakes, a thought so foreign to my nature that I knew I couldn't let those words out of my mouth, especially to the president.

Suddenly an air of excitement swept through the crowd, punctuated by the hushed words, "He's here! He's here!" As we caught our first glimpse of the president, he seemed taller and slimmer than his pictures made him look.

Does he really have that charisma, that mesmerizing look, that handshake? I wondered. As he came closer, gladly shaking each outstretched hand and looking each person in the eye, an unexpected awe swept over me. Whether or not you agree with the man, there is something inspiring about standing in the presence of the president of the United States.

As he reached for my hand, his eyes looked straight into mine as if no one else mattered. I offered my hand, opened my mouth, and surprised myself by saying, "Mr. President, I want one of your sexy handshakes."

I heard my husband gasp at my request as Clinton clasped my hand and put his left hand on my shoulder. He leaned over and whispered in my ear, "Wasn't that awful? My face was red for days after she wrote that." He worked over my shoulder, gave my hand a final squeeze, beamed, and winked at me.

Yes!

I had received the full-body experience! I could see why people were swayed to change their votes after a few minutes with Bill Clinton.

Carl Mays lifted the level of the conversation by admonishing Clinton to "Keep God first!"

"I do," the president replied. "Just this morning I sat up there on the porch," he added, pointing to the White House balcony, "reading the Psalms."

As Clinton moved on, Carl asked, "Which is your favorite Psalm?"

Clinton stopped, looked back, thought a few seconds as we waited, and then said, "The twenty-seventh."

Carl and I looked at each other. *The twenty-seventh?*

As the president moved on, pausing to listen to Nido Quebien's comments on the plight of the Lebanese, we tried to remember the twenty-seventh Psalm. We came up with the twenty-third, but we were foggy on the twenty-seventh.

At that point, the helicopter started its rotors, the president ascended the steps, the marine guards saluted, and Clinton turned and waved good-bye as if we were good friends he hated to leave. As he headed off like Mary Poppins, we all stood in the downdraft, clutching our hairstyles until the helicopter was out of sight and the president had turned his thoughts to charming the state of New Jersey into wanting government-controlled healthcare.

As soon as our bus dropped us back at the Hilton, Carl ran for a Gideon Bible. Clinton either made a lucky guess or he really knew the twenty-seventh Psalm, for when we read it we found it to be appropriate for his embattled position on healthcare and Haiti—and for all presidents and leaders in a wide variety of other situations.

> The LORD is my light and my salvation—
>   Whom shall I fear?
> The LORD is the stronghold of my life—
>   of whom shall I be afraid?
> When evil men advance against me
>   to devour my flesh,
> when my enemies and my foes attack me,
>   they will stumble and fall.
> Though an army besiege me,
>   my heart will not fear;
> though war break out against me,
>   even then will I be confident. (vv. 1–3)

> Hear my voice when I call, O LORD;
>   be merciful to me and answer me. . . .
> Do not reject me or forsake me,
>   O God my Savior.
> Though my father and mother forsake me
>   the LORD will receive me.
> Teach me your way, O LORD;
>   lead me in a straight path
>   because of my oppressors.
> Do not turn me over to the desire of my foes,
>   for false witnesses rise up against me,
>   breathing out violence.

> I am still confident of this
>   I will see the goodness of the LORD
>   in the land of the living. (vv. 7–13)

Using the Personality's Natural Strengths

As someone who is intensely interested in human personalities, I was fascinated to see Bill Clinton face to face. I've read volumes about his personality, his style, and his strengths and weaknesses, and meeting him in person validated everything I'd learned about him. I could see in that one, simple encounter that he has learned to use the strengths of his natural personality to empower himself. He has used those strengths to live the American dream, soaring into the role of ultimate leadership, the presidency of the United States.

Like Bill Clinton, I, too, grew up believing the American dream that anyone can become president. I practiced on every group I attended. In fact, I was reluctant to join any club unless I could see that within a matter of months I could become its president. Being a woman was a deterrent, but I knew someday the times would change and the title would be mine: Florence, the first female president of the United States.

Well, you know that didn't happen. I've never run for any elected office. My kind of personality would like to be in charge, but it would also hold me back from running for fear of losing. Perhaps an appointment as an ambassador to the Court of Saint James would be appropriate. Then I could have the glory without taking the risk.

How about you? You're probably not the president of the United States, either, but maybe you want to be. Or maybe you want to move up the corporate ladder or run for mayor or be president of the PTA. Maybe you just want to develop your natural abilities to be a better, more effective leader of your neighborhood or your family. And what better way is there to learn how to maximize your own leadership potential than by studying some of those people who have made it all the way to the top?

That's what we'll do in this book—take an inside look at the personalities of some of the most powerful people on earth, as well as some contenders, sidekicks, and thorns in the side. In doing so, I predict you will not only learn some secrets about powerful personalities and have fun along the way, but you will also learn how to analyze your own leadership potential and discover how to make the most of your personality traits in whatever role you find yourself. Finally, we'll look at what really makes someone a leader, and we'll consider how we can use what we've learned to select the leaders of our future.

We won't be taking sides but observing people. We won't denounce Democrats or rebuke Republicans. Our trip into the inner world of political leaders' personalities is not for those who have blinders on and can only see value or virtue in their own party's leaders and candidates. This review is for those who can look on the whole political scene with a sense of humor and who want to observe the various personalities of the past and evaluate their own leadership potential.

But before we begin our exploration of personality and power, we'll take a brief look at the four personality types. This will give you a quick idea of your own strengths and weaknesses and your basic personality pattern. Then we'll dig into the fascinating world of presidential personalities as well as some leaders who share the political spotlight.

A chart at the end of each leader's chapter reviews that president's personality profile. Each one of the descriptive statements on the charts is a quote from the media: TV, radio, books, magazines, or newspapers. These phrases are not based on my personal opinion but on what a constantly critical press had to say about the individual during his or her ups and downs along the way to and through the presidency or elsewhere in the public eye.

As you compare your personality with the descriptions in each profile, ask yourself, "If a reporter had followed me through life, which of these words could he or she have said about me?" It's a positive experience to look at our own strengths and be grateful for them, but we learn to make necessary changes when we admit and then assess our weaknesses.

2

OUR FASCINATION WITH LEADERS

From the beginning of mankind, people have been interested in the lives of their leaders, curious to know about their intimate lives and to find out how they achieved success.

We've been fascinated with the lives of our leaders since:

- Moses led his people out of Egypt,
- Julius Caesar controlled the Roman Empire,
- Jesus discipled twelve ordinary men,
- Constantine declared Christianity the official religion of the empire,
- Luther nailed his theses on the church door at Wittenberg,
- John Alden proposed to Priscilla,
- George Washington became our first president,
- Napoleon met his Waterloo,
- Abraham Lincoln gave the Gettysburg Address,
- Teddy Roosevelt carried a big stick,
- FDR gave fireside chats,
- Ike won the war and the presidency,
- Nixon stood on the Great Wall of China,

- Jimmy Carter carried his own suitcase,
- Reagan became the Great Communicator, and
- Hillary (and Bill) tried to handle healthcare.

As we reflect upon these personalities in power, we wonder what made them leaders. Surely these people didn't look alike or think alike. They were obviously from different generations, backgrounds, countries, and political parties. They had unique personalities. What can we learn from them that will enhance our own leadership potential?

Personalities in Power

Twenty-five years have passed since my first introduction to the simple personality analysis I will be explaining in this book. In that time, I've studied and digested the subject, taught the topic in Personality Plus seminars throughout the world, discussed personalities on TV talk shows, counseled hundreds of couples, and written more than twenty books. I have used the knowledge of the four basic personalities to bring understanding to my own marriage, to my relationship with my children, to my business and civic associations, to the speaking profession, and to my Christian ministry.

Several years ago, because of my lifetime interest in politics, I began to highlight all the descriptive words printed about candidates in newspapers and magazines. I jotted down notes about descriptions I heard TV newscasters use. As I analyzed the personal strengths and weaknesses of celebrities, politicians, and presidents, I filed my notes and clippings in a separate folder for each personality pattern.

During the Watergate era, when the personalities of many politicians were being paraded before the TV cameras, I pulled out my research, added the daily exposures, and began to speak on "Personalities in Power." People loved the political application, and this analysis became a staple part of my seminars. Audiences were excited to know the personality differences of Powerful Truman, Peaceful Ford, Perfect Carter, and Popular Reagan.

As the interest in political personalities accelerated during the long primaries leading into the 1988 and 1992 elections, I was asked increasingly about presidents of the past and found that people who didn't even vote wanted to know about the lives of Roosevelt, Eisenhower, Kennedy, Johnson, and Nixon. How had they gotten elected? What made them tick? What kind of families did they have? Could I explain their personalities?

These questions led me into a further study of our past presidents, and soon I was ready to predict some future possibilities. Eventually I realized I must write a book on the four personality styles using the lives of our presidents as examples.

Now you see the result of that writing. In these pages I have aimed to instruct and entertain, to unite history and humor. I have shown how we can use personality analysis for ourselves and for the selection of a president or other leaders. Each chapter also begins with a personality principle all of us can learn from the leader being analyzed. Sometimes this principle is taught by what the person did; in other cases it's illustrated by what he or she *didn't* do. There is no perfect person, for with each set of strengths there are accompanying weaknesses, but as we come to understand the four basic personalities, we can see ourselves and have a quick way to analyze others.

The Elusive Quality of Leadership

To be a leader, by definition, a person must be in front, must march ahead of the others. No matter how bright or right a person may be, he or she can't be a leader if no one else chooses to follow. The elusive quality of leadership is the ability to inspire others to want to do your will. Without this appeal, the intentional leader is a captain without a ship, a king without a country.

What is the difference between a leader and a manager? The word *manager* means someone who has his or her hands on the situation, who moves people around, handles them, puts them in the right spots. A capable manager can direct programs with or without an inspired, magnetic leadership.

In our country we have longed for leadership; we've wanted a king, and we have often been willing to accept a lack of managerial skills or even mediocre performance if we could have a regal leader to inspire hopes beyond belief, to lead us toward an impossible dream, "to see the goodness of the LORD in the land of the living."

We are all managers; each one of us manages something. We direct some phase of life each day. We discipline children, employees, constituents, or congregations. But are we leaders? Do we *inspire* others to do it our way, or do we just insist on obedience? Are we making the most of our leadership potential? Are we functioning in our strengths or plodding along in our weaknesses?

We can all be leaders. We can all put power in our personalities, no matter what our background, education, or talent, if we can find a way to assess our abilities and learn to eliminate our negatives. This book offers a plan of action and personal evaluation that combines self-analysis with real-life examples from history. Here is a measuring stick with which you can examine yourself (or your family, your coworkers, your church leaders, and your elected officials), not to be judgmental but to understand your own or others' leadership potential. This knowledge can help you learn to get along with others so you can progress from managing mediocre moments to leading your troops, whoever they might be, with inspiration and excitement.

My purpose in writing this book is to take a practical personality concept, first introduced by Hippocrates, and use it to explain the triumphs and tragedies of past presidents. As we see that each one was a great man with some inborn weaknesses, we will learn to anticipate similar patterns in ourselves and others and be able to make future choices and improvements with both knowledge and wisdom.

> *Instruct a wise man and he will be wiser still;*
>   *teach a righteous man and he will add to his learning.*
>   Proverbs 9:9

Part II

THE FOUR
PERSONALITY PATTERNS

3

A BETTER WAY
THAN "GROPE AND HOPE"

There are many areas of our lives over which we have no control. We can't choose our parents; they were here when we arrived. We can't choose the color of our skin. We can't pluck our IQ out of an encyclopedia or decide as infants where we will live. In recent years, scientists have come up with impressive evidence that personality fits in this category of inherited inevitabilities as well.

According to an article in the *Journal of Personality and Social Psychology* reporting work done at the Minnesota Center for Twin and Adoption Research, "Heredity has a greater influence on one's personality and behavior than either one's upbringing or the most crushing social pressure. The debate over what has been called 'nature versus nurture' seems to be taking a decisive turn."

These researchers concluded that our personality is determined by our genes and that our environment influences and molds our inborn traits. They brought together 348 sets of twins, including 44 pairs of identical twins, reared apart. After six days of testing and more than fifteen thousand questions, the study showed amazing similarities in the identical twins even though they had not seen each other since infancy and were raised in different environments.

One set of identical twins who had been separated four weeks after birth in 1940 were both named Tim, both drove the same year and same model blue Chevrolet, chain-smoked Salem cigarettes, chewed their fingernails, owned dogs named Toy, and vacationed on the same strip of beach in Florida. One of the investigators in the Minnesota project, psychologist David Lykken, said, "the evidence is so compelling that it is hard to understand how people could *not* believe in the strong influence of genetics on behavior."

Applying this theory personally to our adopted son, we could conclude that when we received him at three months of age, he already had within him the deep, serious nature he has today. His caseworker told me he had never smiled and would lie in the crib and stare at the people around him as if he were analyzing them. We realize now that he had what we've categorized as a Perfect personality right from the start, and he has never changed.

His inborn personality had nothing to do with us, his adoptive parents; but in providing a nurturing environment, we have influenced the finished product by guiding him in becoming business-minded, in giving him basic manners, and in instilling spiritual truth, self-confidence, and bearing.

This principle is also obvious as we review the presidents' personalities. We can see their inherited personalities plus the direction given them by their parents and their childhood circumstances. For example, we'll see that Franklin Roosevelt and John Kennedy had similar birth personalities. The earliest descriptions of their lives show they were both born leaders, and they also had natural charm and a way with words. People were attracted to them because of their obvious magnetism, their optimistic approach to life, and their colorful ability to make every occasion an event.

Their differences came in how they were raised. Even though both were wealthy, FDR was an only child, groomed as a gentleman and educated in the classics, with no great need to go out into the world and make a living. He might have gratefully settled into Hyde Park and become a country squire, or he might easily have lost himself in his books and become a scholar. But because he was born with a powerful urge to lead and a charming personality that made people want to follow him, he left the family comfort zone and ventured out to find purpose in helping those less fortunate.

Kennedy's environmental difference, as we will see, came from the driving family force to achieve both money and status and show those Back Bay Brahmins that an Irishman could get to the top. The family demands for winners and Jack's anointing for the presidency by his father amplified his controlling nature and put him into a perpetual overdrive.

Identifying and Using Personality Power

Learning about our natural-born personalities and understanding the effect of family background can be invaluable to us in making decisions about our own future or in making decisions regarding other people. Without this knowledge, many of us feel a latent sense of futility because we don't know how to make those decisions intelligently. We simply grope and hope.

Some of us enter professions where we have to hire and fire. Without any effective means of evaluating how well the person will perform, we cross our fingers, go with our instincts, and end up putting whatever warm body shows up into the job opening.

When our civic club needs a president to replace Rollicking Ralph, who put on more parties than any other president but retired with the finances on the brink of bankruptcy, should we choose Serious Sam, who can balance the budget and owns a computer but who thinks sociability is a sin? Or should we reach for Laid-back Larry, who's out of a job and would have time to go over the books and find the missing checks and W-2 forms if he weren't too lazy to do it?

Each time there's an election, we have to decide whom to choose for each office. Do we vote a straight ticket of our parents' party, assuming that will bring unity to the nation? Or do we analyze each individual according to his or her strengths, platform, character, and personality, taking into account his or her weaknesses and potential for producing problems in the future? If only there were a simple way to learn to understand people short of going back to college and becoming a psychiatrist.

Well, there is!

More than two thousand years ago, Hippocrates, known as the father of modern medicine, created a system of categorizing that he called the four basic temperaments. Many other personality analyses have been plotted out since then, but most of them have their roots in his theories. Here's how we will adapt Hippocrates' terms to analyze our own and our leaders' personalities:

Hippocrates' Term	What It Means	Our Term
Sanguine	Magnetic personality	Popular
Choleric	Commanding personality	Powerful
Melancholy	Analytical personality	Perfect
Phlegmatic	Low-key personality	Peaceful

No matter what political party a person is from or what platform he or she stands upon, his or her decisions ultimately will be based on personality and instinctive reactions.

Doris Kearns Goodwin, historian-author, said, "In recent years, we have come to understand that even though a man's concerns and opinions may change when he reaches the White House, he remains the same man. His character and personality, the values that guide him, and his characteristic ways of behavior do not change."

The presidents' personalities do not change after they are elected, and our personalities don't either. We come into life with a birth personality, and as we begin to examine the traits that are typical of this personality we can understand our own natures, learn to identify our strengths and weaknesses, and anticipate our future behavior.

It's also important to keep in mind that people often have combined traits of two of the four basic personalities. The combinations tend to round us out and lend balance to our lives.

As you read through this book, remember that whatever personality you may have, you can be a leader. As you accept your strengths and talents and work to overcome your weaknesses, you will grow into your limitless potential and become the leader you were meant to be. Then begin to analyze the people you live and work with, not to become an amateur psychiatrist, but to be aware of their differences so that you can accept them as they are, not as you had hoped they'd be.

In reading each of the chapters describing our leaders' personalities, you will see that all were positive persons with some inborn weaknesses. By examining how their personalities affected their lives and their leadership, we can learn to anticipate similar patterns in ourselves and others and be able to make future choices and changes with both knowledge and wisdom. To paraphrase Robert Burns:

> Would the gift that God would give us
> to see ourselves as others see us.

4

THE POPULARS

(SANGUINES)

Family Motto: Let's do it the fun way.
Family Hymn: "Oh, for a Thousand Tongues"
Family Verse: "A cheerful heart is good medicine." (Prov. 17:22)

The Populars started out in life with winning ways. The little girls knew how to charm their fathers, and the boys knew how to roll their eyes toward Mother. They talked early and constantly, said adorable things, and seemed to attract doting attention. They managed to delight their teachers, gather a retinue of little friends, become class presidents, and be voted most likely to succeed. They starred in the senior-class play, became flamboyant athletes and cheerleaders, and were the life of every party.

As adults they aimed at professions that emphasized glamour over work, creativity over routines, loose hours over schedules, and people over statistics. With their appealing personalities, they were promoted quickly until they reached a plateau where more than an easygoing performance was required for advancement.

Many of the Populars went into teaching, acting, lecturing, or radio and television—anyplace they could talk for a living. An example is Popular Willard Scott, who loves doing the weather on the *Today* show although he often loses his notes and sometimes can't find South Dakota on his map. Many Populars became salespeople; it was undoubtedly the Popular Brothers who first sold a refrigerator to an Eskimo. However, the unit was probably never delivered because they misplaced the order, forgot the Eskimo's name, and couldn't tell one igloo from another when they returned. The Populars can sell anything from cosmetics to a castle, and they get especially motivated when the grand prize is a pink Cadillac or a trip to Hawaii.

Populars in Politics

Throughout history, the Populars have been drawn into politics because it combines talk and work, promises and patronage, personality and position, confidence and charm. Politics provides a platform, the role of favorite son, attention from a continuous audience, bands and banners, and excitement and suspense. The campaign trip becomes a big board game where the candidates move from square to square, and election night becomes the biggest party of all because the Populars are made to be winners and they are always reaching for a prize.

The Populars were brought up on fairy tales where every princess marries Prince Charming and where everything turns out all right in the end. They tend to avoid harsh realities, turn the other way in times of trouble, and flee the pursuit of the Bad News Bears.

As we begin to understand the Popular personality, we will see that with the charm and cheer comes the inability to remember details and to follow through. The Populars have light, fluffy strengths and what they feel are trivial weaknesses. They expect everyone to love them, they enjoy center stage, they gravitate to spotlights, and they all want to be the star of the show!

The Populars are fascinated with themselves and get excited over any minor personal accomplishments. When he was six, my Popular grandson, Jonathan, kicked the ball into the wrong goal in his soccer game and came running off the field, calling out, "Wasn't I great?" For people who don't understand the different personalities, Jonathan's enthusiasm could be considered conceited, but for a Popular it's natural. Self-adoration can be considered a weakness, but it is also a part of the bubbling enthusiasm that gives the Populars their magnetic appeal.

When President Ronald Reagan, a Popular personality, faced a group of reporters in November 1988, he stayed true to form when he told them, "You're going to miss me." Who else could say that and get away with it? *Newsweek*, which reported the encounter in its August 21, 1989, issue, went on to say that even though much of the media disagreed with Reagan, they couldn't help but like him and they *would* miss him:

> During the Johnson, Nixon, Ford and Carter years, the presidency seemed to lose its luster. Reagan restored its dignity, and infused it with a sense of drama. Like FDR, he came along at a time when the nation needed to believe in itself again; and like FDR, he knew how to use his charismatic personality and the symbols of his office to restore America's confidence.

Newsweek was right; we have missed him.

A brief summary of Popular strengths and weaknesses follows. Check the ones that apply to you.

Popular
Let's do it the fun way.

Strengths
___ Magnetic personality
___ Talker with sense of humor
___ Storyteller
___ Entertaining
___ Charming
___ Optimistic
___ Cheerful
___ Enthusiastic
___ Friendly
___ Creative and colorful
___ **TOTAL**

Weaknesses
___ Compulsive talker
___ Exaggerates
___ Cannot remember details
___ Poor follow-through
___ Undisciplined
___ Disorganized
___ Loses things
___ Immature
___ Interrupts
___ Easily distracted
___ **TOTAL**

___ **Total of Popular strengths and weaknesses**

5

THE POWERFULS

(CHOLERICS)

Family Motto: Do it my way *now!*
Family Hymn: "Onward Christian Soldiers, Marching As to War"
Family Verse: "Let all things be done decently and in order."
(1 Cor. 14:40 KJV)

The first time the little Powerful babies yelled for a bottle and Mother came running, they knew they could take control. It was not a matter of could they, or would they, but *when* they would take the whole house away from Mother. The baby Powerfuls invented "demand feeding." They soon found that adults were willing to let them have their own way, and if their wishes were not quickly fulfilled, they could get instant action by throwing themselves on the floor and screaming. This threat of a temper tantrum, especially in front of company or in supermarkets, would bring the entire family to its feet in obedience.

Once control had been established, the little Powerfuls only had to use manipulative skills when faced with defiance from family or friends. Because the Powerfuls were all born leaders, they dictated the rules for every game, made definitive choices for every hesitant person, and were put in charge when the teacher had to leave the room. The Powerfuls won the games and earned the letters; they were outstanding members of the debate team and could argue equally well for either side of any issue.

They always had projects under way, and from childhood they seemed to know how to make money. Because of their constant activities, they had little time for friends. While the Populars needed companions to form an audience and the Perfects needed supporters to cheer them up when they didn't quite reach their own high goals, the Powerfuls needed no one. They were self-sufficient, and often those other people just got in the way and slowed down their progress.

As adults, the Powerfuls looked for opportunities where they could exert control; they preferred occupations where they could start at the top.

The Populars were voted most likely to succeed.

The Perfects were depressed for fear they wouldn't succeed.

The Peacefuls didn't care whether they would succeed.

The Powerfuls passed them all by and succeeded. They became the entrepreneurs, the presidents of Chrysler, the CEOs of the Fortune 500 companies. It was a Powerful female family member who created the concept of women's lib, marched shoulder-to-shoulder with Bella Abzug, and started success magazines for working women, and it was a Powerful woman, Phyllis Schlafly, who almost single-handedly stopped the passage of the Equal Rights Amendment.

Since the Declaration of Independence, the Powerfuls have been influential politicians. Because of their innate desire to lead, they take to political office like the proverbial duck to water. Imagine a whole district to dominate, a whole state to sublimate, a whole country to control!

The Powerfuls grew up with pragmatic principles: If it doesn't work, get rid of it. One Powerful pastor produced an unwanted mutiny when his first move in a new position was to abolish the women's missionary society, which he described as "just so much deadwood."

Powerfuls don't want to spend time thinking about action, as the Perfects do, or talking about action, as the Populars do, or avoiding action, as the Peacefuls do. They want to act *now* and take a chance that their program will work. Powerfuls such as Phil Donahue promote controversy, thrive on opposition, and enjoy cutting comments. They are confident in their leadership, often impulsive in their decisions, and impatient with the dummies. They believe that work is the answer to all problems, and if only the rest of us would get off our duffs, get down to business, and do it their way everything would turn out all right. Vacations and coffee breaks are for the weak and undisciplined who will never amount to much in life anyway.

Great Britain's former prime minister, Margaret Thatcher, is an excellent example of a Powerful woman who made it to the top in a field previously open to men only. Because of her dynamic personality, her drive, and her determination, she succeeded as a respected leader.

Powerful Lee Iacocca, a born leader with the desire to control and no need to rest, made famous the expression, "Lead, follow, or get out of the way." Other Powerfuls, such as news anchor Dan Rather and the *Today* show's Bryant Gumbel, have strong strengths and noticeable weaknesses—with all the talent and ability they possess, they reportedly become bossy, opinionated, impatient, arrogant, and rude.

In the theatrical productions of life, if the Powerfuls can't run the show, they won't be in it.

A brief summary of Powerful strengths and weaknesses follows. Check the traits that apply to you.

Powerful
Do it my way *now*.

Strengths	Weaknesses
___ Commanding personality	___ Bossy
___ Worker with a business mind	___ Impatient
___ Born leader	___ Quick-tempered
___ Excels in emergencies	___ Intolerant
___ Goal-oriented	___ Workaholic
___ Logical thinker	___ Rude and tactless
___ Quick organizer	___ Manipulative
___ Takes control	___ Demanding
___ Dynamic	___ Not a team player
___ Undeveloped emotions	___ Believes end justifies the
___ Stimulates activity	means
___ Motivational	___ Impulsive decisions
___ Confident	___ Unrepentant
___ **TOTAL**	___ **TOTAL**

_____ **Total of Powerful strengths and weaknesses**

6

THE PERFECTS

(MELANCHOLIES)

Family Motto: If it's worth doing, it's worth doing right.
Family Hymn: "When the Roll Is Called Up Yonder, I'll Be There"
Family Verse: "Be perfect, therefore, as your heavenly Father is
perfect." (Matt. 5:48)

The Perfects sensed from childhood that it was better to be right than popular. With an inbred sense of propriety and manners, they became model children who kept their rooms neat, their toys in even rows, and their Monopoly money in the box and sorted by denomination. To their neighbors, they all seemed to be prodigies as they practiced the piano each morning from six to seven and would rather conjugate French verbs than play video games.

They pleased their teachers by raising their hands before speaking, by completing their papers on time, and by turning in the truants. Their parents bought them computers where they stored the grades of their classmates (including the median mark for each exam), mastered the complexities of the Federal Reserve System, and calculated the daily comparative value of the dollar, the peso, and the yen.

One of the Perfects was valedictorian each year and several received scholarships to Yale. As adults they chose careers that took intellectual depth, brilliance, talent, and attention to details. Several of the Perfects became surgeons; others became psychiatrists, professors, artists, musicians, accountants, and tax attorneys.

Because of their perfectionistic natures and their pessimistic bent, the whole family could easily become depressed when people disappointed them and circumstances didn't turn out right. They wouldn't verbalize their feelings, though; if you asked what was the trouble, they'd say, "Nothing."

Although they don't feel they are critical, and they wouldn't want to be quoted, I know they think the Populars are too noisy and superficial, the Powerfuls are too bossy and insensitive, and the Peacefuls are too compromising and indecisive. The Perfects didn't intend to be politicians—the whole system seems so unsystematic—yet as they looked at the shallow intellect of the available candidates, they felt a self-sacrificing call to save the nation from the collection of nitwits trying to lead it nowhere in a hurry.

Once involved, the Perfects couldn't leave the political parties unperfected, and they felt strongly about the punctuation of the platforms and the construction of the Constitution. Because the Perfects have a passion for history, they see all present problems from a broad perspective, and because their minds think in columns, they can memorize dates, figures, details, and allotments, making all those competing around them feel stupid and unprepared.

The Perfects were brought up in ivory towers, giving them a somewhat unrealistic view of the masses below. They believe in the basic goodness of each individual and idealistically look to the day when the slums are slammed shut, the castles closed up, and we all live happily ever after in the suburbs.

Walter Mondale, former vice president of the United States and currently the American ambassador to Japan, is a member of the Perfect family. In 1984 he was quoted in *Newsweek* as saying he felt "he had been blessed with a rare opportunity to speak to America—to stand up for the old Democratic principles that had nourished him and to cry out against what he saw as a new politics of selfishness and greed abroad in the land. His campaign, in its haunted last weeks, had become something more to him than a canvass for votes. It had become a witness, a kind of summing up, he said, of 35 years of public life. He paused then and turned away, gazing out at the sky above the clouds. It was as if he were seeing a time draw to an end."

The Perfects are the dreamers and visionaries. They have high standards for themselves and others and sincerely believe that everyone wants to be perfect like the Perfects are, if only they knew how. But as the Perfects' strengths are deep, thoughtful, and introspective, so their weaknesses are also deep, leading them into depression and despair when nothing seems to be going right.

Although they avoid drawing attention to themselves, the Perfects can become sensitive character actors for they have a unique ability to put themselves into the life of another person and portray that person's innermost feelings. We can easily picture a Perfect person playing the part of Hamlet, the melancholy Dane, standing on a turret of the Castle Elsinore and meditating deeply about the meaning of life and death. As the mist swirls around him, he muses, "To be or not to be . . . that is the question."

A brief summary of Perfect strengths and weaknesses follows. Check the traits that apply to you.

Perfect
If it's worth doing, it's worth doing right.

Strengths
___ Sensitive to others
___ Philosophical and mystical
___ Artistic and musical
___ Organizes on paper
___ Long-range goals
___ Schedule-oriented
___ Sees problems
___ Likes charts and graphs
___ Keeps emotions in check
___ Serious and analytical

Weaknesses
___ Easily depressed
___ Bogged down
___ Too perfectionistic
___ Emphasis on negatives
___ Inflexible
___ Pessimistic
___ Moody
___ Suspicious
___ Too mysterious
___ Slow to action

___ Thoughtful   ___ Too sensitive

___ Intellectual   ___ Withdrawn

___ Detail conscious   ___ Seldom smiles

___ Thinker with great reasoning
      power

___ **TOTAL**   ___ **TOTAL**

___ **Total of Perfect strengths and weaknesses**

7

THE PEACEFULS

(PHLEGMATICS)

Family Motto: Let's not rock the boat.
Family Hymn: "Leaning on the Everlasting Arms"
Family Verse: "Blessed are the peacemakers, for they will be
called sons of God." (Matt. 5:9)

The Peaceful babies were every mother's dream. They seldom cried, slept through the night, and didn't care if they were wet or dry. As toddlers, they smiled pleasantly, played with anything available, and loved naps. When the Popular children came over, the Peacefuls laughed at all their antics. They could get serious and deep with the Perfects and were motivated into action by the Powerfuls. They were responders to the initiators of life.

Their teachers loved them because they were no trouble in the classroom, although they seldom got excited over any project and couldn't decide whether to go outside for recess.

As teens, they got along with everyone. They would laugh with those who laughed and weep with those who wept. They never demanded their own way and were never offensive. Because the Populars had proven to be more talk than action, the Powerfuls had made the rest of the class feel stupid, and the Perfects were sitting back waiting to be coaxed, the Peacefuls were often thrust into leadership. Once in a control position, they were just, fair, unbiased leaders who were not swayed by emotion or the chance of personal gain.

As adults, they liked jobs that didn't demand creative initiative, jobs where advancement was automatic as long as they did their best and didn't cause trouble. They were drawn to education, the military, administration, counseling, and personnel, areas where objectivity and compliance were more important than creativity and self-motivation. They became excellent mediators in other people's problems but avoided personal conflict at any cost. They resisted change.

The Peacefuls didn't intend to go into politics as it appeared to them to be fraught with difficulties, conflicts, and stress; it obviously demanded decisions, new ideas, and endless effort. Since they aren't flashy people and tend to resist responsibility, the Peacefuls didn't want to be in charge of anything, but often they won by default; they became the compromise candidate. Their greatest strength was their lack of obvious weaknesses.

As political leaders, they tried to keep everyone content, avoided controversial issues, and healed party rifts. Because they didn't have a thirst for Power and didn't need to be Popular or Perfect, they became the comfortable choice in a contentious selection of candidates. Historically speaking, the Peacefuls weren't noted for innovative legislation but for healing the hurts and binding the wounds.

As an excellent example of the Peaceful who made it to the top, ex-president Gerald Ford exemplifies the Peacefuls' low-key strengths: He had an easygoing nature and was inoffensive, loved by all, and had no obvious weaknesses. Like Ford, Peacefuls are passive with low creativity, a lack of brilliant ideas, and little ability to excite crowds; but they do behave, stay out of trouble, and heal the hurts of others.

The presidential campaign of 1988 spawned a host of Peacefuls, including candidates George Bush, Mike Dukakis, and Lloyd Bentsen. *Los Angeles Times* columnist David Shaw suggested in the August 14, 1988, issue that because of the intense media scrutiny of the eighties, we have chosen leaders who are hard-working, conscientious, and dull, in other words, "increasingly uninteresting people—gray, bland centrists and technocrats unlikely to drift very far from the middle of the road, either stylistically or ideologically. . . . If you were having a dinner party and wanted witty, lively, charismatic guests—rather than merely famous, powerful guests—to insure an evening of sparkling conversation, it's not likely that any of these gentlemen's names would be on your invitation list."

The Popular wants the fun way.

The Powerful wants "my" way.

The Perfect wants the right way.

The Peaceful wants the easy way.

The Peacefuls don't often care whether they're in the show, but if they're cast in a supporting role, they'll do their best and not cause any trouble. The Peacefuls have a low-key sense of humor and a dry wit that sometimes produces a Jack Benny, a Will Rogers, or a George Burns.

A brief summary of Peaceful strengths and weaknesses follows. Check the traits that apply to you.

Peaceful
Let's not rock the boat.

Strengths	Weaknesses
___ Cooperative	___ Indecisive
___ Diplomatic and low-key	___ Unenthusiastic
___ Dry sense of humor	___ Fearful and worried
___ Patient	___ Compromising standards
___ Well-balanced	___ Not self-motivated
___ All-purpose person	___ Procrastinating
___ Agreeable and pleasant	___ Underlying will of iron
___ Inoffensive	___ Lazy and laid back
___ Team-oriented	___ Dull and bland
___ Administrative	___ Too accommodating
___ Steady and easygoing	___ Blocks out problems
___ Hidden emotions	___ Sarcastic
___ Mediator with listening skills	___ Passive
___ **TOTAL**	___ **TOTAL**

___ **Total of Peaceful strengths and weaknesses**

Now record the totals of your strengths and weaknesses on all four personality patterns. Then record your overall totals.

Strengths

Popular	Powerful	Perfect	Peaceful
_____	_____	_____	_____

Weaknesses

Popular	Powerful	Perfect	Peaceful
_____	_____	_____	_____

Total

Popular	Powerful	Perfect	Peaceful
_____	_____	_____	_____

You should now have an idea of your personality pattern. As we continue, we will examine the personalities of our leaders during the last sixty years. In doing so, I hope you will be able to discover the leadership potential in your own personality.

Part III

POLITICAL
PERSONALITIES

8

THE FIRESIDE CHAT

FRANKLIN DELANO ROOSEVELT

President: 1933–1945
Personality: Popular-Powerful
Principle to Learn: Listen to both sides of an issue.

The first president in my memory was Franklin Delano Roosevelt, who came to power in 1932 when I was four years old. Without television and its army of political prognosticators, we had to get our election-eve predictions via light beams that flashed from one home to the other through the darkness of the night. Although I can't remember the election code, I do recall sitting at the window with my father and counting flashlight beams that foretold the 1932 victory for Roosevelt and the loss for Herbert Hoover. There in New England, the process was reminiscent of Revere's signal, "one if by land, two if by sea."

Roosevelt came from aristocratic stock and could trace his family back to colonial days. His father was over fifty when Franklin was born, and the boy became the darling of his Powerful mother, Sara. As a child, he had long, blond curls until he was five; he was exceptionally bright—a born leader among his peers—and he had a broad scope of interest. Brought up alone, young Franklin never attended public school but was taught by a governess-tutor until he was fourteen, when he went away to prep school in Groton, Connecticut. Even though he had been raised in affluence, at Groton he was required to live in a six-foot-by-ten-foot cubicle with sparse furnishings; he began each day at dawn with a cold shower.

Roosevelt was a dedicated student in such subjects as German, French, Latin, Greek, English, and history. Although he was wealthy, he was impressed with Dr. Endicott Peabody's fiery sermons that pronounced it the duty of the privileged to go into public service and raise the standards of the poor. This basic philosophy was the impetus for Franklin's life of political action and care for those less fortunate.

Because he was slight in stature, Franklin never excelled in team sports, but he did immerse himself in books. He not only loved to read books, he just loved books—period. Because he was so frequently alone, he substituted books for people. He would hold a book before him and look at it with the pleasure of someone gazing into the eyes of a friend. In that way, many of the classics became comforting companions to him, and in later years he was able to quote from them freely.

As a child, he was excited over the sight of ships and dreamed that someday he might be a naval commander. He studied naval history and waged imaginary battles. His mother told him tales of the family's fleet of sailing ships that went to China, and he played with the remnants of sailing paraphernalia found in Grandpa Delano's old sea chest in the attic.

He enjoyed possessions that had special meaning, and he became a collector of stamps, first-day covers, gadgets, flags, cigarette lighters, ship models, Christmas cards, and figures of donkeys, dogs, and pigs. In his presidential years he kept many of these items on his desk where he could pick them up and reminisce over their origin. He dabbled in architecture, enjoyed drawing house plans, and designed two wings that were in fact built on to the Roosevelt home in Hyde Park, New York.

Charm and Control

From these brief bits of his biography, we can see Roosevelt came from a background of security, self-worth, stability, and intelligence. His personality was a combination of Popular and Powerful; he wanted to charm and control those around him.

One clue to show that his Powerful personality was evident in childhood is this anecdote from Enos Perry's book *The Boyhood Days of Our Presidents*. According to this story, one day Franklin's mother told her little son he was becoming bossy. "My boy, don't give orders all the time. Let the others give them too." In the words of a true Powerful child young Franklin answered, "Mummie, if I don't give the orders, nothing would ever happen."

Although Roosevelt's studious nature and collecting craze initially might seem to put him in the Perfect family, a closer look would show that he liked his collections, not to file them away in a systematic order, but to have them on display before him as friends. He loved to hold the figurines, stroke them, and show them to guests.

Some people in Franklin's position in life would not have been drawn to a career in public service, but his Popular personality and Powerful drive for achievement combined with his Popular love for people and the direct influence of Dr. Peabody made him a natural for political life.

Roosevelt had all the social skills of a Popular and was described as having a jaunty flirtatiousness, a winning and inspiring personality, and a cavalier and regal attitude. As a young man, Roosevelt loved laughter, liked to tell stories, and was the life of every party he attended. His secondary Powerful side was shown in his ambition, his self-discipline, his confidence, his sense of fairness and justice, and his boundless energy.

His mother doted on his charm and humor and spent her lifetime controlling his drive and ambition and trying to keep him tied to her side as long as possible. Any woman he married would have had difficulty with Powerful Sara, but the one he chose, young Eleanor, was absolutely overwhelmed by her.

Developing a Mind of Her Own

Shy, insecure, and homely, Cousin Eleanor had lost her mother during her childhood years and had been raised by her grandmother because her Popular father was a roustabout—irresponsible and unreliable as a parent. Eleanor worshiped her father for his charisma and wished she could be more like him. Even though he forgot to come home and see her when he said he would and even though he disappointed her frequently, she idolized him and was devastated when he died as a dissipated alcoholic. His letters were magic to her, and she carried them with her to read and reread for the remainder of her life.

Quiet, moody, sensitive, and lonely, Perfect Eleanor was attracted to Franklin as a replica of her father's virtues without his destructive weak-

nesses. She transferred her sense of worship to Franklin, and her insecure nature couldn't believe he would want to marry her. His acceptance
of her just as she was lifted her confidence in spite of Sara's control over
where they lived, what they spent, and how they raised the children. It
was rumored that Sara let the children know they were "her children"
and that their mother had "only" given birth to them. If they stepped out
of her prescribed pattern for their behavior, she would threaten them
with being disinherited.

As Eleanor tried to placate her mother-in-law and keep up with her
husband, she found out he was having an affair with the lovely Lucy Mer-
cer, her social secretary. Lucy had everything Eleanor knew she lacked:
charm, grace, beauty, ease with people, giggles, magnetic appeal, and a
way with men. Poor Eleanor, who had been abandoned by her father
whom she worshiped, found herself rejected by her magnetic husband
whom she adored.

Even though Sara was flattered by Lucy, she would not allow a divorce
to taint the family, and Eleanor would not allow the affair to continue.
Lucy was sent packing, and the marriage was preserved, but Eleanor never
got over the feelings of rejection caused by her husband's infidelity. However, she made the best of a bad situation and decided to become an independent person on her own in case such a situation should ever arise
again. Little did she know that a quirk of fate would bring paralysis to this
fascinating, lively, attractive man, placing him under her control.

In 1921 Roosevelt, already active in the New York Democratic Party,
was stricken with infantile paralysis (polio). Suddenly Eleanor was in
charge; leadership was thrust upon this woman who had wanted to stay
in the background. Roosevelt couldn't move, and he needed her. While
Eleanor dedicated herself to helping her husband recover, Sara took this
disaster as a time for her to tighten her hold on the children, even taking some of them to Europe while Franklin was lying in pain.

He emerged from this attack crippled and with the probable progno-
sis that he would never walk again. Many others who were stricken at
that time fulfilled the depressing prediction, but as a Powerful person,
Roosevelt determined to beat the odds. With Eleanor's round-the-clock
attention and care, he began to improve. He took therapy in New York
and later at a sanitarium. He grew to love the healing waters of Warm
Springs, Georgia, a place that was to become his second home in future
years; he died there in 1945.

Enduring painful therapy that many other victims could not have tolerated, Roosevelt improved to the point where he could walk with the aid of heavy metal braces on both legs. During his lengthy recovery, Eleanor's secondary Powerful personality, which she had not even realized she had, came bursting forth, and she became a political personality in her own right. Initially, she got into the New York Democratic Party to keep her husband's name before the people. She talked about him, expressed his opinions, and brought people to see him. She believed he had presidential possibilities, and she was not going to let his paralysis make him a forgotten man. She achieved her goal so perfectly that soon people were quoting *her* opinion and not what she reported from the recovering Franklin. From that time on, Eleanor's stature grew until later she even dared to express views in public that differed from her husband's.

In spite of his physical handicap, Powerful Franklin Roosevelt ran for governor of New York, forced himself to travel and campaign, and was elected in 1928. He learned to accentuate his positives and overcome his weaknesses. History books and biographies describe him as Popular; he had a winning personality, he loved laughter, and he was a spellbinding storyteller. He was loquacious, gregarious, and hospitable as well as inventive, imaginative, and inspiring. Aided by Eleanor's constant public relations, Franklin's popularity in New York spread to the nation, and in 1932 he was nominated for president on the Democratic ticket.

This choice was not a gift because at the time the nation was at a disastrous crossroads. The Roaring Twenties had come unwound in a depression, and on the very day Roosevelt was inaugurated, he closed all the banks in the nation. Who knows what another man might have done in the crisis Franklin met, but he was an overcomer and a creative genius who stood up in his braces and told us we could make it.

In 1933 in his first inaugural address, he gave us hope by stating, "All we have to fear is fear itself." This simple sentence reverberated throughout the country, and even we children could repeat it.

Time correspondent Walter Shapiro wrote in the November 9, 1987, issue, "The Democratic candidate for president during the dark days of 1932 had few firm economic ideas. Buffeted by conflicting advice, he lamely tried to split the difference. His speeches were a study in contradiction, combining hints of bold spending programs with cries for a balanced budget. If Franklin Roosevelt's approach was inconsistent, even intellectually dishonest, it helped produce a landslide victory over Herbert Hoover and ultimately the New Deal."

Adventurous, Daring, and Confident

FDR seemed to make sense, and he was Popular enough to win our support and give us hope for the future, but he was also Powerful. Once in office, he showed his frightened, hungry nation that he was in charge. He was decisive, straightforward, courageous, adventurous, daring, and self-confident, all traits that were sorely needed by a depressed society.

FDR cultivated one additional trait that was unusual for his personality. He was a good listener, and he invited others' opinions. As a highly educated and creative person, he was able to conceive of plans to help pull the country up by its bootstraps, but he didn't just dream them up and dictate their implementation. He would always run his ideas by his closest advisers, who, ironically, did not include any of his vice presidents. He felt all of them were intellectually unable to provide wise counsel. He listened to his advisers' feedback, and when they had ironed out the specifics, he would take the next step, inviting opinions from those he expected to oppose his idea. Bringing them in one by one and expressing sincere interest in their personal opinions, he would nod in affirmation, saying, "Why didn't I think of that?" or "Why didn't one of my staff come up with that?"

Occasionally, Roosevelt would adopt someone else's suggestion, but he prepared them ahead of time in case he couldn't. "I certainly agree with your point, and I hope I can use it," he would say. "But you must realize," and here he would lean forward as if to share a secret, "I'm not in this alone. I have Congress to deal with and all those other politicians to convince, but you can count on me to do my best."

This conciliatory approach of giving his opponents their moment alone with the president enabled Roosevelt to make massive changes with what appeared to be minimal resistance. He created the New Deal and cooked up an alphabet soup of government agencies and acts such as the CCC (Civilian Conservation Corps), the AAA (Agricultural Adjustment Act), the NIRA (National Industrial Recovery Act), the SSA (Social Security Act), the FHA (Federal Housing Act), the WPA (Works Progress Administration), and the TVA (Tennessee Valley Authority).

When FDR was reelected in 1936, I was eight, one brother was four, and the other was a new baby. My father was fifty-eight, and my Peaceful, frightened mother was thirty-eight. The company my father had worked for and had expected to retire from had closed during the depression, and he was left an unemployed older man with no way to support his young family. Roosevelt's WPA created public service jobs, and my father became a timekeeper on a road construction gang. I was the recipient of little WPA-created dresses worn identically by all the "poor girls" at school. I remember going to a charity Christmas party where an elegant lady presented me with two books of Shirley Temple paper dolls. Even as a child I knew I was on the wrong side of the stage. *Someday I'll be the one on the stage giving out to others, not the poor child receiving,* I promised myself.

Just because the New Deal, Roosevelt's recovery reform, was providing employment and clothing to those in dire need did not mean that all of his programs were met with universal enthusiasm. Many recipients, such as my family, who were not used to being charity cases, sometimes resented being on the dole and kept up a murmur of dissent, calling the New Deal a "raw deal." Many believed that Roosevelt's policies prolonged the depression.

Despite the criticisms, FDR was passionate in his beliefs that history would prove him right, and he was willing to assume responsibility for the outcome of his programs. In order to keep his popularity intact, he instituted what became known as his "fireside chats," informal radio programs in which he took his problems straight to the people. He spoke from the Oval Office in the White House, and in the next day's newspaper we would see his picture, taken as he "chatted" with his radio audience while seated at the desk laden with his favorite figurines. Even without television, we were able to picture him in our minds as we listened to him. These series of frank conversations with the American public gave even his detractors confidence that he really cared.

Our National Father

FDR had a way with words, a talent that's innate with the Populars, and one of his writers once said, "Franklin Roosevelt is a better phrasemaker than anybody he ever had around him."

In his second inaugural address he stated, "I see one-third of a nation ill-housed, ill-clad, ill-nourished."

In vetoing a tax bill in 1944, he wrote, "It is not a tax bill but a tax-relief bill providing relief not for the needy but for the greedy."

FDR's clever use of his communication skills set him above presidents of the past and increased his popularity to the point that he became our national father. Even those who wouldn't vote for him had to admit his personal appeal.

Not everyone considered him a brilliant orator; some accused him of being arrogant and lacking in humility, especially when he gave speeches such as the one on October 31, 1936, in Madison Square Garden where he claimed eloquently, "I should like to have it said of my first administration that in it the forces of selfishness and of lust for power met its match. I should like to have it said of my second administration that in it these forces met their master."

By 1940 Hitler was marching through Europe, and our fearful focus had shifted from starvation to war. We were afraid to change horses midstream, so we elected FDR to an unprecedented third term. He promised in his campaign that he would give assistance to the British: "All aid short of war."

No one wanted war; we had hardly pulled out of the depression. However, on December 7, 1941, Japanese bombers attacked the American naval base at Pearl Harbor without warning. The attack came as a shocking surprise to the American people and showed that our desire to stay neutral had resulted in wishful thinking and willful blindness.

FDR instantly became commander in chief, and he fit his role well. I remember the pictures of him sitting regally on the deck of a ship wrapped in his dark navy cape. It wasn't until I studied history in college that I realized his cape was not only for drama but also a convenient cover-up for his wheelchair. He didn't want us to be reminded that he was physically weakened and couldn't bear to wear his heavy braces.

With his keen sense of history and his lifetime study of naval operations, FDR became a commanding legend who met many times with Winston Churchill, a Popular-Powerful himself.

Throughout his time as chief executive, FDR maintained his broad interests in life, never succumbing to self-pity; he exhibited valiant energy in spite of physical debilitation and inspired the world to admire and respect him—and his country. He was also able to withdraw from the crowds, personally inscribe each book he was given as to which library it should ultimately belong to, and select some of his major speeches to be bound as gifts for his family and friends.

Although his strength decreased, his mind remained clear; his memory was remarkable, and he continued his amazing powers of concentration. He obviously possessed exceptional leadership skills, but some people denounced him as a hypocrite for putting us into war after he had clearly stated in a campaign speech in Boston on October 30, 1940, "Mothers and fathers, I give you one more assurance. I have said this before, but I shall say it again and again and again: Your boys are not going to be sent into any foreign wars."

He was impatient when things didn't go his way, and when the party didn't approve of his choice of Henry Wallace for vice president, he countered, "Well, damn it to hell. They will go for Wallace or I won't run, and you can jolly well tell them so."

He got angry at those who made mistakes or didn't agree with him. When Cactus Jack Garner, his first vice president, didn't totally support his plans, Roosevelt left him out of the inner circle that gathered after cabinet meetings; Garner was not consulted about any important decisions. Fuming about his relegation to the sidelines, Cactus Jack, a Popular Speaker of the House, said, "I gave up the second most powerful job in the government for one that didn't amount to a hill of beans . . . or a bucket of warm spit."

Roosevelt was considered unconventional in his political approach, and when the conservatives were overruling his programs, he added six new judges to the Supreme Court, causing him to be accused of "packing the court." He seemed to enjoy controversy and once said, "There is nothing I love as much as a good fight." Truly, a Powerful statement.

Although he was noted for the intellectual quality of the advisers he chose and the talent he attracted, FDR spent little time in the selection of a vice president to run with him for his fourth term in 1944. He had better things to do than interview prospective candidates, so his advisers were left to find someone who would bring political balance to the ticket. In doing so, they pulled an unknown senator, Harry S. Truman, out of the backwoods of Missouri.

Roosevelt and Truman had very different backgrounds, and although they won as a team, they never developed a close relationship. Truman, like Garner, was not included in many of the high-level discussions; the treatment left him ignorant of important decisions and policies when Roosevelt died in April 1945.

The Unrelenting Eleanor

In retrospect, it seems obvious that Roosevelt's health was so poor, he shouldn't have even considered running for an unprecedented fourth term. The toll of the war and his constant effort to move had so depleted his energy that he hardly ever got out of his wheelchair. Friends who hadn't seen him for a while were shocked at his appearance and begged Eleanor to keep him from running. Instead she encouraged him to go for it because she sincerely believed the country needed him, and she also thought a new campaign would brighten his spirits.

And it did. During the campaign, he put aside his pain and fatigue and showed us once again he could rise above almost any set of circumstances. The applause of the crowds gave him renewed vigor, and he even regained enough use of his legs to occasionally stand at the rear of his campaign train and speak to the people. Eleanor pushed him to go on and seldom let him rest. When he won his fourth term, Eleanor became almost a second president, instructing him until he had to push her away. She would bring him papers to sign at the end of a long day when all he wanted was a moment of peace and some uplifting words. In frustration, he soon turned to his daughter, Anna, as a confidant and adviser.

Joseph P. Lash, a Roosevelt biographer, wrote in his book *Eleanor and Franklin,* "Eleanor was too independent, too strong ethically, too unrelenting to provide him with the kind of relaxed, unjudging company that he wanted. 'The one thing she was not able to bring him,' wrote her son, James, 'was that touch of triviality he needed to lighten his burden . . . she was a woman of commanding dignity and of an almost saintly selflessness, whom all admired and some even loved.'"

FDR spent his last days in Warm Springs in the company of pleasant friends, including Lucy. He was posing for a new portrait when he told the artist, "I'll give you exactly fifteen minutes." At the end of fifteen minutes he grabbed his head and collapsed, dying shortly of a massive cerebral hemorrhage.

The only president in American history to be elected four times left a legacy of warmth, fatherly concern, and inspiration. While controversial, he was never boring, and in the face of attack he never lost his sense of humor.

When he was accused during his last campaign of using taxpayers' money to transport his dog, Fala, he countered, "These Republican leaders have not been content with attacks on me, or my wife, or on my sons. No, not content with that, they now include my little dog Fala. Well, of course, I don't resent attacks . . . but Fala does resent them. . . . I think I have a right to resent, to object to libelous statements about my dog. . . . When Fala heard these stories, his Scotch soul was furious. He has not been the same dog since."[1]

Franklin Delano Roosevelt had the obvious assets of the charming, witty Popular personality combined with the potent strengths of the commanding Powerful, and his unique skill was being able to use his winning ways without letting us see many of his temperamental weaknesses. Few leaders in history have been able to present such a consistent personality over the years.

FDR's personal secretary, Grace Tully, summed up his sense of mission, "He simply felt that he had been given a grand opportunity to do something about the problems that beset the nation."[2]

I remember the day when the news came across the wires and we gathered around our arched Zenith radio in the kitchen to hear the awful announcement: "The president is dead." He'd been the only president I'd known. Whether or not we agreed with all his programs, we loved him as a father. There was security in knowing he was there in times of poverty and in the throes of war.

Of all our modern presidents, Roosevelt was the one who made the very most of his strengths, overcame his physical weaknesses, and rose above his handicaps and pain. Eleanor also was able to put the hurts of infidelity behind her, get beyond her lack of physical beauty, and bravely march forward to become the most influential first lady we had ever known.

We can all learn from the Roosevelts to accentuate our positives and eliminate our negatives. As leaders, we must learn to make the best of adverse circumstances and rise above our problems.

Franklin D. Roosevelt
Popular-Powerful Personality

The following lists of strengths and weaknesses include words and phrases used in newspaper articles, magazines, books, television, and radio to describe President Roosevelt's personality, a combination of Popular and Powerful traits. Check the characteristics that could also apply to you.

Popular Personality

Strengths
___ Spell-binding orator
___ Jaunty flirtatiousness
___ Winning, inspiring
    personality
___ Amusing, life of the party
___ Loved laughter
___ Happy, friendly, and warm
___ Loquacious and gregarious
___ Loved to tell stories
___ Good mimic
___ Hospitable
___ Beloved by all
___ Never boring
___ Imaginative and inventive
___ Encouraged all he met
___ Gave hope to the hurting
___ Articulate and entertaining
___ Phrase-maker
___ Vibrant voice
___ Dramatic and debonair
___ Cavalier attitude
___ Able to attract talent
___ **TOTAL**

Weaknesses
___ Too dramatic
___ Played to the audience
___ Pulled out rhetorical stops
___ Practiced storyteller
___ Stretched the truth
___ Deceptive
___ Feather duster of fluff
___ Mama's boy
___ Unfaithful

___ **TOTAL**

Powerful Personality

Strengths
___ Learned to listen
___ Self-confident and decisive
___ Overcame adversity
___ Willing to accept
    responsibility
___ Straightforward
___ Sense of fairness and justice
___ Courageous and adventurous
___ Passionate in beliefs

Weaknesses
___ Arrogant leader
___ Irritated by others
___ Impatient
___ Looked down on dummies
___ Angry at incompetence
___ Unconventional
___ Enjoyed controversy
___ Insisted on his own way
___ Frank and abrupt

___ Active in spite of pain   ___ Manipulated people
___ Aggressive   ___ Intellectually dishonest
___ Daring and brave
___ No self-pity
___ Valiant energy
___ Extraordinary political skills
___ Energized by the people
___ **TOTAL**   ___ **TOTAL**

Total of your presidential profile of Popular-Powerful strengths and weaknesses: _____

Are You a Leader Like Roosevelt?

If you have many of Roosevelt's strengths, you have the potential for inspired leadership. His combination of charm and confidence kept him in power longer than any other president in the history of our country. His ability to speak clearly and to tell stories that were amusing and made a point appealed to the masses. He never talked down to people, and he listened to what others had to say, giving them an uninterrupted opportunity to express their opinions.

So many of us in leadership have no time for "the little people." We tend to forget the old saying, "Even the dull and ignorant have their point."

Another great strength was that FDR did his homework. He studied history, battles, and political procedures all his life, and he functioned out of a depth of knowledge. So many of us want to be leaders without doing any background study. We want to win the prize without preparation.

FDR surrounded himself with intelligent and competent advisers. In contrast, some of us associate with people who agree with us and make us look good instead of being willing to seek diverse opinions. Our minds are never stimulated to greatness when we are surrounded by smiling "yes men" and "yes women."

FDR had a sense of humor even in drastic circumstances, and his most important gift was his ability to give hope to the hopeless. These are traits we should all emulate, but if you are a combination of the outgoing Popular personality and the confident Powerful, you will be more able than others to give believable encouragement to those who look to you for leadership.

When people observe your behavior, can they see that you have a passionate belief in your own agenda? Can they be sure your walk matches your talk? Do they have confidence that you will listen to all sides of an issue before making a decision?

Those who were critical of FDR felt he was too glib, too dramatic, too impressed with himself. They felt he wanted his own way, no matter what, and he manipulated people for his own desires. Some found him arrogant and impatient, but historically speaking he was a man for his time, a man with the courage of his convictions and one who was willing to make hard choices even when they weren't popular. He listened to both sides of an issue before making a decision, and he knew how to amplify his strengths and minimize his weaknesses. We would all do well to follow his example as we aim to fulfill our presidential potential. Look and listen before you leap!

9

"GIVE 'EM HELL!"

HARRY S. TRUMAN

President: 1945–1953
Personality: Powerful
Principle to Learn: Speak the truth.

On April 12, 1945, Harry S. Truman became president, and the next day he told reporters, "When they told me yesterday what had happened, I felt like the moon, the stars, and all the planets had fallen on me." So did many of us.

Suddenly we found ourselves without the commander in chief many of us had know for an entire generation. Franklin Roosevelt's obscure substitute was called a "dirt farmer" or "the haberdasher from Kansas City." We had the same feeling of disappointment we might have had if we had gone to the theater to see the great actor Lionel Barrymore and found out he was being replaced that night by an unknown understudy.

Even the staunchest Democrats were inwardly shaken when they saw what they had on their hands. From the aristocratic, articulate Roosevelt they went to the brash, earthy Truman, who cussed automatically and was ready to "give 'em hell." He had never attended college and was considered to have a chip on his shoulder because of his humble beginnings.

Although Harry had been in the Senate, he lacked knowledge or experience in foreign affairs. As Robert Donovan wrote in his book, *The Tumultuous Years,* "Roosevelt largely ignored him and excluded him from the innermost discussions of strategy and diplomacy as the second World War was nearing a climax."

Truman was angry that Roosevelt had left him in such a predicament, and he let us all know his feelings. Truman described vice presidents as being "about as useful as a cow's fifth teat." All they do, he said, is sit around "waiting for a funeral."

There is little doubt that Truman started from below zero in a job that was considered far too big for him; however, we didn't realize that Harry came from a long line of Powerfuls, people who know how to sprint into action when the chips are down and are energized by the phrase, "It can't be done."

If the Populars heard those words they would respond, "Good, it didn't sound like much fun anyway." The Perfects would say, "Oh, really? I had just figured out how to do it right." The Peacefuls would answer, "I'm relieved; it sounded too much like work." Only the Powerfuls would state, "That's what you think. Just watch me!"

Confidence and Determination

One of the most consistent Powerful traits is the confidence that anything can be solved with the right person in charge. The words "It can't be done" just spur Powerfuls on to victory. The impossible just takes a little longer. Once at work on the impossible, Powerfuls will not quit, even if the facts show they can't succeed. This trait is a positive in that the Powerfuls can and do accomplish more than others in a shorter time, but it becomes a weakness when they will not listen to advice and insist on fighting to the death.

Harry Truman is a fascinating example of a man with humble beginnings who wouldn't take no for an answer.

Because Harry's father, John Truman, was a short man nicknamed "Peanuts," he had to exert his Power in feisty ways. John Truman grew up in the late 1800s in Missouri, where the family literally fought for its life in border warfare. He became scrappy and defensive at a very early age. He would wheel and deal in anything, and at one point he made an exchange that put five hundred goats in his backyard. He dabbled in local politics and didn't let anyone push him around. One day when John was a witness at a trial, the lawyer accused him of lying. John jumped out of his seat and chased the big lawyer out of the courthouse, ending the case. Looking at his father, it is obvious where Harry Truman got his taste for politics and his incendiary nature.

Harry's mother, Martha, was less controversial but still a hardy soul with a true pioneer spirit. She taught her children that waste and laziness were tools of the devil and that hard work was next to godliness. She called herself a "light-foot Baptist," meaning she was devout but not legalistic and saw nothing wrong in a little dancing if the beat were right, no matter what the deacons thought.

From childhood, Harry was extremely nearsighted and his having to wear glasses excluded him from athletics in school. Instead he read books about heroes and leaders, and by the time he was twelve he had read the Bible through twice. Although he never went to college, he read the classics for pleasure and digested Plato and Cato.

His mother played the piano, and she began teaching him when he was a child. At age thirteen he started with two lessons a week and rose at five o'clock each morning to practice for two hours before school. This Powerful family believed strongly in the work ethic, and Harry learned that if you didn't work you didn't eat. Each child had specific jobs, and it never occurred to them not to complete their chores.

Harry's first official job was with L. J. Smith Construction Company, earning thirty-five dollars a month. The tough-talking men made fun of his thick glasses and his love of classical music, and it was from this crude group that Harry learned his salty language and became determined to be a winner.

During World War I, the Kansas City National Guard was called up, and Harry was sent to Germany where he was part of heavy fighting. As a captain and later as a major, he was in charge of an undisciplined group he soon brought under control. Harry learned in the military to strike first before the enemy finds you, and he carried over this practice into politics. Once he became president and emerged from the uncomfortable role as underdog with no control, he came into his own Powerful personality. He decided once again to show who was boss.

Exhilarated by the sense of combat, Harry came out swinging. When the eightieth Congress refused to rise to his leadership, he branded them as a "good-for-nothing, do-nothing" group. These words did not inspire them to cheerful support when he ran for reelection, and he found himself having to frequently eat some of his more salty sentences.

Scorned as a "little man" and a "misfit," he had a contempt for his critics that led him into impulsive actions typical of the Powerful personality. His decision to drop the atomic bomb has been debated ever since it exploded on Hiroshima, and it so incensed his stolid Peaceful wife, Bess, that she packed up and went back to Kansas City as a sign of her disapproval. But Harry was buoyant when the bomb brought the war to an end, and he continued to bounce back after other defeats as well. He had remarkable stamina and was determined to do the impossible. Being hit over the head just made him emerge taller.

When it was time to run for reelection, even his own party wasn't consistent in its support of him. He was disgusted with the lot of them and determined he would run and win. The governor of New York, Thomas Dewey, who had previously been defeated by Roosevelt, was to be his opponent, and few gave Truman much of a chance.

I remember being on the Dewey side of the issue when I was part of the debate team in college, and I came up with what I thought were brilliant statements on why Harry couldn't win. I pointed out that Dewey ran a Peaceful, nonconfrontational campaign, maintaining the dignity of a sure winner, while Harry, on his three-thousand-mile whistle-stop campaign, got out and gave 'em hell again.

Somehow his vintage-American, earthy character quietly caught on, and with the headlines "Dewey Wins!" already printed, we woke up to find that the country had gone wild about Harry. He let us know, "I told you so" and made it clear he had been vindicated. The impossible just took more determination, and Harry made it happen.

Was there ever a Powerful who laid it on the line so clearly? We never had to worry about what Harry was thinking; he told us. While FDR's Powerful traits were modified by his refined upbringing and lightened by his Popular personality, Harry's lack of finesse and his forthright phrases defined his feisty spirit, and his insecure sense of worth caused him to rattle his cage loudly and sometimes overstep his normal presidential bounds.

Robert Donovan wrote in *The Tumultuous Years,* "He had a weakness for rushing into action without fully weighing the consequences."

His strong Powerful need for control showed up all too clearly when he locked horns with another Powerful, General Douglas MacArthur, who took pleasure in making policy statements without checking them first with the president, for whom he had little personal respect.

While the debate of who was right will go on into political history, the way in which Truman chose to dismiss MacArthur for insubordination turned the sympathies toward the general, who had a great sense for theatrics. Afraid that MacArthur would resign before he had a chance to fire him, Harry told an aide, "The S.O.B. isn't going to resign on me! I want him fired!" Harry canceled his plans to use the proper military channels and gave out a press release from Washington before informing the general of his decision. A soldier picked up the news on the wire, called the general's wife, who then broke the news to her husband. Even those who sympathized with the president's decision deplored the manner in which it was executed, and Senator Robert Taft called for Truman's impeachment. By the time General MacArthur gave his "old soldiers never die; they just fade away" speech before Congress, the American public was sitting tearfully in the palm of the general's hand.

Harry said of his MacArthur situation, "You have to decide what is right to do and then do it, even if it is unpopular." And of his time in office, he explained, "I have tried to give it everything that was in me."

When critic Paul Hume gave the Trumans' daughter Margaret a poor review after her maiden vocal concert, Harry sent him an angry, handwritten note, complete with unprintable expletives.

On April 8, 1952, Truman, in a tussle with a lengthy strike by steel workers, seized the steel mills in what he declared a national emergency. Lyndon Johnson, a fellow Democrat with eyes on the White House, declared, "Truman's order showed a trend toward dictatorship."[1]

The press called him a Caesar, an American Hitler, Mussolini, an author of evil, a bully, a usurper, a lawbreaker, and an architect of a labor dictatorship. The issue went to the Supreme Court, which declared his order unconstitutional. Bombastic Harry had struck out.

Truman's Fall from Power

While much of the public found Harry's hot tongue and trigger-quick replies to be a humorous relief after FDR's almost god-like image, his own party cooled on his short fuse and spread the word that he would not be supported again as a candidate. Truman, in disbelief and disappointment, knew his days were numbered when his own party, whom he had served faithfully, rejected him, an incumbent president, for Adlai Stevenson.

Although Harry's heart wasn't in it, he agreed to a whistle-stop tour for Stevenson, and as the train progressed, Harry's love for declamation warmed him up to such a degree that the people's response to him was more enthusiastic than to the candidate himself. Thousands yelled, "Give 'em hell, Harry!" and I wonder if the Democrats wondered whether they had made a mistake in their selection.

After the defeat of Stevenson and the inauguration of General Dwight D. Eisenhower, Truman said in an interview with John Snyder, "Two hours ago I would have said five words and been quoted in fifteen minutes in every capital of the world. Now I could talk for two hours and nobody would give a damn."

While Harry's clear words were not considered on a par with Roosevelt's or Churchill's, he was a prolific writer. Walter Isaacson commented in the August 31, 1987, issue of *Time* magazine about this part of Truman's life:

> The last president to leave a cache of candid correspondence was Harry Truman, who wrote more than 1,200 letters just to his wife. Not only do they reveal his delightful personal style, they provide convincing insights on matters ranging from his dealings with Stalin to his decision to drop the atom bomb. There is even a book filled with letters that Truman wrote in moments of pique, then wisely filed away unmailed. His diaries, though intermittent, are no less revealing. In June 1945, as General Douglas MacArthur was closing in on the islands near Japan, Truman's entries fore-shadow the bitter personal battles that lay ahead. He describes the general as "Mr. Prima Donna, Brass Hat Five Star MacArthur" in one entry and adds, "He's worse than the Cabots and the Lodges—they at least talked to one another before they told God what to do."

When Harry looked back on his time as president he said, as a true Powerful, "I never did give anybody hell; I just told the truth, and they thought it was hell."

A Modern Revival

Although Harry left office as a questionable leader, history has been kinder to him than his own party was. His words are often quoted today as brilliant, and Paul Simon, a candidate for president in 1988, called himself a Truman Democrat and revived interest in Harry as a folk hero. If Harry were here, he'd state proudly, "I told you so."

It happened again in the presidential campaign of 1992, when all three major candidates—George Bush, Ross Perot, and Bill Clinton—at one time or another laid claim to being like Harry Truman. Clinton claimed Truman's country-boy roots and his take-charge talent, Perot professed that he was the only candidate telling the truth and having the guts to lay it on the line like Harry did, and even Bush, a Republican, said he'd surprise all and come from behind as Truman had done in 1948.

Suddenly there was a nostalgia craze for the "improbable president." Why? According to Benedict K. Zobrist, director of the Truman Library, "In 1953, when Truman left office, he was at a low, rock-bottom ebb of popularity. . . . By 1969, Americans practically had forgotten him." He points out that Watergate brought a longing for a Truman-type honest leader and now, "Wow! All of a sudden this boom in interest." What has brought this new fascination for a dead leader whose missteps as president led critics to coin the phrase, "to err is Truman"? Zobrist responds that Americans are worried about their nation and yearn for a leader who will speak plain and straight to them. "Through the distillery of time, Truman has come to personify such a figure."[2]

Was Truman the last honest president? Was he the last one to leave office poorer than when he went in? Was he the last one with no spin doctors or sound-bite creators? Was he the only one who didn't like to spend time "flattering, kissing, and kicking people to get them to do what they are supposed to do in the first place," as he would say?

Truman didn't try to humor the masses or charm the country into compliance. He used his Powerful decisive strengths even when they were perceived as weaknesses, and he let the chips fall where they might. "This is no popularity contest," he said more than once.

It was General George C. Marshall who said of Truman, "The full stature of this man will only be proven by history. It is not the courage of his decisions that will live but the integrity of the man."[3]

Harry S. Truman
Powerful Personality

The following lists of strengths and weaknesses include words and phrases used in newspaper articles, magazines, books, television, and radio to describe President Truman's Powerful personality. Check the characteristics that could also apply to you.

Strengths	Weaknesses
___ Frank and outspoken	___ Bombastic
___ Loyal and honest	___ An American Hitler
___ Punctual and decisive	___ Dictator
___ Goal-oriented	___ Seized authority
___ Delightful personal style	___ Cussed automatically
___ Hard worker	___ Impulsive and erratic
___ Gutsy	___ Outspoken and abrupt
___ Secure and self-confident	___ Lacking in finesse
___ Theatrical	___ Bully, usurper
___ Buoyant	___ Chip on his shoulder
___ Good-natured	___ Irritated and angry
___ Remarkable stamina	___ Trigger-quick replies
___ Courageous	___ Short-tempered
___ Strong-willed	and hot-tongued
___ Earthy	___ Vindictive
___ Sincere	___ Disdainful and brash
___ Shrewd	___ Ridiculed opponents
___ Aggressive	___ Wanted revenge
___ Excited by challenges	
___ Didn't need to be popular	
___ **TOTAL**	___ **TOTAL**

Total of your presidential profile of Powerful strengths and weaknesses: _____

Are You a Leader Like Truman?

Did you find some similarities between yourself and Truman? It's popular to relate to Truman today, for "give-'em-hell Harry" has become a 1990s folk hero. What looked brash and earthy after the charm and dignity of Roosevelt has mellowed out to be seen as courage and honesty today.

If you are the Powerful personality, you can be grateful because you are a born leader. You have it within you to succeed. You have the driving spirit to walk in where angels fear to tread and to take charge whether or not you are asked to do so. You can set goals realistically and pursue truth without fear. People have confidence in your leadership because you seem so sure of yourself and so excited about the future. You don't get discouraged easily and you stick to your guns no matter what others think.

These are all leadership strengths that should catapult you to success beyond the norm. However, as with each personality, there are possible weaknesses that can prevent your reaching your potential. The first one is your tendency to think you don't have any weaknesses! You tend to believe all problems are someone else's fault. You are a creative genius in quickly proving yourself right and others wrong. Your personality type takes credit for success and rationalizes away responsibility for failure.

Powerful people feel that admitting mistakes shows weakness, and yet the opposite is true. It takes a mature person to say I'm sorry. History has proven that the American public will forgive almost any leadership error if the person will honestly admit, confess, and repent.

Conversely, we don't trust the leader who denies involvement and covers up the truth.

What made Harry Truman remarkable was his willingness to accept responsibility for good or bad. "The buck stops here," he adamantly announced. He is not remembered for his charm or finesse, for his style or clever repartee, but for his forthright honesty in all he did and for his willingness to shoulder the blame in times of trouble.

Could this be said about you? Are you able to admit when you are wrong and say, "I'm sorry. It was my fault. I'll try to do better in the future"? If a biographer were to write your life story, could he or she conclude, "It's not just the courage of his (or her) decisions but the integrity of the man (or woman) that we'll remember"?

10

"WE LIKE IKE"

DWIGHT EISENHOWER

President: 1953–1961
Personality: Peaceful
Principle to Learn: Find the middle road.

After twenty years of Democratic Party rule led by two Powerful presidents, the country was ready for a change. We'd been disheartened by the depression and worn down by the war. We wanted to put it all behind us and be normal again. Who better to lead us to national peacetime victory than genial General Dwight D. Eisenhower?

So often at the end of a certain era we look for someone who is totally different in personality from what we've had. We'd lived with the forceful personality of Roosevelt, who had controlled an entire generation, and we'd adapted to Truman's forthright command. We'd had the New Deal followed by the Fair Deal; now Eisenhower offered an Honest Deal. "Let's drive out the crooks and the cronies." Let's keep it "clean as a hound's tooth."

We'd had hot, and we wanted cool. Ike was typical of the Peacefuls who quietly do what is expected of them, walk the middle line of life, and manage to offend no one. They smile, nod in agreement, and pacify the contentious. They will agree with either side of an issue if it will keep people happy. Their low-key personality doesn't mean they have nothing intelligent to say; they just reserve their wit for the right time and have no need to add a comment to every conversation. Peacefuls are content to listen to others and give at least token agreement, two traits that make them very popular with the Populars. They are willing to do what pleases others and not buck authority, so they are also favorites with the Powerfuls, who usually marry one of them. The Peacefuls are able to sit quietly for hours and work on plans, impressing the Perfects. Everyone gets along with the Peaceful personality, and indeed, we all liked Ike.

The general had come from humble midwestern beginnings, as Truman had. The Eisenhower family originally came from Germany to Pennsylvania in 1732 to find freedom of worship. Although the word *Eisenhower* means "iron ax," they were pacifist Quakers who lived by the Golden Rule and felt self-reliance and hard work were the basics of life.

As a child, Ike peddled the family's surplus vegetables, and twice a week he got up at 4:30 A.M. to build the fire in the woodstove and cook the breakfast. In high school, his father got Ike a job stoking boilers in the creamery where he worked, and in between the shoveling, Ike would read and doze. Even though his parents were Peacefuls and were against war, Ike studied history and was fascinated with military heroes. Much to the family's dismay, he took the examinations for West Point and Annapolis, and his score of 87.7 was the highest one earned. He chose West Point, where his class of 168 graduates included 56 men who ultimately became generals.

He was promoted steadily and recognized for his rational reasoning abilities. He could keep his head while all around him were losing theirs. In typical Peaceful fashion, he had always quietly done the right thing at the right time, pleased his superiors, and not caused any shock waves anywhere along the line. He had a sense of how to get along with others, and he didn't need to have his own way. His easygoing nature, wide grin, and willingness to compromise made him a hit with the hotheads, and Truman even suggested him as a possible Democratic candidate for President. He had lunched weekly with Churchill, and he personally knew Roosevelt, as well as Josef Stalin, Konrad Adenauer, and Charles de Gaulle. He was in a league with Generals George Marshall, Omar Bradley, and Douglas MacArthur, but Eisenhower alone was considered the peace-loving man of war. As the old Latin saying put it, Ike was "gentle in manner, strong in deed."

In the book *Ike the Soldier*, author Merle Miller compared Ike with General Ulysses S. Grant.

> Both Eisenhower and Grant maintained a consistent calmness amid either triumph or adversity; Ike's command of himself is a much-repeated theme among those who recall him. In both Ike and Grant, this quality sprang from a complete self-confidence that underlay an apparent modesty. In both, furthermore, self-confidence sprang in turn from a consistency and fixity of purpose that would not let them be diverted from their goals. . . .
>
> Throughout the discouraging early phases of the battle, Ike maintained the calmness and underlying confidence that were so characteristic of him, while many other Allied leaders grew nervous and testy.[1]

The Aura of a Hero

Eisenhower's grandson, David, in his book *Eisenhower: At War, 1943–1945*, said the general was "known for his affability, his abilities as a negotiator and his talent for reconciling differences among strong personalities." All these traits are typical of the Peacefuls, who are always willing to mediate between people who are at opposite extremes.

Playing upon Truman's inability to end the Korean War that had erupted just before the European conflict had been put to rest, Eisenhower promised in his campaign that he would go to Korea and see firsthand what was going on. We were so tired of war, hardships, and scrap drives that we praised his willingness to make the trip and knew that with his experience as a general he would settle the issue of war once and for all time.

In his uniform, Eisenhower had the aura of a hero, and we were in need of one. We handed him the country to take care of, then we all settled in for a long winter's nap.

Charles R. Morris said of Eisenhower, "He was a president shrewd enough to know when the country was on a winning streak, and self-disciplined enough to keep his hands out of the machinery."[2]

We all wanted peace, and Peaceful Ike became our balm of Gilead. While we all liked him, he was never known for exciting or creative ideas or for many innovative programs. But then again, we asked little of him, only that he leave us alone and let us return to normal.

Calming the Tempest

Eisenhower was an all-purpose, middle-of-the-road president whose greatest strength was his lack of obvious weaknesses. As a typical Peaceful, he avoided personal confrontation. When his chief of staff, Sherman Adams, admitted that he had accepted a vicuna coat and some blankets from merchant Bernard Goldfine, Eisenhower looked the other way. Compared to the immoral hijinks we have seen in the more recent political arena, the gift of a coat and blanket seems trivial, but in the climate of 1958 the headlines made Adams sound like a member of the Mafia.

All Peacefuls resist change, and Eisenhower was typically reluctant to part with Adams. When asked why, he answered simply, "I need him." When discipline was demanded by party leaders, Eisenhower eventually sent his aides to do his dirty work, and Adams resigned.

Later Adams wrote in his memoirs, "Any presidential appointee whose presence in the administration becomes an embarrassment to the president for any reason whatsoever has no choice but to submit his resignation."[3]

Although Eisenhower could plan an invasion, his vision began to dim in time of peace. Nelson Rockefeller, who served under Presidents Roosevelt, Truman, and Eisenhower, felt that the Eisenhower administration "was drifting from crisis to crisis, was preparing its plans and managing matters of state on a month-to-month, year-to-year basis, while America's position in the changing world required planning that reached from today over 5 years, over 10 years, into the farthest foreseeable future."[4]

Other critics murmured that Ike was a remote and detached manager who didn't have any idea what was really going on. When Lyndon Johnson was senate majority leader, he looked down on Eisenhower's ability and didn't think the president knew what a bill was or even if he had any in mind. One night after a frustrating visit with Eisenhower in which he had been unable to get a definitive answer from him, Johnson roared, "That man does not deserve to be president!"[5]

Truman disliked his successor, but according to Tip O'Neill's report, he was very protective of Mamie Eisenhower and her reported problems with alcohol. In typical direct style, Truman said, "Let me tell you something. Some of the newspapers are making snide remarks about Mrs. Eisenhower, saying she has a drinking problem. Now it wouldn't surprise me if she did, because look what the woman has to put up with."[6]

Referring to the rumor, which was not confirmed until years later, that Ike had an affair with his chauffeur, Kay Summersby, Truman blew up. "I've got no use for the man, and I don't give a damn what you say about him." Truman also stated, "The general doesn't know any more about politics than a pig knows about Sunday."[7]

A Man for His Hour

The majority of the public looked at Eisenhower's strengths and not his weaknesses. Although he was relaxed, witty, and appealing, Eisenhower never had the Popular charisma of FDR. He was able to win the European war, but he was no fighter on the home front. As Gerald Ford was to be in the future, Dwight Eisenhower was a man for his hour: no more and no less.

One of Eisenhower's most winning Peaceful traits was his humility. From his experience in directing the movements of troops in and out of battle, he had been constantly aware of how small a cog he was in the vast wheel of war. When honored in London in 1945, Eisenhower stated, "Humility must always be the portion of any man who receives acclaim earned by the blood of his followers and the sacrifices of his friends."

After years of Franklin Roosevelt, the ultimate commander in chief who easily controlled with confidence, and the feisty Harry Truman, the Peaceful, humble, relaxed, and smiling Eisenhower was a welcome and restful change. He became president, not because of lifelong political ambitions, but as the quiet answer to the call of duty.

Another attribute Eisenhower had was patience. He didn't need it all done yesterday as the Powerful would have demanded. He didn't want to offend, and he was willing to wait until the time was right to move.

Had Eisenhower been a Powerful personality instead of a Peaceful one, he might have hastily, upon inauguration, thrown out the "welfare-state psychology" of the New Deal. Instead he applied an objective, businesslike point of view to the transition and refused to be influenced by outside pressures. He possessed persuasive powers typical of the Peaceful personality, and when he couldn't win a quiet victory, he would resort to the veto.

On one vetoed bill, he wrote to Congress, "This kind of legislation, this expectation of something for nothing, weakens our national fabric and with each occurrence leaves it more seriously impaired. The spread of this expectation and its reflection in our increase of such legislation are profoundly disturbing for the future of America."

Eisenhower was not influenced by party bosses; he was an outsider and had no future political goals. He just wanted to do a good job and go home. When he was given the use of Shangri-la, a retreat in the Catoctin Mountains of Maryland, he winced at any place with such a fancy name and changed it to Camp David in honor of his father.

Even though Eisenhower was a successful general, he never liked war's effects, and he turned away from personal conflict of any type. In his 1953 inaugural address, he said, "Since this century's beginning, a time of tempest has seemed to come upon the continents of the earth."

He wanted to use his strategic skills to calm the times of tempest, not to fight eternal wars. He was willing to give a little here and there to avoid upsetting anyone, and he didn't need the credit for his own ego, a rare trait in a political hero.

He believed strongly in the delegation of authority, and he surrounded himself with the ablest team of men he could acquire. He wanted businesslike methods of government, and he based his choices on "experience, ability, character, and standing in their own communities." With quiet resolve, Eisenhower and his business associates steered the country away from the welfare state it had become to the free-enterprise system we accept as the norm.

Although the benign general did not want involvement in any new wars, conflict around the world kept creeping up before him. The Korean truce talks bogged down, and Eisenhower had to decide whether to push North Korea back to the Yalu River, a venture that would call for the involvement of more American troops at a time when the country was longing for peace, or accept the divided country. Thirty-four thousand Americans had already died in Korea, so Eisenhower signed the Panmunjon Peace Treaty on July 27, 1953.

Next, Eisenhower aimed for some cooperative control of the atom bomb, and after much delay, the Russians became part of the International Atomic Energy Agency. They refused, however, to approve Eisenhower's "open skies" plan of mutual inspection of military establishments.

Next came the Vietnam problem, which had been growing more critical with each passing year. The French were tired of battling the Communist invaders, but Eisenhower knew that allowing Vietnam to fall would lead to the demise of Laos and Cambodia and the spread of Communist control. He was faced with the same type of decision he had made in Korea: either go all the way or accept the division. On July 21, 1954, the Geneva Agreement was signed, creating North and South Vietnam. Even though Eisenhower never sent troops to the area, he did all he could to support the Saigon government, including the sending of a thousand American "advisers."

Hardly had the ink dried on the treaty when the Communists began shelling Quemoy, an island off Formosa where Chiang Kai-shek and two million anti-Communist Chinese had fled in 1949. To preserve a free Formosa, Eisenhower took a hard line, asked Congress to support his stand, and let it be known he might use atomic weapons if provoked. The president's decisions met with severe criticism and verbal attacks from a war-weary country, but his strategy worked: The enemy invasion never took place.

The question of whether Eisenhower should run again was asked repeatedly from the moment he was elected. His heart attack of September 24, 1955, seemed to provide the answer, but he recovered from the attack quickly, reviving hopes. Then he required surgery for ileitis.

Another Landslide

The odds were that he wouldn't run, but his underlying stubborn streak, so typical of the Peaceful, and an OK from Mamie caused him to say, "Why not?" His slogan was "peace, prosperity, and progress." The campaign itself was far from peaceful; the Democrats launched a ferocious campaign against him. But in spite of the attacks made on him, Eisenhower stayed above the fray and won the day. He surpassed his own previous landslide.

We still liked Ike.

Eisenhower had yet to face the crisis that erupted when Egypt seized control of the Suez Canal, the American defense of the Lebanese government against a potential coup, the scare caused by the Russians' launch of the satellite *Sputnik*, the shooting down of an American U-2 spy plane over Russia, Castro's gaining control of Cuba, and the criticism for sending troops into Little Rock to enforce desegregation. He always did what he felt was right whether or not it was popular. As the old soldier, he marched straight ahead, played according to the rules, and always responded to the call of duty.

Contrary to Roosevelt and Truman, who were both Powerful and who kept their vice presidents at a long arm's length, Eisenhower was not concerned with power for its own sake, and he gave Richard Nixon authority in many areas. Eisenhower often asked for Nixon's opinion; he seated Nixon across from him at meetings of the cabinet and the National Security Council, and he sent him on international missions. Many historians believe Nixon was the best-utilized vice president of this century.

When Nixon campaigned against Kennedy, a young Democratic Catholic, logic made Nixon the winner. Eisenhower gave him his low-key blessing and even did some campaign appearances for him, but many thought Eisenhower's help was too little too late.

A New Look at the Old General

The American public loved the genial general, but when his time was up, they were ready to replace age with youth, wisdom with vigor, and a Peaceful personality with one of Popularity and Power.

Just as Truman was revived in the 1990s, so Dwight Eisenhower was brought back from eternity to grace the cover of *Time* on June 6, 1994. In uniform and with the look of painful responsibility on his face, Eisenhower appeared under the title, "The Man Who Beat Hitler."

With the fiftieth anniversary of D-Day at hand, historians took a new look at the old general. The invasion of Normandy became Eisenhower's plan, his war, his great crusade. "Only the Supreme Commander could give the order to attack," the article reminded us. With a favorable weather report in hand, Eisenhower had conferred with the other generals and admirals involved and gave the simple statement, "OK. Let's go."

In reviewing D-Day and the war that followed it, reporters refreshed our memories on the genial general who ran the military operation like a large business. What Churchill talked about, Eisenhower accomplished. He inspired loyalty in his troops because he treated those below him with respect and let them know he had faith in their ability to win the war.

In spite of criticism from British General Bernard Montgomery, who felt Ike was "no real director of thought, plans, energy, or direction," Eisenhower made the coalition work and became the man who beat Hitler.

Eisenhower represents the ultimate in the Peaceful personality, friendly and low-key with a single-minded purpose and a high level of motivation. Under the intensity of the circumstances, he became a forceful leader with a stubborn will and determination to win.

One of his greatest but unsung achievements was his ability to hold together the other Allied commanders, few of whom liked each other and all of whom thought they should have had his job. "Prima donnas, all of them!" he was once heard to say.

Add this ability to Eisenhower's need to keep in touch with a dying President Roosevelt, to humor Winston Churchill, and to not antagonize Josef Stalin and you begin to realize just what he achieved. Only a Peaceful personality could have held it all together, turned the other cheek, and completed the task at hand.

Now, with a fifty-year perspective, we can stand in awe of what the Peaceful man of war accomplished for our benefit. "He may not have handled his crusade in Europe perfectly because nothing in war goes precisely according to plan," the 1994 *Time* article stated. "But those who look back and say he could have defeated Hitler sooner are playing games with history and hindsight. In the tumult of battle with colleagues second guessing him and comrades dying by the hundreds every day, Dwight Eisenhower made decisions that won the war in Europe and established a peace that prevails today."

Dwight Eisenhower
Peaceful Personality

The following lists of strengths and weaknesses include words and phrases used in newspaper articles, magazines, books, television, and radio to describe President Eisenhower's Peaceful personality. Check the characteristics that also apply to you.

Strengths
___ Humble and modest
___ Courageous
___ Will of iron
___ Nerves of steel
___ Calm and casual
___ Honest
___ Good listener
___ Spoke cautiously

Weaknesses
___ Indecisive
___ Hesitant
___ Detached and inattentive
___ Content to reign, not rule
___ Drifting and dreaming
___ Avoided confrontations
___ Weak
___ Remote

___ Persuasive
___ Open to other opinions
___ Straightforward
___ Compromising
___ Willing to delegate
___ Candid yet tactful
___ Able to accept criticism
___ Engaging grin
___ Self-disciplined
___ Mantle of popularity
___ Affable
___ Aura of a hero
___ Negotiator
___ Reconciler
___ Soldier-statesman
___ Million-volt personality
___ Instinctive good will
___ Fundamental
___ Middle-of-the-roader
___ Consistent calmness
___ Quiet self-confidence
___ Apparent modesty
___ Fixity of purpose
___ **TOTAL**

___ Unsure and confused
___ Deceptive
___ Unyielding
___ A waif with a winning smile

___ **TOTAL**

Total of your presidential profile of Peaceful strengths and weaknesses: _____

Are You a Leader Like Eisenhower?

Probably few of you reading this book are generals, but many of you may identify with Eisenhower's Peaceful personality. Perhaps you didn't relate to Roosevelt's suave way with words or Truman's forceful personality. Instead you're the quiet type with no compulsive need to be in control. You get along well with people and adapt to whatever situation arises, and you know how to mediate in contentious circumstances as long as you're not closely involved.

You have a cool objectivity about you, and when you make a statement, it is usually right. You don't have a need to talk, direct, or correct, but that doesn't mean you don't have opinions. You know what's going on even though others sometimes feel you're tuned out. By nature, it's easier for you to be a follower or even to stay out of the way than it is for you to become a leader. "Let those other people take charge," is your modus operandi.

But you have traits that can produce effective leadership and can elevate you above some of the more obvious controllers. Eisenhower wasn't pushy, bossy, or belligerent. He went into the army to get an education and found he had qualities of leadership he had not thought about before. He was a good listener, open to all options, willing to compromise, and able to delegate responsibility. He considered all possibilities and made inoffensive, middle-of-the-road choices that united opposing factions.

Do you have these same skills? Can you keep your balance while those around you are losing theirs? You may never be called upon to beat Hitler, but you can be the consensus builder in your business; you can reach out the hand of peace when others are inciting rebellion. Your inoffensive, friendly, balanced nature is your greatest asset. Don't waste it.

Possibly you are your own worst enemy. Perhaps you weren't praised as the cutest or smartest child in the family, so you believed the lie that you didn't have as much talent as the others. Put that thought to rest and begin to search for the best in yourself. Start functioning in your strengths instead of wrapping up warmly in your weaknesses. Dare to go out in the cold and take a chance! A peaceful leader is the best kind.

11

CAMELOT

JOHN F. KENNEDY

President: 1961–1963
Personality: Popular-Powerful
Principle to Learn: Keep a sense of humor.

The obvious heir to the Eisenhower throne was Richard Nixon, his dutiful vice president. However, even though Eisenhower utilized Nixon as a busy vice president and included him in governmental strategy meetings more than Roosevelt did with Truman, he never appeared comfortable with Nixon. He couldn't bring himself to wholeheartedly endorse him, and he seemed to leave Nixon stranded on the front step of sociability.

At the beginning of the 1956 campaign, a Nixon friend journeyed with Nixon to the Eisenhower farm at Gettysburg for a major press conference kicking off the campaign. According to historian Theodore White in his book *The Making of the President,* "When the ceremony was over, President Eisenhower jovially beckoned to two of his cronies and invited them into the farmhouse with him. Nixon, standing beside his friend on the lawn, watched the little group enter the farmhouse, then turned to his friend and remarked bitterly, as the friend remembers, 'Do you know he's never asked me into that house yet.'"

Because Nixon saw himself as being left on his own, he wanted desperately to win the presidential plum all by himself. As a Perfect-Powerful, he was determined to do it right and show everyone he didn't need to ride on anyone's coattails.

Running against the vice president with his years of governmental experience was an unlikely opponent: John Fitzgerald Kennedy. In *The Making of the President,* White wrote, "He and his men had planned them a campaign that seemed utterly preposterous—to take the youngest Democratic candidate to offer himself in this century, of the minority Catholic faith, a man burdened by wealth and controversial family, relying on lieutenants scarcely more than boys, and make him president, one that would sweep out of the decade of the sixties America's past prejudices, the sediment of yesterday's politics, and make a new politics of the future."

Indeed a preposterous plan! Yet in Eisenhower's last years we'd seen the president age through heart and stomach problems and a small stroke. He was no longer quite the macho hero he had been after the war we were trying to forget. He was a general no longer in command of any troops. It was time for the old soldier and all he stood for to fade away.

Vigor and Vitality

In contrast, we were excited by Kennedy's youth; we loved the way he ran up the stairs to any waiting plane and turned at the top to wave a personal farewell to each one of us. We felt as if we were part of the family football games, and we all wanted to have fun and feel young again.

In *A Time of Passion—America 1960–1980,* Charles Morris explained, "Kennedy offered an attitude, a sense of omnicompetence that had been missing during the Eisenhower years, a style of problem solving—cool, pragmatic, non-ideological to be sure, but brimming with confidence that the world could be made a much better place than it was. . . .

"Kennedy was acutely aware that he was the adventurous alternative, and he and his entourage self-consciously adopted a coolly heroic mien."

The Kennedy-Nixon debate in 1960 gave a national television platform to the challenger on which he could demonstrate his charm and vigor, youth and vitality. Although the debate was short on significant substance, it was long on Irish style and wit.

In the wake of Peaceful Eisenhower, we were happy to hear the Kennedy war cry, "I will get the country moving again," and just enough of America fell into line.

Perfect Princess

With the close victory of Kennedy over Nixon, we packed up the depression and the wars in an old kit bag and, along with our new president, we smiled, smiled, smiled. We were transported into a fairyland.

Not only did we have a Popular-Powerful president, but we also had a Perfect princess. Following Eleanor, Bess, and Mamie—hardly a beauty pageant lineup—we had elegant, charming, classy Jackie. We watched everything she wore with covetous attention, and before we knew it, we were all wearing pillbox hats.

Jackie had an air of mystery about her, as every fairy princess must have, and she seemed solidly secure in any social situation. We watched her standing so elegantly next to the queen of England and the wives of assorted European prime ministers, and we were proud of her designer gowns that put the others to shame. We didn't even blame her when she took one look at the White House and knew it had to be done over before she could feel at home. Jackie dressed perfectly, charmed dignitaries perfectly, decorated perfectly, and entertained perfectly. She was Perfect, and we could understand why she didn't want to get messed up playing football with the family. No one thought of asking how much she spent on clothes or whether she borrowed her gowns from French designers.

The White House became Camelot, the setting for lavish state dinners and the stage for a continuous stream of Hollywood celebrities. The front door was always open, and there was a new style, elegance, and zest for life, or *joie de vivre*, as Jackie, who preferred French, would say.

When our princess tired of entertaining, she would vacation on the yacht of a Greek shipping tycoon, Aristotle Onassis, and we would pretend we were with her, cruising the Mediterranean Sea. In retrospect those little trips may not have been so innocent as we assumed they were, but we weren't looking for trouble. We trusted our princess and wanted to live happily ever after.

Sense of Humor

Jack Kennedy's presenting personality was Popular; he was fun-loving, charming, even intoxicating. He exuded sex appeal whether he was wearing a T-shirt or a tuxedo. He had a sense of humor, was a spontaneous storyteller, and was always the center of attention. He was able to look presidential without being pompous, and he could shine brightly while standing next to superstars.

In her book *Among Those Present*, Washington reporter Nancy Dickerson said Kennedy took "unabashed delight at being at the summit." His whole life had been spent in preparation for "the summit" even though his family had humble beginnings.

The president's great-grandfather, Patrick Kennedy, had emigrated from Ireland in 1848 during the potato famine, arriving in Boston penniless. He took a job as a barrel-maker and let his children know they had to work hard to overcome their immigrant background. In those days, Boston was a bastion of "Back Bay Brahmins," and the poor Irish newcomers were looked down upon as slaves. For employment they could find only menial tasks, and it soon became fashionable for the wealthy to have an Irish maid or two.

Patrick's second-generation son, P.J., couldn't accept his nonacceptance, and he determined to rise above his lowly status. He quit high school to go to work, first as a stevedore and later as a bartender. By hard work and with a good personality, he soon owned a saloon and later went into the wholesale whiskey business. He raised his family with the iron hand fathers exerted in those days, and no one dared buck his authority.

The fastest way for an Irishman to raise his community status was to enter politics. P.J., who was assumedly a Popular-Powerful, got into ward politics in East Boston, and soon people knew if you needed a favor, you went to see P.J. He was on the rising crest of ward-boss politics, and he was a natural.

He was elected to the state House of Representatives at the age of twenty-eight and later became a state senator. With these positions came a certain amount of local power and the chance to be respected as a leader.

P.J. never lost any opportunities to move up the Irish social ladder, and he taught his only son, Joseph, how to manipulate people and control cash. Joe made the rounds with his father and often saw how the one-man-one-vote rule meant little in Boston. He would attend the celebration parties for the victors and cheer for the citizen who had been able to vote the most times in one election.

The Irish felt because they were the underdogs that any tactic was ethical and any opponent fair game. P.J. often said, "There's only room for one at the top."

Young Joe grew up with an insatiable thirst to be that one. He wasn't content to be a hero only to the Irish; he wanted to move into the mainline society, a daring thought that was far beyond the dreams of his immigrant grandfather, Patrick. Joe embraced his father's willingness to work and inherited his zeal for making money. As a child he sold the pigeons he captured in the park and peddled candy on sightseeing boats.

A major step up the social ladder was Joe's acceptance into Harvard. He was not only the first Kennedy to go to college, but it was to *Harvard*. Nothing less would have done for him or his ambitious father. P.J. got Joe part of a sightseeing-bus franchise in Boston to help with the money needed to finance his education.

After graduation, with no experience but ample influence, young Joe was appointed as a state bank examiner. As a Powerful blend like his father but with the Perfect's grasp of figures, Joe grabbed this opportunity and became an immediate expert in Massachusetts banking. Where his father had the additional engaging Popular Irish personality, Joe was a Perfect who devoured facts and figures and didn't care as much about charm as about cash.

At age twenty-five he saved his father's own bank from devastating losses, then took it over and became the youngest bank president in Massachusetts. Joe's single-minded devotion to wealth and power brought him both of them plus the attention of the mayor's daughter, Rose. Mayor "HoneyFitz" Fitzgerald, a true Popular, was the epitome of the typical Irish politician; he was an extrovert who loved to sing, dance, give speeches, and attend wakes. Rose was socially above Joe, and he was aware of the advantages he received as the mayor's son-in-law.

While Rose raised the children, Joe learned more about banking, business, and the stock market. His keen sense for finance and his political contacts moved him ahead rapidly.

According to biographer Nancy Clinch in her book *The Kennedy Neurosis,* "Joe Kennedy amassed a personal fortune, and Boston became too small an arena for his monetary and social ambitions. Realizing that he could never crack the social snobbery of the New England aristocracy no matter how brilliant his business successes, he packed the family aboard a private railroad car in 1926 and moved to New York, where the Irish *nouveau riche* family might be more acceptable. Perhaps, too, he wished to succeed on his own away from his father's native city."

Lust for Success

Once settled into New York, Joe headed for the excitement of Wall Street and soon managed to move the market to his advantage. Conscience was never a deterrent to Joe's lust for success. When the stock market crashed in 1929, no one who knew Joseph Kennedy was surprised to find that he had cashed out a few weeks before. While others were jumping out of windows, Joe was counting his money. He bought into Hollywood film companies, owned a chain of theaters, and began his real estate business.

Through his political contacts and support of FDR, he became friends with James Roosevelt, and while on a trip with him to England just happened to pick up liquor franchises that appeared to be useless because of Prohibition. Months later Prohibition was repealed, and he was instantly in a very lucrative business. What cost him a hundred thousand dollars to set up in 1933 he later sold for eight million dollars.

Along with Joe's material successes came the deep desire for his children to achieve and receive the social acceptance that had eluded him. He taught them maxims such as "Don't play unless you can be captain," "Win at all costs," and "Second place is failure." When Joe told his children, "If you don't win, don't come home," he meant it.

With Joseph's success in the financial world and in Hollywood came his own allowance to himself to have relationships with women outside of marriage and to pass this permission on to his sons.

Pearl Buck wrote in *The Kennedy Women,* "Rose Kennedy showed for years a steadfast loyalty to her husband while he continued a long relationship with a beautiful film actress (supposedly Gloria Swanson). Outwardly she maintained a proud silence. But the inner struggle must have left its mark on the children. . . . The Kennedy men were never celebrated for their faithfulness to their wives, but their wives found it worthwhile to continue as wives and mothers."

Whatever it took to keep the Kennedys climbing up the ladder—looking the other way, tampering with the system, manipulating others—Joe was all for it. Since winning was all, he had to make his sons winners. After a lackluster term as ambassador to the Court of Saint James, Joe knew he'd gone as far as he could go in the political world, and he turned all of his single-minded attention to his sons.

He chose Joe Jr. to become his alter ego, and he personally groomed him to be president. Joe Jr. was set up as a model for his younger brothers, and he was allowed to discipline them if he felt the need. He actually was a junior version of Joe Sr., and the father looked to the future in excited expectation of the time when he could live the presidency vicariously through his son. In August of 1944 that dream came to a drastic end when Joe Jr. was killed on a dangerous mission in the war. As Pearl Buck described it in *The Kennedy Women*, "The son he had molded in his own image and on whom he had lavished the greatest care was dead. The news was like a sword thrust deep into Joseph Kennedy's heart, an agony from which he never fully recovered."

Charisma and Style

As with royalty, the presidential mantle fell on Jack, and his father quickly groomed him as the replacement, insisting he run for the U.S. House of Representatives from Massachusetts. Jack had looks, charisma, and style, so, with Joe's strategy, money, and influence, they made a winning team. Within two years of young Joe's death, Jack had been elected to national office.

Six years later Joe got the sweet taste of revenge when he pitted his son against Henry Cabot Lodge, the incumbent, aristocratic senator, and Jack won. Perfect-Powerful Joe managed every detail superbly, and the campaign went down in Massachusetts history as the most methodical and scientific ever. Joe's mind moved meticulously, and he managed a campaign that defied the odds and paved the way for his son's road to the presidency.

About Jack Kennedy's win over Lodge, Joe Kennedy said proudly, "When you've beaten him you've beaten the best. At last we've evened the score."

The Perfect part of Joe's personality believed the world was a jungle where only the fittest could survive. His Powerful side determined that the Kennedys would be the fittest and they would not only survive but be the big winners.

In his book *Man of the House,* Tip O'Neill, the former Democratic Speaker of the House, tells that old Joe Kennedy handed out cash-filled briefcases to politicians who would do his bidding and kept a careful watch on the progress of his sons. "The old man," O'Neill wrote, "even had a maid in Jack's Washington house who reported to him."

Although the Kennedys had little similarity with the Trumans and Eisenhowers, there were some parallels with the Roosevelts. While the Kennedys were considered *nouveau riche* versus the long heritage of the Roosevelts, both Franklin Roosevelt and Jack Kennedy were aristocratic, well educated, affirmed by their parents, financially secure, and able to fit into any strata of society. They were both rich men who were noted for their compassion for the poor. They both felt anything was possible once they were in control, and they were both Popular and Powerful.

Jack Kennedy's Powerful nature made him a fast mover in spite of back trouble; he was a quick and intellectual thinker and a highly competitive opponent. When he walked into a room, he had instant control, and he used his ability to manipulate skillfully and without effort. His father had put an emphasis on ability and the pursuit of excellence, and he endorsed these principles wholeheartedly.

In *The Making of the President,* Theodore White wrote, "John F. Kennedy, in his 14 years in politics, has had many servants, many aides, many helpers. As he has outgrown each level of operation, he has gently stripped off his earlier helpers and retained only those who could go on with him effectively to the next level. . . . In the personal Kennedy lexicon, no phrase is more damning than, 'He's a very common man,' or 'That's a very ordinary type.' Kennedy, elegant in dress, in phrase, in manner, has always required quality work." Although this statement was made before Kennedy's election, it was also to prove true while he was in office.

Kennedy was Popular and Powerful: He wanted it done his way *now*. His demand for excellence was often carried to the extreme. In *Among Those Present,* Nancy Dickerson said of his competitive nature that his motto should state, "Be tough and have trophies to prove it."

His quest for the best caused him to be impatient with those not meeting his standards, to be irritated by those who didn't move quickly, and to be annoyed by the "dummies of life" with whom he occasionally had to deal. His desire for action covered a fear of boredom, and he was uncomfortable whenever he was not in control. He looked in disdain at those who did not see it his way, and he could make people feel guilty if he caught them at a time when they were not doing anything. Today his *machismo* attitude might be looked upon as chauvinistic, but then women saw it as virility and strength.

Illusion versus Reality

How did Kennedy's personality pattern and his family background affect his limited time as president? When we look at the Popular part of his personality we see the inborn traits of making life fun, looking through rose-colored glasses, desiring the adulations of the crowd, and wanting everyone to love him. With these strengths came his overemphasis on illusions versus reality and his deceptive way of making us think he was accomplishing more than was actually going on. Indeed, many political pundits recognize that Kennedy's popularity is rooted more in fiction than reality. Author and political observer George Will, in his book *The New Season,* commented, "John Kennedy . . . became a permeating presence in the nation's imagination only after, and because of his death."

Kennedy's Powerful side gave him the innate drive for success so easily harnessed by both his father and mother, the need to be a winner and not a runner-up, and the obsession with masculine strength and control. When we add these personality patterns together and stuff them into a handsome, dynamic man with an abundance of charisma, we can see the product old Joe had created to package and sell to the American public.

Jack Kennedy came into power like a king, and in his efforts to get us moving again, he set aside his "first thousand days" to effect long-lasting results.

Quick Decisions

As with most politicians, Kennedy found that exciting change looks easier from the outside than it becomes when faced with the reality of compromise and Congress. Since he came into office as a hero, Jack wanted to act like one, and when it was suggested that he help a group of Cuban exiles invade their homeland, he had to give the idea serious consideration. The CIA had made the plans, and the Joint Chiefs of Staff were willing to act. The quick invasion of an apparently Communist country by its own native exiles seeking to be restored sounded like movie stuff and appeared to have few risks. If, in spite of careful planning, the operation failed, it would not be a major defeat. Kennedy rationalized optimistically, "If we have to get rid of these eight hundred men it is much better to dump them in Cuba than in the United States."

The invasion failed miserably and Castro's forces rounded up not eight hundred men but approximately twelve hundred to fifteen hundred exiled Cubans. "Kennedy had been indecisive, neither intervening to call off the attempt nor providing the support that would have been necessary for success."[1]

"Cyrus Sulzberger, the *New York Times* columnist, lamented that the United States 'looked like fools to our friends, rascals to our enemies, and incompetents to the rest.' It was hardly an auspicious way for the new president to demonstrate his mastery of foreign policy."[2]

In his book *Right from the Beginning,* columnist Pat Buchanan expressed the opinion of many Americans: "The Bay of Pigs disaster had shown a hesitancy, a timidity, and a confusion on the part of President Kennedy, in the use of military power, that were ominous. Strike hard, or not at all, was among the oldest of military maxims. That is the way America had fought and won World War II."

Shoot for the Moon

Kennedy seemed better at winning elections than at winning wars. His Irish luck had failed, and he needed to turn over a whole new four-leaf clover. New adventure came in response to the first manned orbital space flight of Yuri Gagarin launched by the Russians the same week as the Bay of Pigs fiasco. Kennedy sent a memo to Lyndon Johnson, head of the National Space Council, and asked if we could go to the moon and how much it would cost. The answer of cost didn't seem to matter, and Kennedy announced his all-out space program in May of 1961. We had little time to mourn the Bay of Pigs as our attention was diverted in a flurry of activity to reach the moon: "Fly me to the moon!"

Despite this excitement, a year after the Bay of Pigs it appeared that Kennedy's honeymoon was beginning to wane. "Khrushchev posed another challenge, this time not on the exposed periphery of American power but near its heart, ninety miles off the coast of Florida. Kennedy's unwillingness to commit the forces necessary to overthrow Castro and his acquiescence in the Berlin Wall seemed to signify a failure of will, and the Russians apparently reasoned that they could install missiles in Cuba with relative impunity," wrote George Brown Tindall in *America, A Narrative History.*

This time Khrushchev underestimated Kennedy. Our president, determined to be Powerful, insisted that the Soviets remove their missiles. Khrushchev agreed and entered into an agreement to remove the missiles in return for an American commitment not to invade Cuba.

On March 5, 1987, twenty-five years after the crisis, a group of former Kennedy advisers met for a class reunion to relive the two weeks of the Cuban missile crisis. Sponsored by Harvard University's John F. Kennedy School of Government, the gathering included former Secretary of Defense Robert McNamara, presidential aides Theodore Sorenson and Arthur Schlesinger, former Undersecretary of State George Ball, and many others whose purpose was to discuss the events in retrospect and see how they might bear upon current crises. On August 30, 1987, the *New York Times* reviewed the need for this meeting, stating about the missile crisis, "Perhaps no event since World War II so preoccupies the makers and critics of foreign policy as those '13 days' when the world seemed to tremble on the brink of nuclear apocalypse."

Crisis-Prone

Kennedy seemed crisis-prone as he bounced from problems ranging from the Bay of Pigs to Berlin to the space program to missiles in less than two years. And behind these up-front problems was the boiling question of Vietnam. Presidents Roosevelt and Truman had been involved in the determination of whether France should be in control of this misbegotten country. From 1946 through 1954, the United States had poured some two billion dollars into France's support of the country, only to have the Communists defeat the French in May 1954.

Peaceful Eisenhower, with support from Congress and then-Senator John Kennedy, refused to intervene, and a line was drawn between South and North Vietnam. We were willing to aid South Vietnam, and we sent Ngo Dinh Diem from this country to be the temporary leader. He must have been a Powerful person because he loved power and he took over for good. He had no interest in elections, and his regime became about as repressive as Communist leader Ho Chi Minh's government was in North Vietnam.

Even though our support was conditional on fair, democratic elections that never happened, we looked the other way and continued contributing to the Diem government while growing numbers of guerrillas were opposing the regime.

Kennedy first tried for a truce in Laos, sent troops into Thailand, and then looked at Vietnam. Had no action been taken, the same North Vietnamese that are now in control probably would have won—only it would have been sooner and without so many American losses. But at the time, "counterinsurgency," or limited intervention, seemed to be the direction.

From 1961 through 1963, American involvement grew from 2000 men to 15,500. On November 1, 1963, Diem was captured and shot by a military junta that seized control of Saigon. Three weeks later Kennedy was assassinated.

We will never know whether the future of Vietnam would have been different if Kennedy had lived; instead the seemingly endless war became the burden and ultimately the downfall of the next president, Lyndon Johnson.

In his 1984 book, *America, A Narrative History,* Clarence B. Carsen summed up the general belief about Kennedy's administration. "Kennedy had not been a very effective president during his first two-and-a-half years or so. He had not been able to get what he reckoned to be his major legislation through a [friendly] Democratic Congress. His administration had in general been crisis-ridden. Foreign action, if any, tended to be decided in the midst of crisis, which might not have occurred if his policy had been known in advance."

The Aura of Leadership

In retrospect, every president could have done better, but surely Kennedy, young, Popular and Powerful, was faced with a series of crises that kept him from establishing a sound legacy. But we liked his looks, his charm, and his aura of leadership. As he put out fires around the world, we watched the parties the Kennedys hosted and the glamour of the family.

We weren't analyzing his personality as a subject at the time, but in retrospect we can see two important traits that exemplified Kennedy's aura of leadership: his sense of humor no matter what the situation and his ability to bring out the best in others. He didn't waste time on those he considered losers, but he was willing to put his time and effort into the future of those he deemed to have potential. He didn't keep secrets of success; he shared them. He gave away what he had and kept smiling that smile that magnetized men and women alike.

Biographer Richard Reeves called Kennedy a "surpassing cultural figure" and compared him to an artist. "Kennedy painted with words and images and other people's lives, squeezing people and perceptions like tubes of paint, gently or brutally, changing millions of times. He focused

Americans in the directions that truly mattered—toward active citizenship, toward the joy of life itself."[3]

As a country, we let him pull us to happy-ever-after land because we wanted to believe. We were willing to overlook his mistakes because he'd given us a vicarious vision of royalty, but suddenly it was over. Our hero was gone, murdered before our eyes. Reality hit hard.

Shortly after Kennedy's death in November 1963 Jacquelyn Kennedy, speaking to a reporter, said, "At night we would play records, and the song he loved most came from a current Broadway hit, *Camelot,* based on the legends of King Arthur: 'Don't let it be forgot, that once there was a spot, for one brief shining moment, that was known as Camelot'—and then she concluded wistfully, 'and it will never be that way again.'"[4]

Dignity in Death

Jackie was right. Life has never been that way again. Our king and queen had shown us how to live, and then Jackie showed us how to grieve. At only thirty-four years of age she gave us dignity in death, grace in gruesome circumstances. Again and again we watched the replay of the shooting, Jackie cradling her husband's head as they sped to the hospital. We sat in shock by our TV sets as she stood beside Lyndon Johnson as he took the oath of office. All of us who watched those scenes remember her blood-soaked pink suit, and we remember her answer when aides suggested she change clothes. "Let them see what they've done to Jack," she said simply. And we saw.

We watched as our queen walked down the broad avenues of Washington in the funeral cortege. Even then she set the style for what the grieving widow should wear as she held her head high under a black veil that covered her face and floated gently in the soft November breeze. We cried as Jackie knelt in the Capitol rotunda with her daughter, Caroline, and kissed the coffin of her husband. We ached as little John-John saluted his father's casket after the funeral. A British journalist wrote about the funeral, "Jacquelyn Kennedy has today given her country the one thing it has always lacked, and that is majesty."[5]

Before packing and leaving the White House, Jackie oversaw the answering of 800,000 sympathy letters. In a note to one friend, she wrote, "So now he is a legend when he would have preferred to be a man."[6]

Lady of Sorrows

Jackie became a legend of style and class, a perpetual widow, our "lady of sorrows." Women continued to watch everything she did and copy everything she wore. Our worship came to an unhappy halt five years after she became a widow when she married Aristotle Onassis. Although he was rich and had forty-two telephones on his yacht, he just didn't look right for Jackie. He was short, unromantic, and some of us thought he was downright homely. Money didn't make him Prince Charming. It took us a while to forgive Jackie; even the forty-two million dollars she received as a divorce settlement seemed tainted. We tried to forget that marriage and go back to the memories we admired. We wondered why she went to work editing books when she had all that money, but it did show us she had not lost the common touch and it was fitting in the field of quality literature on the arts and politics. With her Perfect personality, Jackie "had a taste that made you strive to keep up," said Peter Kruzan, Doubleday Publishing Company's art director, who worked with Jackie for five years. "The product had to be absolutely correct. She was always tuned in to the overall visual impact. She had a classical point of view, but it was always couched in terms of the new and different."[7]

Jackie always did what was right and she did it with class. She determined to raise her children well and while other young Kennedys were falling from grace, Caroline and John Jr. grew up to be normal, attractive adults with obvious respect for their mother.

Beautiful Silence

No one was ready for the news that Jackie had lymphoma, and when we heard it in February 1994 we were sure that somehow money could buy a cure. But it couldn't, and Jackie died with the same style and courage with which she lived. A New York schoolteacher standing outside Jackie's apartment was heard to say, "I thought she would be like Guinevere. I thought she would ride off, in her beautiful silence, and never die."

A tourist in mourning held up a sign that said, "Camelot will be united in heaven."

For many of us, the passing of Jackie is the end of an era, an era when it was positive to be polite and acceptable to have manners. Was Jackie the last woman we Americans could idolize? In a time when the real royals are reeking with scandal, when Madonna's picture book gives pornography a bad name, and when Roseanne plunges crudity and crassness to new lows, we're going to miss Jackie.

"We're not allowed to believe fairy tales anymore," wrote Sarah Crighton. "And we demand so much from women now; no one woman can ever embody all our dreams. But we fell in love with Jackie in a simpler time. When we wanted to grow up to be princesses, she was our princess. And later when we wanted to be independent, she was independent. And she was always one step ahead, and one step better. She made it all look so easy, when for the rest of women it always seemed so hard. . . . We all want to live in a fairy tale, sometimes."[8]

There was a mystique about Jackie that fascinated us all, her fragile form, her misty silence, her symbol of serenity in a vanishing era.

"She was a last link to a certain kind of past, and that is part, only part, of why we mourn so," presidential speech writer Peggy Noonan wrote. "Jackie Kennedy *symbolized*—she was a connection to a time, to an old America that was more dignified, more private, an America in which standards were higher and clearer and elegance meant something, a time when elegance was a kind of statement, a way of dressing up the world, and so a generous act. She had manners, the kind that spring from a certain moral view—that you do tribute to the world and the people in it by being kind and showing respect, by sending the note and the flowers, by being loyal, and cheering a friend. She was a living reminder in the age of Oprah that personal dignity is always, still, an option, a choice that is open to you. She was, really, the last aristocrat. Few people get to symbolize a world but she did, and that world is receding, and we know it and mourn that too."[9]

Yes, we mourn what could have been, we grieve for what we no longer have, "a spot, for one brief shining moment, that was known as Camelot."

John F. Kennedy
Popular-Powerful Personality

The following lists of strengths and weaknesses include words and phrases used in newspaper articles, magazines, books, television, and radio to describe President Kennedy's personality, a combination of Popular and Powerful traits. Check the characteristics that also apply to you.

Popular Personality

Strengths
___ Fairy-tale image
___ Optimistic and outgoing
___ Charming and regal
___ Storyteller extraordinaire
___ Sense of humor
___ Center of attention
___ Intoxicating like champagne
___ Open and hospitable
___ Surprising and innovative
___ Captivating to women
___ Aura of glamour
___ Dramatic
___ Too good to be true
___ Encouraging
___ Willing to share
___ **TOTAL**

Weaknesses
___ Aching for greatness
___ Needed to be a hero
___ Afraid of boredom
___ Shows off
___ Womanizer
___ Pseudo-hero
___ Unfaithful
___ Too shallow
___ **TOTAL**

Powerful Personality

Strengths
___ Omnicompetent
___ Competitive
___ Winning is everything
___ Be tough and win trophies
___ Fast-moving
___ Quick and active
___ Used power to control
___ Everything is possible
___ Emphasis on ability
___ Courageous
___ Youthful and dynamic
___ Pragmatic
___ Adventurous
___ Heroic
___ Full of vigor and vitality
___ **TOTAL**

Weaknesses
___ Made unreasonable demands
___ Overwhelming ambition
___ Drive to heroic gratification
___ Indifferent to danger
___ Impatient
___ Manipulated by money
___ Uncomfortable when not
     in control
___ Irritable
___ Male chauvinist
___ Made everyone keep moving
___ Instilled guilt
___ Reckless and impulsive
___ Domineering
___ **TOTAL**

Total of your presidential profile of Popular-Powerful strengths and weaknesses: _____

Are You a Leader Like Kennedy?

Few of us have the magnetism of John Kennedy, and even fewer have his money, but we can learn from his brief time as president. In the previous lists if you found expressions about Kennedy that also could have been said about you, be grateful! These are the magic ingredients for leadership.

Natural charm and an inborn sense of humor are traits that can't be taught or bought. When people enjoy being with you and see that you are having more fun in life than others are, they will be anxious to follow you. They respond to your enthusiasm, energy, and excitement. They want to be like you, look like you, and dress like you. What an awesome responsibility you have not to lead these dedicated people in the wrong direction!

It is vitally important for you to gain depth in your role of leadership and follow through on what you say you'll do. Charm alone is not enough to sustain long-term respect.

Those who attract others easily often get carried away with their popularity and build monuments to themselves. Kennedy could easily have done this, but instead he put his focus on others. He shared what he knew, and he encouraged others to achieve. Successful leaders don't hide their secret ingredients. They give them out to those willing and anxious to learn.

If you have the outgoing and optimistic nature of the Popular personality and also the Power to achieve, you, too, could be president. But it takes discipline to exert leadership worthy of following, and it takes desire and drive to even dare to try. When Kennedy was asked how he had the nerve to run for president of the United States, he replied, "I looked at the others who were considering running and said to myself, 'Why not?'"

Ask yourself, "Why not?" The world is crying out for leadership. Why not you? If you have the charisma of the Popular personality and the drive of the Powerful, you have the necessary abilities to lead.

Is something holding you back? Have you perhaps extended yourself too far? Are you in charge of so many things you can't do any of them well? Are you physically exhausted from trying to do too much? Do you overwhelm others? Do people back up when you approach? Do you need to be in charge to be happy? If your answers are yes, perhaps you should reevaluate your time commitments and your style of leadership. Are you filling needs in the lives of others or are you grabbing for authority to fill a gap in your own life? What is your reason for being center stage? When it's to gratify your own ego, people will soon see that. In an era full of imitations, the public is desperate for the "real thing." Why not you?

12

"ALL THE WAY WITH LBJ"

LYNDON JOHNSON

President: 1963–1969
Personality: Powerful-Popular
Principle to Learn: Be prepared.

There was never any doubt that Lyndon Johnson wanted to be president, but he had not expected to receive the title in such a tragic way. A young Popular-Powerful president had been assassinated, and Lyndon was called up to fill his shoes. He had been preparing for this role for years; he'd done his homework, and he was ready. He'd been an effective Senate majority leader, and he was confident that when he got in control of any situation he could make things happen. He always had.

Like Kennedy, LBJ had an outgoing, optimistic personality but he was first Powerful with some of the Popular added on. However, there was a difference in the manifestation of Johnson's personality, in his childhood background, and in his concept of self-worth. While Kennedy had come from wealthy parents, had a classical education, and was comfortable with prince or pauper, Johnson had not been so privileged. His roots were in the soil, and in spite of his brash behavior, he was insecure underneath. Johnson was sensitive when people made fun of his Texas background, called him a cowboy, or ridiculed his accent. Where Kennedy always seemed to hide his temperament weaknesses from public view by covering his impatience and intolerance for incompetence with a cloak of charisma, Johnson couldn't find a place big enough in all of Texas to encase his enormous ego or hold down his anger when things didn't go his way.

In 1948 when he ran for the Senate, he daringly broadcast his words to the people while whirling around in a helicopter. Because of his known love for dramatic oratory—plus the effect of the circling blades of the helicopter—his machine was dubbed the "Johnson City Windmill."

Climbing the Stepladder to Power

LBJ was his own Horatio Alger story. From the time he was a child he wanted to be in charge, and he was constantly convincing others that his way was the right way. He could see early on that politics was the stepladder to power, and he wanted to spend as little time as possible on each rung.

He married his Lady Bird, who came from a well-feathered nest, and she became a Perfect counterbalance for his volatile Powerful personality. Lady Bird was genuinely gracious in a more homespun way than was Jackie, with her regal style of entertaining. For years at their Texas ranch, Lady Bird had been hospitable to any number of people at any time, with or without advance notice, for when Lyndon said, "Y'all come," he really meant you *all*.

As LBJ was flamboyant, Lady Bird was disciplined and controlled, organized and efficient. As he was Popular, she was willing to give him center stage. As he needed to be the life of the party and carry on monologues to get his message across, she was willing to listen attentively and act as if she'd never heard that line before. As he was prone to exaggeration and had a habitual disregard for the truth, she did her homework, knew her facts, and talked intelligently.

When LBJ was chosen to be Kennedy's vice president, he knew it was not because Kennedy liked him but because Johnson provided balance to the presidential ticket. Kennedy was young and new to national politics; Lyndon had been around forever and had immeasurable influence in Congress. Jack was Eastern Establishment; Lyndon was Texas Southern, complete with drawl.

Even though LBJ had not wanted to be in second place, he was so eager for increased power that he was willing to accept the vice presidency. He felt he would have a strong influence on the new Democratic team, and he often said, "Power is where power goes."

But when Johnson tried to exert power with the young Kennedys and their friends, he found they didn't care for his suggestions; he soon had to admit to himself that he just didn't fit in. Disappointed but undaunted, he set out to design his office in a way to denote power. His choice was a spacious suite so lavishly decorated that it was soon nicknamed the Taj Mahal. Kennedy's youthful team made sport of him behind his broad back, and they took lightly the list of demanding prerogatives he sent to the president. He was always seeking moments when he could be in front, and he desperately wanted to be both Powerful and Popular. He grabbed on to the authority that came with being head of the space agency, and he was his true flamboyant self when riding in an open car down Broadway with astronaut John Glenn.

The Gentle Arm-twister

Because his opinion was not asked for by the young president and he was not allowed to be closely in tune with the inner circle, LBJ set up his own fiefdom in the Taj Mahal. This separation of power kept him from knowing what was really going on, and when Kennedy was shot LBJ was shocked, sympathetic—and released.

After an appropriate time of mourning, Johnson dared to come into his own bigger-than-life image. He was a born politician who knew how to twist arms quietly and give people "the Johnson treatment." He would tell each one, "You are a very important person to me, and I need your help now."

He was a born power broker; he knew how to use his personal contacts for gain and when to call in his markers. He had used this skill with uncanny results in the Senate. He was also a born storyteller, had a legendary charm and wit, and was exhilarated into brilliance by adoring crowds. He would give a lecture on anything to anyone at anyplace at the drop of a ten-gallon hat.

Reporter Nancy Dickerson, who knew Johnson well, praised him for his speaking skills. She watched him become "a full-blown orator," the "image of a Messianic preacher." She said he, above all, made "talk an art." How every Popular person wishes these words could be said of him or her!

Ridicule and Rejection

In their early days in the White House, the Johnsons entertained Texas-style until the press made fun of their ranch beans and quipped that the rose garden had been turned into a barbecue pit. While LBJ liked to kid with others, he had a thin skin when anyone made fun of him.

Popular people have a desperate need to be loved by all, and they can't bear to think there's anyone who doesn't like them. Powerful people try to hold on to control strongly enough that no one will dare turn against them. Johnson, being a bountiful blend of the two, resented any negative comments. He would become like a hurt little boy when the press took him on, saying sadly, "I'm the only president they've got."

For all of Johnson's formidable ego and his apparent confidence in himself, he was always insecure with his Texas origins and his lack of prestigious credentials. He covered his concerns with his outgoing Popular personality, and because he was uncomfortable when not in control, he seized every opportunity to be in charge and to exert his energetic and sometimes exhausting power.

Jimmy Carter once said of him, "Johnson never felt secure inside, especially around the Eastern Establishment—the professors, experts, writers and media people—and that's why they got him in the end."

Nancy Dickerson suggested that LBJ felt anyone's rejection of him or his policies denoted a lack of patriotism. With LBJ, everything was black or white; you were either for him or against him. As a correspondent assigned to the White House, Dickerson said in her book, *Among Those Present,* that Johnson made three mistakes with the press that came to haunt him.

1. He showered the reporters with gifts as a manner of control. They took it to mean that if they'd play the game by his rules, they'd get along just fine. However, "LBJ's lack of subtlety backfired. His blatant attempts to influence sometimes forced reporters into being overly critical just to preserve their independence."

2. He toyed with the press by not telling the whole truth, a lifetime habit that he did not see as dishonesty. He twisted words to imply meaning that wasn't correct and then was relieved when the press drew their own wrong conclusions.

3. He tried to manipulate press conferences by planting questions, and when the reporters didn't come through with the topics he wanted, he berated them.

This combination of press control by the president was sufficiently upsetting to the reporters to cause them to ridicule his background, his lack of style, and his Texas accent. For a man who dearly wished to be loved, he turned the most vocal force in the country against him.

Johnson also loved to have his picture taken, and his craving for attention sometimes caused his better judgment to go astray. In 1963, after a gallbladder and kidney-stone operation, he happily lifted his shirt to show off his scar for the photographers. The resulting picture that spread across the nation was so offensive it produced a cry of outrage. He laid himself out for further ridicule and rejection when he offered his excised gallstones to the Smithsonian Institute and it refused to display them. In 1964 he allowed himself to be photographed while lifting his pet beagle, named Her, off the ground by her ears, causing animal lovers across the land to protest loudly.

Another Arm's-Length Vice President

When it was time for Lyndon to choose a vice president to run with him in 1964, he stalled and teased many potential candidates to draw out the procedure and keep the country in suspense. He believed in any tactic that would keep him on the front page.

Ultimately, he selected Horatio Hubert Humphrey, who felt he deserved to be president, but in lieu of that option he was willing to accept second place, as Johnson himself had done when Kennedy had extended the offer. Humphrey was a true Popular, and whatever came in his ears went out his mouth without staying around long enough to ferment. He always looked wide-eyed and innocent, and he had a quick answer for every question—not necessarily based on fact. Neither HHH nor LBJ ever let the truth stand in the way of a good story.

Once, when asked about his exuberance in talking endlessly on any topic, Humphrey replied, "I do—I like every subject. I can't help it—it's just glands."

And so it was with both Humphrey and his boss. The vice president's constant chatter annoyed LBJ, who no doubt missed their similarities, and he quipped about Humphrey, "If I could only breed him to Calvin Coolidge."

Although Johnson had resented Kennedy's excluding him when he was vice president, he evidently didn't learn much from this neglect because he kept gregarious and garrulous Hubert at arm's length. Before the president would accept Humphrey, he had to pledge absolute loyalty and agree never to disagree. He was to try to keep his mouth shut, never upstage Lyndon, and avoid making headlines. "No deviation from administration policy would be tolerated."[1] When Humphrey later dared oppose the bombing of Vietnam, he was excluded from Johnson's inner circle as punishment.

Isn't it amazing that the cloak of authority we consider unacceptable when others are wearing it we put on quickly when we get to sit in their chair!

During the 1964 campaign, opponent Powerful Barry Goldwater, viewing the war of attrition in Vietnam, called for us to go in there and finish off the enemy. His tough talk branded him as an incendiary warmonger, and LBJ with his political instincts capitalized on this view of Goldwater and appeared to be the peace candidate. After all, the last thing anyone wanted was a real war.

Then, on August 4, 1964, in the midst of the presidential campaign, North Vietnam was reported to be attacking U.S. warships in the Gulf of Tonkin, and Johnson made his most famous speech, calling for retaliation. This moving message led to the Gulf of Tonkin Resolution, granting Johnson freedom to act in South Vietnam. His lust for power seized this aggressive attack as a reason to accelerate the nonwar.

Imagine Goldwater's emotions as he was defeated in a landslide election while being labeled trigger-happy by a president who was sending troops to an undeclared war and launching air strikes against the enemy.

As the situation in Vietnam worsened, civil rights issues boiled, and the hippies and flower children experimented with new drugs, Johnson, after an overwhelming win, found himself in a no-win position. His Powerful nature recoiled at anything he couldn't control, and his Popular personality was infuriated by any kind of criticism. He wanted obedience and adoration, and he was getting neither.

In an article in the November 1976 *Ladies Home Journal,* political writer Doris Kearns Goodwin said of this situation, "Even though one could not have predicted the disaster of Vietnam, it would have been possible to foresee LBJ's difficulty in dealing with any situation that would not yield to his enormous talents for persuasion and compromise."

By March 1968, President Johnson finally had to admit to himself that he couldn't get out of Vietnam. He tried his Popular best to get the people to go along with him, but his most-pleading exhortations fell on deaf ears and he lost face with the friends who had reelected him in faith that he would put out the fires. His natural optimism faded away, and his craving for positive attention went unfed. He felt deserted and unloved.

In *Among Those Present,* Nancy Dickerson wrote, "He went into the White House thinking that he could do better than anyone else; he left knowing that only another president could end the war. . . . No man could have tried harder."

LBJ believed anything is possible if you just work hard enough. When he couldn't end the Vietnam War, his life-long work ethic fell apart. He was so proud of the Great Society he was creating out of the fragments of the New Frontier, and he couldn't believe people wouldn't accept his strengths and overlook his weaknesses.

Bob Pierpoint of CBS wrote, "Johnson was probably the most qualified president I've covered. He really understood how the American system should work. He was colorful and unpredictable. He had experience and background, knew all the inside angles. But he couldn't work himself out of the Vietnam war. He had three different press secretaries —George Reedy, Bill Moyers, George Christian—all good, but they couldn't prevent Johnson from putting his foot in it."[2]

A Powerful who has no power and a Popular who is no longer popular become depressed. The photographers showed a Johnson who was drowning in despondency. One captioned a picture of a downhearted Johnson, "You love me or I'll leave."

Although he wanted another term, Johnson couldn't stand the thought of a possible defeat, so he decided not to run. He accepted the typical Powerful theory, "If you're not sure you'll win the game, it's better not to play."

He was a man whose strengths, when carried to extremes, became weaknesses. Because of his underlying insecurity, he forced himself to be more than charming, more than dynamic, more than successful. He became somewhat of an exaggeration of himself. FDR and JFK each functioned as about 50 percent Popular and 50 percent Powerful, but LBJ came across as 100 percent of each. His overwhelming personality made him a 200 percent man. There was a lot of Lyndon!

When Strengths Become Weaknesses

With each personality type, there is the possibility that the strengths can go too far and become weaknesses. For example, the Perfects are addicted to the facts; their greatest strength is that they delve deeply into every subject, analyze every alternative, push for perfection, and deliberate every decision. Carried to an extreme, however, they become dulled by details; they also tend to be too deep to be understood, they nitpick others to perform better, and they easily become depressed when things aren't perfect.

Another personality type, the Peacefuls like Eisenhower, wouldn't hurt a soul. One of the Peacefuls' greatest strengths is the natural ability to heal the wounded and bring hope to the downtrodden. They avoid any kind of trouble and will withdraw rather than take a chance of stepping on anybody's toes. Carried to an extreme, though, Peacefuls become so passive as to be colorless, so indecisive as to appear weak.

In contrast, the Populars' greatest strength is the ability to talk anywhere at anytime on any subject with or without information. Carried to an extreme, Populars such as LBJ talk all the time, interrupting others on subjects they know little about, spouting proclamations that may bear only a distant relationship to the truth.

Powerfuls are also born leaders; as LBJ did when Kennedy was assassinated, Powerfuls can take charge of any group without having read the bylaws, make instant decisions without research, and correct the mistakes of the inept without asking for input. These excellent abilities, when carried to extremes, make the Powerfuls appear bossy and arrogant and make others feel indecisive and weak. These tendencies also cause the Powerfuls to take control of situations that are none of their business, leaving a trail of wounded victims in their wake.

As we look at the life of Richard Nixon in the next chapter, we will see another example of a man whose greatest strengths ultimately became his weaknesses.

Lyndon B. Johnson
Powerful-Popular Personality

The following lists of strengths and weaknesses include words and phrases used in newspaper articles, magazines, books, television, and radio to describe President Johnson's personality, a combination of Powerful and Popular traits. Check the characteristics that also apply to you.

Powerful Personality

Strengths

___ Gave "the Johnson treatment"
___ Always in charge
___ Stood "tall in the saddle"
___ Wanted to run everything
___ Power-balancer
___ Constantly convincing others
___ Went first class
___ Liked to exhort the masses
___ Just like a fox
___ Took instant control

___ **TOTAL**

Weaknesses

___ Insisted on total
    commitment
___ Irritated by delays
___ Crude wheeler-dealer
___ Two-faced
___ Demanding of others
___ Exhausting to be with
___ Bossy and bragging
___ Had temper tantrums
___ Infuriated by critics
___ Formidable foe
___ Restless volcano
___ Manipulative
___ Impulsive

___ **TOTAL**

Popular Personality

Strengths

___ Grandiose style
___ Running monologue
___ Legendary charm
___ Open, friendly, generous
___ Natural host
___ Loved uniforms and
    costumes
___ Full of surprises
___ Made talk an art

Weaknesses

___ Enormous ego
___ Blatant demonstrations
___ Largest press badge
___ Disregard for truth
___ Prone to exaggeration
___ Needed an audience
___ Insecure with Texas
    background
___ Loud and garrulous

___ Messianic preacher
___ Constantly lecturing
___ Gabbing vigorously
___ Liked to have his
      picture taken
___ Loved attention
___ **TOTAL**

___ Twisted words to suit
___ Exasperated by
      interruptions
___ Desperate need for love

___ **TOTAL**

Total of your presidential profile of Powerful-Popular strengths and weaknesses: _____

Are You a Leader Like Johnson?

"Be ready for the surprise visits of God," wrote Oswald Chambers. "A ready person never needs to get ready. Think of the time we waste trying to get ready when God has called."[3]

Getting ready is good advice for all of us, and yet so many of us, especially the Powerful and Popular personalities, don't want to spend time preparing for something that may not happen. Johnson got ready. His whole life was built around controlling today and preparing for tomorrow. As Shakespeare said, "Some are born great, some achieve greatness, and some have greatness thrust upon them."

LBJ had already achieved stature in the Senate, but by the death of Kennedy he had permanent greatness thrust upon him. Who knows if he could have made it on his own?

Are we ready to have greatness thrust upon us? In getting ready, we have to question our motives. Do we want success for our own ego, or do we want to exercise our gifts for the benefit of others?

When achieving becomes a necessity for our own self-worth, we have to ask ourselves, Why? Where do our insecurities come from? Our poor upbringing, our lack of education, our association with people from classier backgrounds? Secure individuals don't *need* to be in charge, don't *need* to be on center stage, don't *need* to always be right, don't *need* to have the last word. Leadership based on our own emotional needs will ultimately fail.

Did you check off many of Johnson's strengths as being applicable to yourself? How about his weaknesses? Do you have a compulsive need to be in charge? Do you have to be more prepared and smarter than everyone else to feel good about yourself?

If you are ready and if your motives are pure, watch out for one tendency that could bring about your downfall. Because the Populars want everyone to love them and the Powerfuls are sure they are right, this combination of personality finds it close to unbearable to cope with criticism.

How about you?

Are you open to the valued opinions of others? Can you step back and look at yourself objectively rejoicing in your strengths and working to overcome your weaknesses? Being prepared for the big opportunity is essential for success, but only someone who is willing to accept and work on his or her weak points can stay on top. Learn to listen today from LBJ.

13

KNOWLEDGE IS POWER

RICHARD NIXON

President: 1969–1974
Personality: Perfect-Powerful
Principle to Learn: Know more than the others.

There was a poignant sadness about the death of Richard Nixon in 1994. With all of his exceptional accomplishments and his brilliant mind, he was never quite able to wash away the stain of Watergate. In his years as an ex-president he was always willing to give wise counsel to those in the position he had been forced to vacate, no matter what their party or opinion.

Like several presidents, Nixon had come from humble beginnings and had to work hard to become somebody. Like all the presidents, he came into the presidency on his strengths and left on his weaknesses.

Nixon was an exceptional example of the deep, analytical perfectionist with an underlying need for control; his strengths and weaknesses were both exaggerated because of a frustrating childhood of insecurity. His father, Frank Nixon, was a man who wanted to succeed but never could pull all of life together at one time. He struggled with various occupations as diverse as carpentry, storekeeping, and operating a trolley car. He also struggled with the mental image he had of himself as the typical male head of the household. Father Frank was no more successful in shepherding a family than in running a business, and his failure factor frustrated him into bursts of anger and violence. He learned that a temper tantrum taught all those around him to toe the line, and he controlled his family by intimidation.

Because he could not deal consciously with his occasional feelings of childhood rebellion, young Richard buried his emotions. This repression satisfied his Perfect nature, which did not want to face the facts that he was surrounded by imperfection, legalism, uncertainties, rejection, and the death of two brothers. His Powerful personality rose to take control of his life. He suppressed grief and guilt and was determined to succeed. His strong aggressive impulses were unacceptable to his domineering, religious mother, Hannah Milhous Nixon, and to his pacifist Quaker grandmother, who spoke in "thee's" and "thou's," and to his insecure yet authoritarian father.

Dr. Eli Chesen, who analyzed Nixon and wrote a book describing Nixon's psychiatric profile, said that young Richard "functioned in this rigidly controlled emotional straight-jacket."[1]

Psychologists tell us that when our real feelings are repressed, they come out somewhere else at some other time. As an adult, Nixon's Perfect mind remembered every hurt and rejection, and he could burst out like a lion and pounce upon those who had triggered his hidden anger.

His brother Donald remembered, "He couldn't argue much with me. But once, when he had just about as much of me as he could take, he cut loose and kept at it for a half hour. He went back a year listing things I had done. He didn't leave out a thing. I've had a lot of respect ever since for the way he can keep things on his mind."[2]

A Master of Detail

Young Richard learned early in life that he was not popular or particularly handsome, so he opted to develop his mind. He became obsessed with the mastery of details and needed to know everything about every subject. He found that Perfect knowledge is Power, and when you have

Perfect control of facts you can soon control people and situations and have more Power.

Nixon's childhood was not a happy one. His brother Harold's fatal illness occupied much of his mother's time, and to help her out he was relegated to what he considered female tasks. When he did the dishes he was so afraid someone would see him that he pulled the shades. He had an intense fear of being thought a sissy or weak in any way, and this concern kept him from allowing any friends to get to know him. He stayed remote and emotionally uninvolved with people and was nicknamed "Gloomy Gus." His desire to hide his true self from others as a youth stayed with him as an adult; he kept his emotional shades pulled much of the time.

Young Richard had ambivalent feelings about his parents. He wanted to be masculine like his father, but Frank was a failure, and his son was obsessed with the vision of success. He related more with his domineering mother, who was ambitious, but he feared her female influence.

When Richard was twelve his mother left him in charge of the household for two years while she took Harold to Arizona in search of a cure for his tuberculosis. Richard felt abandoned, rejected, and unloved. He also felt as if he were the "woman of the house," and when both brothers, Harold and Arthur, died, he somehow thought it must be his fault. *If only I'd known what to do,* he told himself. He determined never to let anything get beyond his control again.

His combination of guilt for his brothers' deaths, fear of not being masculine or strong, anxiety over insecurity and rejection, and need to keep people from knowing who he was or how he felt drove him into an inferiority complex and a life-long fear of failure. A little resident black cloud seemed always to hover over him. Eli Chesen called Nixon's anxieties "a feeling of vague impending doom. . . . While all of us experience anxiety in a multitude of forms, few people have been able to harness this energy as effectively and as efficiently as Richard Nixon. This accounts for much of this man's greatness as well as weakness."

Nixon was a clear example of the principle that a strength carried to extreme becomes a weakness. The strengths of his anxieties led him to study deeply, memorize facts, train his brilliant mind, win debates, and get a scholarship to law school. The weaknesses manifested later caused him to have a compulsive need to win, even if he had to bend the rules to do so.

114

Political Personalities

Richard's youthful insecurities grew along with him for a lifetime. In his book, *A Time of Passion,* Charles Morris wrote, "The constant pricking of his inferiority was like picking off a scab." His emotional wounds never healed, but he successfully covered them with a large band-aid of knowledge and control. These childhood problems, when not dealt with in a healthy way, sometimes lead to what is called the obsessive-compulsive personality.

The *American Psychiatric Association Diagnostic and Statistical Manual* defines the obsessive-compulsive personality as a behavior pattern, "characterized by excessive concern with conformity and adherence to standards of conscience. Consequently, individuals in this group may be rigid, over-inhibited, over-conscientious, over-dutiful and unable to relax easily."

Chesen wrote, "This definition, while accurate, is incomplete. The outward characteristics of this personality (overinhibition, compulsivity, overconscientiousness, and striving for perfection) are all mechanisms used by the obsessive-compulsive. These mechanisms are used by such a person to gain control over himself and his environment. In this way, he will not lose control of himself—and his environment will not be able to control him."

A Passion for Facts

Richard Nixon wanted to be in control and be Powerful; he had a passion for facts, a need to know it all, an ability to take advantage of others, and an obsession to be Perfect. With his Perfect-Powerful personality, he decided to go into politics.

Time magazine wrote of him, "An unlikelier politician would be hard to concoct. Reserved, secretive, glowering, as awkward at backslapping and gladhanding as an android at a stag party."[3] When questioned later on his tactics, Nixon answered, "I had to win. That's the thing you don't understand. The important thing is to win."[4]

And win he did! As the junior congressman from California, Nixon arrived in Washington during a brief period of Republican control and was put on the House UnAmerican Activities Committee at a time when Joe McCarthy was bent on purging the country of Communists.

Nixon biographer Stephen Ambrose wrote in *Nixon: The Education of a Politician,* "McCarthy's charges were so extreme, his inability to back

them up so obvious, that he made Nixon look like a scholar and statesman in comparison."

Nixon's compulsion to get the facts put him in a positive position when
in pursuit of Alger Hiss, a government official accused of espionage. His
attention to detail and persistence led to Hiss's conviction, and Nixon
suddenly became a new young star for the Republican Party. When
Dwight Eisenhower was convinced to run for president and the old general needed a young lawyer to do his dirty work, Richard Nixon fit the
prescription. He freed Eisenhower up to be presidential and fatherly.
While Ike grinned, Nixon glowered.

Unfortunately, success often turned into a crisis for Nixon. Some of
his California friends raised eighteen thousand dollars for him, and when
the New York Post caught wind of it the story ran under a headline that
proclaimed "Secret Nixon Fund." At that time, the thought of any improprieties in Perfect-Powerful Nixon shocked us all, and I remember lis-
tening as he came on TV to explain emotionally how poor and humble
he really was. He told us how his wife, Peaceful Pat, wore a "respectable
Republican cloth coat" and how he hoped we would let him keep the gift
of a little cocker spaniel named Checkers. He had us all in tears with him
as he concluded his plea followed by Ike giving Nixon his blessing of
"You're my boy."

We were all convinced "Tricky Dick" had been picked on, and we were
grateful for Eisenhower's paternal support. However, as time went on,
Peaceful Ike became less enchanted with Nixon's penchant for controversy and conflict, and by the time Nixon was ready to face Kennedy for
president, Ike suggested that he wasn't "presidential timber."

When a reporter asked Eisenhower what Nixon's major vice-
presidential decisions had been the president answered, "If you give
me a week, I might think of one."[5] Perhaps this was Eisenhower's Peaceful, low-key sense of humor, for biographer Ambrose wrote that Nixon,
"became the most visible vice-president of the 20th century, and the most
successful."[6] Nixon inferred that life with Eisenhower in his sunset years
was confusing and indecisive. "After ordering Nixon to take the low road
while he stayed on the high road, Eisenhower would admonish Nixon
that he had gone too far—and then once again order Nixon to go after
the Democrats."[7]

The frosty relationship between these two was a natural personality clash. The Peaceful Ike held down the Powerful Richard and let him know that he wasn't yet Perfect.

Nixon went from being vice president to suffering an unexpected loss to Jack Kennedy followed by another defeat when he ran for governor of California, a job that seemed an easy win for such a national figure. After losing the California race, the anger he had repressed since his teen years refused to stay under control, and he told off the press in another moving moment by saying, "You won't have Nixon to kick around anymore."

He stayed out of sight, at least for a while. It was in this interim period that I met Nixon at a party honoring him in Milford, Connecticut. My husband had the food-service contract at the Schick headquarters, and when they asked Fred to put on a spread for their top executives as well as Richard Nixon, Barron Hilton, and company president Patrick Frawley, I volunteered to be the hostess. The pictures I'd seen of Nixon made me feel he only came in black and white, but when I met him I was surprised to see a well-tanned, attractive man in living color. He greeted me most cordially, considering he wasn't running for office at the time, and he seemed at ease with his business peers.

Ready for Change

By the time Nixon announced he was again available to run for president and salvage Johnson's unpopular war, the country was ready for a change. We'd had enough of brash promises and exaggerated stories. We'd been a little embarrassed when LBJ, on a whim, invited a camel driver from Pakistan to visit the White House—and he'd come.

We were sick of flower children, druggies, and criminals who had more rights than the victims. We'd given up on the New Frontier that had become old, and we were disenchanted with the Great Society that hadn't gotten better.

Nixon promised to end the war in Vietnam, and he took a tough stand on law and order, saying the Supreme Court under Chief Justice Earl Warren had gone too far in favor of the criminal.

As president, Nixon was at his best. His whole life had been a rehearsal for such a time as this, and he faced the nation with confidence. His personality patterns shone in their strengths, and he put his weaknesses to bed for a season. In *Among Those Present,* reporter Nancy Dickerson said of Washington at that time, "The city gamely tried to discover virtues in Richard Nixon that had never been perceived before."

In *Nixon's Psychiatric Profile,* Eli Chesen stated, "His tendency to over-prepare has made him a master of political capability and diplomatic awareness. He is almost always well-researched and exhibits an impressive ability to recall detail . . . he tends to be a genius of interpersonal diplomacy and expert in his forte—foreign affairs."

Charles Morris, in *A Time of Passion,* wrote that Nixon had "daring and imaginative pragmatism," "unusual sweep and clarity of mind," and "bold courage for the brilliant stroke."

Judging by these words of praise and considering his landslide reelection, we could assume that Nixon would go down in history as one of the greats, a genius, a foreign-policy expert.

So what happened? Where was the fatal flaw?

When we understand the basic personalities, we can see how little it takes to move persons from their strengths to their weaknesses. Nixon's underlying fear of ever losing again and his consistent need to gather every possible fact led to the creation of the Plumbers, a unit of special investigators designed to stop news leaks that slipped out of the Nixon administration. Daniel Ellsberg had infuriated Nixon with his publication of secret Pentagon papers, so the Plumbers entered his psychiatrist's office to find damaging evidence. Tapping telephones of newsmen gave Nixon advance information to fortify any weakness before things got out of control. Investigating Ted Kennedy's Chappaquiddick fiasco gave Nixon an unused stockpile of information for the future. Nixon's need for omniscience allowed his Plumbers to eagerly apply wrenches to any dripping pipeline they saw. Nixon would have won without any subterfuge, but he wanted to win big.

"A Nonsense Thing"

In retrospect, he said himself of the break-in at the Democratic headquarters at the Watergate office complex: "There was no way McGovern was going to win the election. So we should have faced up to [Watergate] very early and said, 'Look, who did this thing, and so forth and so on, we're sorry that it happened.' When you try to compare the deed itself [the break-in], rather than the cover-up of the deed—the deed itself was a nonsense thing. It didn't produce anything.

"Without the Watergate episode I would be rated, I should think, rather high. Without it. But with it, it depends on who's doing the rating."[8]

Yes, without Watergate Nixon would have ranked as one of the most brilliant and successful presidents. He will still be remembered as a Shakespearian-style hero, a great man with a tragic flaw. His childhood insecurities and inferiorities taught him that knowledge was power and that he needed all he could get. Experience showed him that even with a mastery of the details he could still lose, so he took no chances.

From his childhood on, his fear of people knowing his inner thoughts and his pulling down the shades on life grew into a compulsion in his presidential years. He was so afraid someone would tap his wires while he was taping their words that he had nine separate private offices all with full communications equipment: The Oval Office and the Lincoln Study, one in the Executive Office Building, two at Camp David, one at Key Biscayne, one on Grand Cayman Island, and two in San Clemente, California.

His obsessive need to know all caused him to install eavesdropping equipment, and his sense of his place in history added to his pre-occupation with detail. He wanted to be sure his words were preserved for history so nothing would be left out of his memoirs. As a result, when he talked with an unsuspecting person, he could weigh his words while the guest said what came to him naturally. This deception created some-what of a *Candid Camera* situation. He always had to have the upper hand, to know more than the enemy. He was a man whose fearful emotions never grew up with his body.

As Nancy Dickerson wrote in *Among Those Present*, "He was a prisoner not so much of his position as of his own personality."

Doris Kearns Goodwin added, "The administration of Richard Nixon demonstrated most dramatically of all that the greatest powers are vulnerable to the most sordid defects of personal character and understanding."[9]

After leaving office in 1974, Nixon spent ten years of reclusive life interspersed with occasional forays into the political arena; then he began his well-planned emergence back into public life. He made himself available as a consultant wherever his vast knowledge seemed useful, and he was considered as the top foreign-relations expert in either party.

Nixon accepted that he would never be officially selected for a government position, but he carefully promoted himself as an elder statesman who was well received in other countries. Without public knowledge, Nixon quietly mediated between Soviet President Mikhail Gorbachev and American President Ronald Reagan, and in July 1986, he presented Reagan with a twenty-six-page document expressing his views of Gorbachev as "a velvet glove with a steel fist," giving suggestions on future relationships and diplomatic accommodations.

Because of his forced resignation and the confiscation of forty-four million pages of presidential material and four thousand hours of audiotape, Nixon was for several years unable to establish a library or museum to house what he did have available. After waiting for the city of San Clemente to debate for four years whether to build a Nixon library, Nixon gave up and moved his request to Yorba Linda, his birthplace. Yorba Linda now has the distinction of having the only presidential library without presidential papers.

A Driving Dream

It was there that Nixon's funeral took place, in front of the little white house his father had built with his own hands. No one could look at that setting—the small, frame house with the flag-draped casket resting quietly before it—without realizing the wonder of the American dream, without seeing the proof that anyone *can* grow up to be president. With enough knowledge one can achieve power.

Looking toward the little house, President Bill Clinton stated in his eulogy for Nixon, "From those humble roots, as frame so many humble beginnings in this country, grew the force of a driving dream."

The presence of the current president as well as four ex-presidents and their wives—the Fords, Carters, Reagans, and Bushes—in the front row during the funeral was evidence of the inner respect they all had for Nixon.

Until his death, Richard Nixon had an unprecedented comprehension of government intricacies and foreign policy, even though his vast knowledge could produce only limited power. He was a brilliant man, a tragic hero with a near-fatal flaw. And like those other men sitting in the front row during his funeral, he had come into the office of the presidency on his strengths and left on his weaknesses.

Nixon used his vast knowledge of foreign affairs to fill his books with memories of great achievements and to provide historical perspective for the post-cold war era. Yet he will go down in history as the only president to be forced from office because of the cover-up of a crime that in itself would not have brought him down. He hadn't learned that the American people will forgive almost anything if you can apologize and move on, but for the Powerful personality those words of confession stick in the throat, and Nixon died with the words "I'm sorry" still inside him.

Richard Nixon
Perfect-Powerful Personality

The following lists of strengths and weaknesses include words and phrases used in newspaper articles, magazines, books, television, and radio to describe President Nixon's personality, a combination of Perfect and Powerful traits. Check the characteristics that also apply to you.

Perfect Personality

Strengths
___ Brilliant mind, a genius
___ Amazing ability to judge others
___ Master of details
___ Efficient and analytical
___ Sobering influence on others
___ Programmed body movements
___ Introspective to the extreme
___ Idealistic and perfectionistic
___ Premeditated responses
___ Publicly pious
___ Memory for details
___ Passion for facts
___ Scholar and statesman
___ Well-researched
___ Guarded, self-contained
___ **TOTAL**

Weaknesses
___ Devoid of charm
___ Reserved, secretive, glowering
___ Split personality
___ Male Greta Garbo
___ Paranoid about the press
___ Uncomfortable host
___ Reclusive and remote
___ Mercurial mood changes
___ Mentally erratic
___ Mean streak underneath
___ Brooding and depressed
___ Cut off from reality
___ Suspicious and untrusting
___ Deceptive
___ Searching for solitude
___ **TOTAL**

Powerful Personality

Strengths

___ Conveyed image of being
    in charge
___ Penchant for notable firsts
___ Daring and imaginative
    pragmatist
___ Unusual sweep and clarity
    of mind
___ Bold courage for the brilliant
    stroke
___ Extraordinary
___ Harnessed energy
___ Confident
___ Loyal
___ Didn't need friends
___ Goal-oriented
___ Law and order
___ All-powerful
___ All-knowing
___ **TOTAL**

Weaknesses

___ Monarchical vision
___ Grandiose stance
___ Couldn't say "I'm sorry"
___ Volatile, quick-tempered
___ Refused counsel
___ Critical of opposition
___ Self-conscious
___ Pretensions to greatness
___ Desperate need to win
___ Vulgar language
___ Above the rules
___ Ruthless

___ **TOTAL**

Total of your presidential profile of Perfect-Powerful strengths and weaknesses: _____

Are You a Leader Like Nixon?

Richard Nixon is the first president we've examined whose major characteristics belong to the Perfect personality. Later we will see some of the same Perfect traits in Jimmy Carter.

Nixon's secondary personality was Powerful; he wanted to be in charge and do things perfectly. He took the statement, "Knowledge is power," first attributed to Francis Bacon in 1547, and adopted it as his personal motto.

He believed if you know more than everyone else in your business or profession you will become the one with the power. This is a sound premise and a natural pattern for those who have the Perfect/Powerful personality.

Is this anything like you? Do you want everything done your way and perfectly? If so, you have the greatest potential for business success. The

122 Political Personalities

majority of CEOs we read about in success magazines fit this pattern. They know more than everyone else in their field, and they know how to get others to do it their way.

Nixon spent his life gathering knowledge and reaching for power. He didn't become president on his charm or gentle spirit but because the public saw his breadth of information and his strength and power to govern.

With this ability to store up a wealth of knowledge and take control of everything in sight comes the temptation to reach too far. Cult leaders and dictators often have this personality combination. They appear to have knowledge from some higher power, and they are gifted in the skills of manipulation.

If you have these extraordinary abilities, use them wisely to achieve and share, not to overwhelm and control. Nixon reached one step too far in his search for knowledge that would keep him in power. This brings us to the second problem for this type of personality: the inability to admit wrong actions and apologize.

It was the combination of these two weaknesses that brought a Perfect-Powerful president to a humiliating end of what could have been a historically memorable two terms.

One other area that Nixon's life brings to our attention is the adult response to childhood rejection and insecurities. No matter what our personality pattern, if we grew up feeling unloved and insignificant, we tend to overextend our strengths as adults. We need affirmation so badly that we reach out in unhealthy ways to receive the acceptance we've always desired.

The Popular personality will do anything for praise, attention, acceptance, and love. The Powerful personality will compulsively grab control and force others into submission. The Perfect personality will obsess with the need to have every detail in order and will become an annoying perfectionist. The Peaceful will bend over backward to please everyone and will sublimate his or her own opinions.

Whatever our personality, the long-term results of childhood trauma can be destructive. Nixon learned to pull down the shades as a child and not let anyone get too close. As an adult he became secretive, lonely, and deceptive. How about you? Have you dealt with your childhood issues? Have you done your homework? Are you open and above reproach? Are your shades up?

14

A TIME FOR WAR AND A TIME FOR PEACE

GERALD FORD

President: 1974–1977
Personality: Peaceful
Principle to Learn: Stay out of trouble.

If ever there were a president whose personality fit the need of the hour, it was Gerald Ford. Having just said farewell to a Perfect-Powerful whose motto, "Knowledge is power," had been carried to extremes, we wanted Peace: Just leave us alone and let us recover from Watergate.

We didn't want any New Frontiers or Great Societies; we just wanted to tune out for a while. We didn't need a person of great vision and expanded horizons; we just wanted a decent, honest man we could trust.

And just when we needed him, there was Gerald Ford with his Peaceful personality. Not since the election of Dwight Eisenhower at the end of the war had we been looking for a man of Peace who would take us in his arms and rock us to sleep. When Ford was inaugurated as the thirty-eighth president, he even had the Bible open to an appropriate verse, Ecclesiastes 3:8: "[There is] a time to love and a time to hate, / a time for war and a time for peace." He told us our "long national nightmare" was over, and he was ready to give us "conciliation, compromise, and cooperation," all words that express the virtues of the Peaceful personality.

The All-Purpose President

Gerald Ford came in on his strengths: his quiet, low-key, noncontroversial nature. He was well-liked by all, calm, cool, collected, and totally inoffensive. He came in as the all-purpose President, a man for all seasons, a team player.

He didn't have the impulsive nature of Kennedy, keeping us on the edge of our seats with a combination of fear and excitement. He didn't have an ego that cried to be stroked as Johnson did. He didn't have the compulsive nature of Nixon, desperately needing to know and tape every thought. He was just happily surprised to be president after all those years of steady performance in the House of Representatives.

Gerald Ford was almost too good to be true.

Ford grew up in the depression days and didn't find out until he was in high school that he had originally been named Leslie King Jr. His parents were divorced when he was two, and his stepfather had adopted him and changed his name to Gerald Ford Jr.

One day while Jerry was working in a restaurant as a busboy, a stranger came in and identified himself as his real father. He obviously had more money than the Ford family, but after taking Jerry out to lunch he disappeared and only showed up one more time, when Jerry was in Yale Law School. That time he brought along his son by his new marriage. We can imagine the hurts that these rejections put upon the young Ford.

Because of his Peaceful nature, Jerry was able to accept his situation and not let adverse circumstances bring him down. Jerry worked hard to get through law school, then he settled into law practice in Grand Rapids, Michigan. As is often the case, he married his opposite, choosing Powerful Betty, who was strong, decisive, brave, dramatic, talented, attractive, forthright, and fearless.

In 1948, Senator Arthur Vandenberg was looking for a young, likable lawyer to run for Congress on the Republican ticket, and Jerry fit the profile. He had no enemies, he carried no negative baggage, and he won. In 1965 he became the minority leader for the same reasons.

Author Doris Kearns Goodwin sums up his political pattern this way:

"At each significant advance in his career Ford's primary qualification was not that he demonstrated superior leadership ability or oratorical skill but that because he was well-liked and had very few enemies, he suited the purpose of others."[1]

When Nixon announced before the assembled Congress that his choice to replace Spiro Agnew, who had resigned as vice president, was "a man who had served for twenty-five years on the Hill with great distinction," the audience knew who it was and everyone seemed thrilled with his selection. People from both parties applauded the choice. Gerald Ford was a team player, whether in football or in politics. He never tried to be the star or do flashy footwork; he just wanted to do his best and be well liked.

Ford was the ideal vice president. He was willing to go from being leader in the House to being in Nixon's long, dark shadow.

We saw many pictures of the Ford family, all beautiful and camera-ready, and we read warm and glowing biographies of the new vice president and his first lady. Hardly had we adjusted to the departure of Spiro Agnew and the acceptance of the "fair-haired boy" as a replacement, when the rumors increased that Nixon was going to be forced to resign and *Voila!* we had an instant president.

Truman, Johnson, and Ford all were instant presidents. Like instant rice, all three were dropped into a pot of boiling water and had to expand to fill their roles. No one would choose to become president under adverse circumstances, but Ford was ready. His public life had been a preparation for such a time as this. Reporters searched for new depths and found little information. Some looked for skeletons in old closets and found none.

Ford was nicknamed "Mr. Clean" and "Goody Two-shoes" because no one knew of anything he'd done wrong. His ability to mediate opposing forces and to smooth down any ruffled feathers was an asset as he headed into the most crucial political position in the country.

No one doubted his obvious decency, although some wondered about his leadership qualifications. "Is he big enough for the job?" they mused. "Can he carry the ball?"

Smart Enough to Handle the Job?

Some even questioned his intelligence. Many of us were shocked when NBC correspondent Tom Brokaw asked Ford if he felt smart enough to handle the position. As others gasped, Ford calmly answered with no touch of anger, "I was in the upper third of my class at Yale Law School."[2]

When reporters could find little color in Ford's life to write about, in desperation they resurrected Lyndon Johnson's old quip, "Gerald Ford is so dumb he can't walk and chew gum at the same time."[3] When Ford would bump his head on an aircraft door or trip on a stair, some wag would quote Lyndon again.

Ford's honeymoon lasted just one month, from August 9, 1974, when he was sworn in, until September 8, 1974, when he surprised the press and the nation by granting Nixon a "full, free, and absolute pardon." Acting out of his forgiving spirit and wanting to avoid investigations that might be damaging to his administration, he cut off any further disclosure of Nixon's involvement in Watergate. In doing so, Ford immediately dropped sixteen points in the popularity polls.

Many political writers felt his early pardon of Nixon was a mistake from which he never recovered, but Ford felt it was something he had to do in good conscience, and the sooner the better.

When the Cambodians seized the merchant ship *Mayaguez,* Ford acted swiftly by directing a naval task force to the area. The rescuers saved the ship and thirty-nine men, and Ford was hailed as a "decisive" leader, a term that had not previously been applied to him.

After the proper and formal entertaining of the Nixons, the casual, open warmth of the Ford family was a welcome change. The Fords loved people and parties, and Betty, a former dance instructor, looked radiant as her husband twirled her around on the dance floor while the band played on.

Betty Ford: Frank, Witty, and Vulnerable

Betty was a refreshing alternative to her more guarded predecessors, and women related to her as a real person. Many applauded her frank stand on women's rights, although some were shocked when she said she assumed her children had tried marijuana. She let it be known that she did not intend to sleep in a separate bedroom from the president, and when interviewed for *McCall's* magazine and asked how often she slept with her husband, she quipped, "as often as possible."

The public rallied to her support when she had to undergo a mastectomy because of breast cancer. Ironically, Happy Rockefeller, wife of Vice

President Nelson Rockefeller, had a double mastectomy within a few months of Betty's surgery, opening up the subject for free discussion, articles, and TV reports. This attention to the topic of breast cancer generated public awareness of the need for preventive examinations and testing, something that was revived again in 1987 when Nancy Reagan had a modified radical mastectomy.

Gerald Ford's dignified and compassionate response to Betty's surgery encouraged other women facing similar situations and belied the myth that once you've had this surgery your husband won't love you anymore.

In later years when Betty admitted she had alcohol- and drug-dependency problems and checked into a rehabilitation center, she again showed her open frankness and encouraged others to get help. After her successful treatment, she founded the Betty Ford Clinic near Palm Springs, California. Those of us who live in the area are kept informed in the daily paper of each celebrity who enters—the news gathered, I assume, by some eager reporter in a palm tree with a telescopic lens.

As Betty sparkled and the children were shining examples, the president kept a soft, steady glow. His low wattage never ignited any fires in his people, and he became somewhat of a baby-sitter, a temporary parent.

Just as Eisenhower, a fellow Peaceful, had been the direct opposite of Truman, so Ford was totally different from the presidents preceding him. Where Johnson was larger than life, entertaining, hilarious, hugging, laughing, manipulating, brash, and controlling, Ford was reserved, open-minded, unpretentious, sympathetic, soft-spoken, and totally inoffensive in nature with a dry wit and a pleasant smile.

Short on Details

Ford was opposite from Nixon in that the latter had a total control of facts on every important subject, and Ford was often caught short on the details. Nor did Ford have Roosevelt's classical background; he was considered an intellectual lightweight by some commentators. Since the press could find little substantial criticism to make, they grabbed on to misstatements such as his reference to Paul Revere's signal as "one if by day and two if by night."

Ford was different from Kennedy in that he did not *need* to win. He liked being president but he wasn't threatened by Powerful people around

him. He was not an initiator in Congress or in the White House, and his
campaign to Whip Inflation Now, ironically dubbed WIN, never quite
won. Ford was more manager than innovator, and he gave us a feeling
of quiet contentment rather than of dynamic leadership.

When it was time for Ford to run on his own for reelection, the public accepted the prospect that he would be voted in. He had done nothing wrong—but he had also done little that could be considered inspirational. He had been inoffensive and had no enemies; however he'd
never succeeded in getting us to march to his drumbeat, mainly because
he wasn't beating any drums.

Ford's Peaceful strengths became weaknesses as he limped through a
lackluster campaign with little commanding oratory. His detachment
from the facts was brought to our attention when, in a debate with Jimmy
Carter, he stated that in his eyes the Soviet Union most certainly did not
control the nations of Eastern Europe.

After that, the campaign coasted downhill to Ford's defeat at the polls
by an upstart peanut farmer who had organized his bid for national attention Perfectly.

Gerald Ford came in on his Peaceful strengths and, after 895 days, left
on his weaknesses. He just never got out of the chair and ran. He took
his defeat calmly, gave no negative condemnations to any of his staff,
blamed no one but himself, graciously turned his position of power over
to his successor, packed his bags, and retired to Rancho Mirage, near
Palm Springs, California.

New Life After the Presidency

As an ex-president, Ford had no goals and no wealth, so when agent
Norman Brokaw offered to make a few financial contacts for him, he
accepted. Suddenly Ford became a hot property. As the calls came in,
Ford was amazed. "I never had that experience before, so it was quite
surprising," he said.[4]

NBC paid Ford about a million dollars to appear in documentaries.
Harper and Row, with *Reader's Digest,* paid another million dollars for the
Fords' memoirs. Betty got a half-million dollars for two NBC specials, and
suddenly their financial picture took on a brighter look. Offers for con-
sulting with different businesses and for serving on various boards of direc-
tors came flooding in, and Ford found himself in a whole new line of work.

Both Betty and Jerry Ford were honored at the 1988 Republican National Convention in New Orleans, and he gave the most dynamic speech of his life, saying that he would not stand by and let somebody pick on his friend George Bush. In that setting, there was a new confidence and assurance about Gerald Ford, the successful businessman, the director of boards, the consultant in demand.

Gerald Ford came into office as an unelected president on his Peaceful strengths and left on his few weaknesses. Since then he has entered a new stream of life and like Ole Man River, Ford just keeps rolling Peacefully along.

Gerald Ford
Peaceful Personality

The following lists of strengths and weaknesses include words and phrases used in newspaper articles, magazines, books, television, and radio to describe President Ford's Peaceful personality. Check the characteristics that also apply to you.

Strengths
___ Quiet and peaceful
___ Perennial good guy
___ Refreshing, natural
___ Genuine, honest and true
___ Obviously decent
___ Reservoir of goodwill
___ All-American boy made good
___ Eagle Scout in the White
     House
___ Well-liked
___ No enemies
___ Aimed for long-term
     solutions
___ Didn't want to be in control
___ Talked simple sense
___ Comfortable and relaxed
___ Naturally sensitive
___ Friendly, courteous,
     and polite

Weaknesses
___ Didn't understand urgencies
___ Slow in decisions
___ Avoided problems
___ Didn't seem to take charge
___ Couldn't face confrontations
___ Had a do-nothing aura
___ Didn't get up and run
___ Indecisive
___ Dull speaker
___ Plodding
___ Pedestrian
___ Inarticulate

___ Skilled at negotiations
        and compromise
___ Inspired affection and trust
___ Uncomplaining and forgiving
___ Unbiased
___ Avoids conflict
___ Affable and of good cheer
___ Not haughty or proud
___ Clear conscience
___ Cool under fire
___ Team player
___ Noncontroversial
___ Content
___ Available
___ Unassuming
___ Normal
___ Well-balanced
___ Easygoing
___ **TOTAL**   ___ **TOTAL**

Total of your presidential profile of Peaceful strengths and weaknesses: _____

Are You a Leader Like Ford?

There's an old expression, "Sometimes just showing up is enough to win." Gerald Ford kept showing up throughout his political career and proving the point that you don't have to be flashy and chauvinistic, dynamic and controlling, or deep and perfectionistic to be president. Sometimes just dependably showing up and being well-liked and having no negative baggage *is* enough.

But Ford did more than show up; he also stayed out of trouble. He didn't try to amass wealth or accept bribes or extend his congressional perks. He didn't carouse, make a fool of himself, or have affairs. He didn't neglect his family for the fast life. He turned away from the temptations of the political scene and seemed genuinely happy as the middle-of-the-road, all-American Mr. Nice Guy.

If your nature is similar to Ford's—quiet and peaceful, genuine and honest, noncontroversial, and with a clear conscience, you could be the greatest leader of them all. So few people know how to stay out of trouble, and so many believe being good will get you nowhere; but Ford gives all Peaceful personalities the hope of high achievement and the motivation to make the extra effort.

It's that motivation that makes the difference. It's so much easier for the Peaceful personality to not make the extra effort, to stay home, to fail to show up. No matter what your goals may be at this moment, realize that your weaknesses can prevent you from achieving them. Your negatives don't show as visibly as the other personalities' weaknesses do. You're not too loud, too pushy, too negative; you just don't always show up. You're slow to make decisions and prefer to let others bear responsibility. You don't like problems and hate confrontations, so you look the other way until the eye of the storm reaches out and engulfs you.

What stands between you and success? The determination to make a greater effort, to get up earlier, to eat correctly, to learn all you can, to reach out to others, to go the extra mile could make the difference for you. With your pleasant, easygoing, relaxed manner and your willful desire to stay out of trouble bolstered by some renewed motivation, you can be a winner.

Just remember to show up!

15

JIMMY WHO?

JAMES EARL CARTER

President: 1977–1981
Personality: Perfect
Principle to Learn: Plan ahead—way ahead.

James Earl Carter came into office somewhat like a schoolteacher bringing the class back to order after recess. As a nation we'd been somewhat out to lunch, and it was time to get organized again. We'd dealt with the crises of Kennedy, the Vietnam escalation with Johnson, and the Watergate scandal with Nixon. We'd needed a rest time with Ford to regroup our thoughts, and now we were after a restoration of order and ethics. No wonder we were intrigued by Carter's obvious morality and his serious-minded desire to get us organized and on the move again.

The political insiders had disappointed us, and the idea of a new intelligent and spiritual outsider seemed to refresh us. When Carter first emerged in the Democratic caucuses, few of us had ever heard of him. "Jimmy Who?" the headlines asked. Could anything good come out of Plains, Georgia?

Jimmy had indeed come out of little, unknown Plains, a town of only six hundred people. His personality fit the Perfect profile right from the beginning as he was an excellent student, loved to read, and was fascinated by engineering. Admiral Hyman Rickover took him as a protégé and trained him on nuclear submarines. Carter had intended to make the navy his career until his father died and he had to return to Plains to save the family peanut business.

Rosalynn had also grown up in Plains and was a friend of Jimmy's sister Ruth. She felt poor and insecure as a teenager, but she set high standards for herself, got all A's in school, and became the valedictorian of her high school class. She had the drive of a Powerful personality, and she remembers that she always wanted to win. She had always looked up to Jimmy in awe but had not dared approach him.

When she saw a picture of Jimmy in his naval officer's uniform, she fell in love and set a goal—completely unrealistic at the time—to marry him. She held her emotions inside and didn't tell anyone her thoughts. When Jimmy came home on leave, Ruth invited Rosalynn over to visit, and a romance started that quickly blossomed into a lifetime love affair.

After moving frequently with the navy, the couple settled back in Plains, against Rosalynn's wishes. As Jimmy fit into his home community again, he became director of the county chamber of commerce, a member of the library board and the county school board, a scoutmaster, a deacon in the Baptist church, state president of the Georgia Crop Improvement Association, state chairman of the March of Dimes, and district governor of Lions International. What was left to do?

Superb Self-Confidence—and Deep Depression

Jimmy was well known in Plains and had already built a reputation for fair leadership across the state through his civic positions, so he ran for state senator and won. During the early sixties, when the integration problems hit the South, Jimmy began to work on behalf of civil rights for the African-Americans.

Jimmy's stand was immediately unpopular with many southerners and led to a confrontation in his own church. An African-American man wished to attend, and the deacons made a ruling, hardly a spiritual decision, that no blacks could come to their church. When the vote came before the church body, Jimmy stood up and spoke against the measure; his moral sense of justice would allow him no other choice. But the vote passed, and his fellow church members were angry with him and his stand.

Even though the state had been predominantly Democratic, the party loyalty split in 1964. So many Georgians were against integration that the Democrats couldn't even find a chairman for Lyndon Johnson's campaign, so Jimmy's widowed mother, fondly known as Miss Lillian, took the position despite threats made against the Carters if they didn't pull away from their "liberal integration stand." Georgia was one of the few states that Barry Goldwater carried in 1964 when he ran against Johnson.

The Carters did not retreat from what they knew to be a fair and just freedom for African-Americans, and this strong stand cost Jimmy many votes when in 1966 he ran for governor of Georgia against incumbent Lester Maddox, a staunch segregationist who owned a restaurant. Maddox had already chased African-Americans out of his establishment and had been pictured wielding an ax handle at his front door. The Carter family campaigned day and night, crossing the state and speaking at every possible stop.

Rosalynn worked days in the peanut warehouse, did Jimmy's senate correspondence at night, kept files on every voter who helped Jimmy, and did the housework in between campaign trips. Powerful Rosalynn, nicknamed the Iron Magnolia, gave Jimmy's bid for nomination all she had while he systematically plotted out every move on paper. When the votes were tallied, Jimmy had lost. The state of Georgia in 1966 preferred an ax-swinging governor to an integrationist.

In an interview with Doris Kearns Goodwin, Carter said, "I've always had superb confidence in myself, but since 1966 it's been different. I was always thinking of myself. I had to prove myself to others. I had to win every battle, which meant when I lost the race for governor of Georgia in 1966, it was horrible. . . . When I had failures it was very upsetting. Even the smallest failures seemed like calamities to me. Life had no purpose."[1]

It was at that time that Jimmy's sister, Ruth Carter Stapleton, shared with him how the Lord had healed her of depression. Carter made a spiritual commitment to Christ that changed his attitudes of pessimism in defeat to the peaceful acceptance that God had a plan for his life.

Joke by Number

The next time Jimmy ran for governor he was even more organized than he had been before. He blocked out the state in zones, noted everyone he knew in that area, and systematically went out to win friends and votes. Rosalynn wrote personal notes to each individual who had responded to Jimmy's messages each day, and Jimmy started a file of speeches and usable jokes, coded by number. Jimmy knew he didn't have a ready sense of humor like the Popular politicians, so he wrote down funny stories and filed them. If he spoke in your town today and told jokes 1, 14, and 110, when he returned he would check his cards and be sure not to repeat his stories.

Can't you imagine Jimmy and Rosalynn driving toward a motel after a long day of campaigning. To lighten the load and save energy he might say to her, "Number 8!" She'd laugh heartily and counter with "Number 62!" Such great fun with such little effort!

Just as Nixon had believed "knowledge is power," so Carter knew his potential was in the Perfect assimilation of details. He constantly studied the issues so he would know every possible fact, and he consulted experts on each current topic.

Perfect Jimmy made perfect plans, kept perfect files, and won. When Rosalynn moved into the governor's mansion she felt all her dreams had come true. She'd gone from being a plain little girl in Plains to becoming the bride of Prince Charming, eventually living in a mansion and being the governor's wife. Surely she would live happily ever after. Although she had been brought up in a poor family with no emphasis on the social graces, Rosalynn made a quick study of protocol and became a confident and gracious hostess. She even trained inmates from the penitentiary to be waiters at her formal dinners. She planted new roses and enjoyed working in the yard. Jimmy even did some gardening and planted a row of peanuts to frame the rose garden and remind them constantly of their humble beginnings.

Jimmy scheduled every day, including time for a bathroom break, and he usually kept to within five minutes of his detailed plan. In 1972 he began working on his organizational charts for his presidential bid in 1977. While few knew what he was planning, he had it all mapped out.

According to Doris Kearns Goodwin, he had "a strategy that called for 250 days of campaigning with visits to 40 states and 200 cities. Carefully allotting a precise amount of time to each state, Carter worked six days a week from 6 A.M. to midnight. And when it all worked out exactly as he had calculated, even down to the number of delegates he had estimated he was likely to win from each state, most of us—but not Carter—were taken by surprise."[2]

Once "Jimmy who?" had won the election in 1976, he began to study all the inaugural addresses of the past presidents so he could compose his from a wealth of background. He had no pretensions of grandeur, and he wanted his message to be simple and his demeanor to be humble. He wanted to be a leader on the level with the people, not a lofty king above the crowds. To demonstrate his servant's attitude, he chose to walk in the inaugural parade instead of riding in a limousine as was the usual custom. He had read where Thomas Jefferson had walked to his inauguration, and he felt this change would symbolize an open and accessible atmosphere for his new administration. As another touch of basic humility, the parade featured a huge helium-filled balloon shaped like a peanut. Carter never strayed far from his peanuts.

Jimmy Carter came into office partly because of America's longing for morality in government. Columnist William A. Rusher wrote, "America in the last decade has been shaken to its roots by the most divisive war in over a century, then shocked by revelations of corruption and lawbreaking at the highest levels of government and in both major parties.

"It is not only unsurprising but downright healthy that, at such a time, the American people should seek fresh contact with the bedrock of religious faith, and look for leaders who are doing the same."

Strong Beliefs

Carter's strong beliefs and his open willingness to talk about God made him different from the passively religious presidents before him, some of whom would well have blushed if asked to give the blessing at a banquet.

The words of Episcopal rector Frederick Rapp of Port Washington, New York, were published by the Associated Press in 1976. "There is a yearning for spiritual and moral leadership in high places, a yearning to be able to trust our government and not have our trust misplaced," he said.

Carter came into the Oval Office on his morality, his firm confidence, his amazing self-discipline, his studied knowledge of major issues, his refusal to compromise his standards, and his appeal as an honest outsider.

Although his morality was never seriously questioned, his lack of guile once caused him to open his mouth without thinking of how his statement could be used to ridicule his virtue. In an interview with *Playboy*, hardly a religious experience, Carter was asked about his fidelity with Rosalynn. Not wishing to seem prudish to the *Playboy* readers, he said he had not committed adultery, but he had looked upon women with lust in his heart. Had Jack Kennedy made such a statement, it would have been taken lightly and with no surprise, but coming from the mouth of Moses, it provided the reporters with a rare opportunity to make fun of the president's morals.

Jimmy was actually quoting from Matthew 5:28 where Jesus said, "I tell you that anyone who looks at a woman lustfully has already committed adultery with her in his heart." But since the *Playboy* reporter didn't know Matthew from Mark, Luke, or John, the concept and comment were attributed to Jimmy and provided humor from then until this very day.

Carter's confidence gradually eroded as he found that not everyone had his Perfect principles or wished to follow his sincere directions. Inflation wouldn't listen to him, recession continued even when he said stop, and the fuel shortage got worse and worse in spite of his threats. He proposed what he called "the most massive peacetime commitment of funds and resources in our nation's history" to develop new sources of energy, but lines kept forming at the filling stations, and angry motorists were honking their horns at him.

Carter's superhuman discipline didn't seem to work on others and his detailed, twelve-point programs appealed to few. *Newsweek* said of him, "Jimmy Carter appears to have been a hard man to work for—demanding, highly critical of inadequate staff work, yet rarely complimentary of a good job."[3] Carter put so much effort into plotting out his schedules that soon critics said he had become a manager instead of a leader. He had to give up some of his noble, idealistic visions so typical of the Perfect personality, and these losses of great plans began to depress him.

Carter hadn't expected the seizure of our embassy in Iran, he didn't know the Ayatollah Khomeini, and he had no idea what to do with the deposed, sick shah of Iran who didn't have a place to stay. No one told him the hottest issues of his administration would focus on Iran and that his inability to release the embassy hostages would bring his reign to a dismal close.

His refusal to compromise sounded brave and noble until Congress disagreed with his plans, and he had to back off in what he felt was defeat.

Crisis of Confidence

Carter's appeal as an honest outsider didn't wear well either. Though no one doubted his basic integrity, his "outsider" mentality caused him trouble because he did not have the usual old-line political cronies to call upon in time of need, and soon he referred to Washington as "poison" to him.

By his third year in power, Perfect Carter's strengths had turned into weaknesses, and the press began to use words such as aimless, drifting, remote, losing touch, depressed, and frightening. Carter created a dismal image when he told us with the heavy heart of the Perfect nature that we were in a national "crisis of confidence," and the news media dubbed his heavy words "Carter's malaise message." What a melancholy word, *malaise!* The dictionary says malaise is "an indefinite feeling of bodily uneasiness or discomfort." As Jimmy lost his comfort, we all became uneasy.

By July 1979, when his presidency had dropped to its lowest ebb in public esteem, Carter did what Perfects do when life becomes imperfect; he retreated to Camp David, where he spent two weeks on the mountaintop communing with God and a steady stream of advisers. His retreat caused the public to consider him a loner, a mystic, or a sick man. His discouraging conclusion at the end of his withdrawal was that we had, according to *Newsweek*, "a sickness of the national spirit—a crisis of faith that makes effective governance nearly impossible for him or anyone else."[4]

And what does any religious man do after two weeks on a mountaintop? Come down and make a speech. The comparison of Jimmy with Moses was so obvious that many cartoonists drew a white-robed Moses with Jimmy's face and large teeth descending the Catoctin Mountains, stone tablets in hand. Ironically, to give the president television time for his speech, CBS had to cancel the episode in its miniseries, *Moses the Lawgiver,* in which Moses descended from Mount Sinai with the Ten Commandments.

As Carter faced the cameras that night, he told the nation, "All the legislation in the world can't fix what's wrong with America." He said in defense of himself, "It's a crisis of confidence. It is a crisis that strikes at the very heart and soul and spirit of our national will. . . . [It] is threatening to destroy the social and political fabric of America." He called for a "rebirth of the American spirit,"[5] which depressed those of us who didn't know it had died.

One of his staff, worried about Carter's unexciting manner of speaking, had suggested he hire Charlton Heston to present his message, but Carter didn't need Charlton that night as he presented his material on the crisis of the American spirit "with an urgency, a passion and an eloquence rare in his or any other recent presidency." He admitted his failures and said we were standing "at a turning point in our history." He looked straight at us and said, "I need your help."[6]

Newsweek reported, "Carter had approached the speech full of melancholy at America's psychic landscape and misgivings about his own hitherto small powers to alter it. . . . But he felt he had to do something to shake the nation free of its malaise."[7]

In his book *A Time of Passion,* Charles Morris summed up how Carter came into his presidency on his strengths and left on his weaknesses.

"Carter's sudden slippage in the last weeks of the presidential race reflected growing doubts about his capacity for office, a concern that turned out to be well-founded. His informality and lack of pomp in his first days in office—his walk to the inaugural, his relaxed official dinners, his jeans and cardigan—were a pleasant contrast to the imperial trappings that had grown up around the White House. But he never succeeded in establishing control over the political process and was from the outset engulfed by events.

"With the exception of the peace agreement he wrung from Israel and Egypt at Camp David, his administration was a failure in virtually every respect. . . . The failure of the helicopter mission to rescue the Iranian hostages was the knell for Carter's administration; from that point, he had no chance to win re-election. Intelligence, goodwill, and simple decency were not enough for a successful presidency."

Sincere Humility or Hokey Gestures?

Columnist Meg Greenfield said that we who put them there are at least partly responsible for the change of attitude that occurs in our presidents. "Those who compose the epitaphs for departed administrations are invariably inconsistent and unfair. The same public that hailed Ford for his down-to-earth good-heartedness and simplicity after the Byzantine Nixon years derided him and his works as 'dumb' by the time he left; it embraced Carter's walk down Pennsylvania Avenue and his homely insistence on reforming the 'imperial presidency' by toting his own suitcase and the like and then decided it hated and was demeaned by all these hokey gestures."[8]

Although Carter's sincere humility was shown in his walking to the inauguration and not wearing a tall silk top hat, this "just one of the guys" attitude came to be interpreted as a lack of strong leadership skills. I'm sure Carter meant well, but he misread the public's concept of what constitutes a leader. And, like it or not, this country inherited from England a penchant for royalty, even though we wouldn't verbalize it. Because of this desire, we had created the Kennedy myth with the Perfect queen and the Popular king living in Camelot. In contrast, the Carter family was basic and real, and we missed the pageantry.

Humorous articles on the meaning of leadership were published during Carter's presidency, and somehow humility wasn't one of the characteristics mentioned. The press ridiculed Carter and seemed to purposefully select pictures of him looking depressed. Here we had a godly, honest man who sincerely thought that he and the Lord could straighten out the problems of the country. He'd done his best, he'd run the race, he'd kept the faith, but he didn't win the prize on his second try.

Devastated by Defeat

In the book the Carters wrote together, *Everything to Gain—Making the Most of the Rest of Your Life,* they expressed their reaction to their unexpected loss to Ronald Reagan. With his deep strengths and faith, Jimmy told how disappointed he was, how he bottled up his hurts, and how he meditated on what he could have done differently. Rosalynn said she was alternately "angry, sad, anxious, and worried."

Although they don't designate their personality types in the book, they describe them accurately: Perfect Jimmy kept calm and reflected deeply on what might have been. Powerful Rosalynn was distraught and upset and was determined they would run again and win. Rosalynn wrote, "There was no way I could understand our defeat. It didn't seem fair that everything we had hoped for, all our plans and dreams for the country, could have been gone when the votes were counted on election day. We had done all we could, and somehow it had not been enough. Events had mocked us. Jimmy said he had always heard that it was harder for a loving wife to accept anything that hurt her husband than it was for the husband to accept it, and I believe that to be true. I agreed that we had been given opportunities and achievements granted to very few, but I had to grieve over our loss before I could look into the future. Where could our lives possibly be as meaningful as they might have been in the White House?"

As Rosalynn grieved, Jimmy pondered and analyzed. "Once I was convinced, correctly or not, that we had done our best, then it was easier to accept the judgment of the voters and move on to other things. Rosalynn was not able to do this. She went about her official duties with her chin up, but she found it impossible to accept the result of the election. Over and over she would raise the same questions: 'How could the press have been so bad?' 'Why didn't the people understand our goals and accomplishments?' 'How could God have let this happen?' Although some of the same questions pressed on me, I did not—or could not—express them, and spent a lot of our private time attempting to reassure her. My arguments and explanations didn't help much. The only thing that sustained her was the hope and expectation that I would run again for president and be elected. She found very little support for this from me or the rest of the family."

Jimmy admitted he maintained "a lot of somewhat artificial cheerfulness during those early weeks. The more Rosalynn was upset, the more I tried to find ways to comfort her. I never admitted how deeply I was hurt, and I still find it hard to do so. We had a few strained and unpleasant moments between us in those early weeks, and now I realize that with my calm and reassuring attitude it seemed to Rosalynn that I didn't recognize her pain."

How difficult it is for people who don't understand the personalities to see why we don't all grieve in the same way!

Jimmy and Rosalynn have put their grief behind them and moved on. Jimmy has written several books about his presidency and his role as a peacemaker. He was honored as an elder statesman at the 1988 Democratic convention in Atlanta, and the following month Bantam published his book *An Outdoor Journal, Adventures and Reflections*. In it Jimmy told of his childhood and of his desire for his father's attention. "He seemed to love me more and treated me as something of an equal when we were in the dove field, walking behind a bird dog, or on a stream."

In an August 18, 1988, review of *An Outdoor Journal* in the *Los Angeles Times,* writer Frank Levering summed up his feelings about Carter and this revealing book. "As president, Jimmy Carter became ensnared in a web of public and media perception—that he was weak, ineffective, too slight a man for the job. But the Carter of this book—the man he wants us to know—is a man's man, tough, durable, courageous. . . . Carter is setting the record straight, combating the lingering image of weakness and salvaging his pride in an imposing exhibition of manly arts. . . .

"Carter the outdoorsman wants us to see him as he wanted us to see him walking down Pennsylvania Avenue at his inauguration; not larger than life but as an ordinary man called to perform extraordinary feats."

"Our Best Ex-President"

In the years since going out of office, Jimmy Carter has become, in at least one writer's opinion, "our best ex-president." He has kept busy building houses with Habitat for Humanity—not just talking about the project but out there hammering, always with a serious look on his face.

Suddenly in June 1994 Carter showed up in North Korea as a dubious emissary from the United States. Supposedly he went as a private citizen, but he met with dictator Kim Il Sung to discuss North Korea's apparent interest in collecting components for nuclear weapons and Carter offered him some official options in dealing with the United States. When reaction to his trip turned sour and people began to ask why he was there, Carter replied that he was trying to help President Clinton, who immediately distanced himself from any connection and seemed somewhat vague as to who Jimmy Carter really was.

Carter claimed success in North Korea although many labeled the trip disastrous. Amazingly, President Bill Clinton later chose him to go to Haiti and offer terms of peace to Lieutenant General Raoul Cedras before the announced American invasion. There he was pictured in the typical Perfect role. As President Clinton's representative he sat at the bargaining table with his own computer and worked out all the details for the agreement.

When he returned to the States he was obviously heavy-laden over the seriousness of his journey. As an ex-president with no elections to pursue, Carter felt free to speak his opinion, similar to what he had done in Korea where he made public statements that differed from what President Clinton had in mind. This time Carter even dared to say that Clinton's foreign policy of crisis management was, in his words, "an embarrassment" to the nation. The *Washington Post* hailed Carter's "freelance diplomacy that pulled the Clinton administration back from the brink of military confrontation . . . but sent officials into a dither of damage control."[9]

At this point in Carter's life, he is speaking the truth and not worrying about what anyone thinks. Perhaps he has at last found his post-presidential niche: as a Perfect private ambassador to promote peace and solve international disputes.

He has redeemed himself from his weak image as a president, is blossoming as an elder statesman and diplomatic troubleshooter, and was nominated for the Nobel Peace prize of 1994. Jimmy Carter is finally receiving the attention and affirmation that his serious, deep, Perfect personality has not enjoyed before.

Jimmy Carter
Perfect Personality

The following lists of strengths and weaknesses include words and phrases used in newspaper articles, magazines, books, television, and radio to describe President Carter's Perfect personality. Check the characteristics that also apply to you.

Strengths
___ Long-range planner
___ Analytical mind
___ Sense of mission
___ Strong spiritual values
___ High moral values
___ Self-disciplined
___ Complex personality
___ Tightly scheduled
___ Engineer's mind
___ Essential loner
___ Missionary zeal
___ Inner-directed
___ Empathy with the poor
___ Highly organized

Weaknesses
___ Saw national malaise
___ Full of melancholy
___ Depressed over failures
___ No sense of humor
___ Secretive and mysterious
___ Withdrawn
___ Rarely complimentary
___ Lost touch with people
___ Bogged down in details
___ Doom-crier
___ Vague and touchy
___ Brooded on the mountain
___ Somber and grave
___ Compared to Moses in meditation

___ Intelligent	___ Hapless
___ Deeply informed	___ Uninspiring
___ Impressive credentials	
___ Immersed in issues	
___ Humble	
___ Unbiased	
___ Dedicated to family	
___ Compassionate to needy	
___ **TOTAL**	___ **TOTAL**

Total of your presidential profile of Perfect strengths and weaknesses:_____

Are You a Leader Like Carter?

Jimmy Carter didn't sit back and let life just happen; he looked way down the line, weighed all the options, and made the best possible plans. Carter was deeply spiritual, but he didn't just sit back and hope God had a wonderful plan for his life. He knew and accepted that "faith without works is dead."

Carter was blessed with a brilliant and organized mind, and he took the responsibilities of life seriously. He left his chosen career to come home and help his mother "keep the farm," but he wasn't content to stay home, grow peanuts, and teach Sunday school.

Carter's outstanding trait that made the big difference was his ability to focus on the future and make long-range plans that might have seemed too distant for many of us. With his analytical mind and his keen sense of mission, he looked for a vocation that took intelligence, depth, and compassion and that called for a humble attitude and a willingness to sacrifice.

In becoming governor of Georgia, Carter didn't seek the limelight or play the starring role. He worked tirelessly to improve the lot of his people.

He saw the possibility of becoming president before the nation knew who he was. He made his charts of the voting districts and his lists of key people he needed as friends. He kept files recording details about every place he went and everyone he met. He made long-range plans that scoffers would have ridiculed if anyone had known he was making them.

By the time Carter's candidacy for president was announced, he had the necessary votes neatly in his notebook. Carter made the most of his personality strengths and did not let his natural tendency toward pessimism and depression get the better of him.

Are you a lot like Carter? Are you serious, thoughtful, introspective? Are you detail-conscious and organized? Are you already a success?

If not, have you let your strengths get carried too far until they have bogged you down? Do you spend too much time thinking without making realistic plans? Are you too wrapped up in your own thoughts to relate to the people? Do you spend so much time in preparing for life that you are letting it pass you by? Are you so pessimistic that you don't think there's much hope for you?

If you relate to any of these questions, it's time for you to take a realistic look at yourself. If you believe you won't succeed, you won't. Jimmy Carter had your nature, but he made specific plans and acted upon them. He built a team of supporters who could see his vision and were willing to help him achieve it. He didn't waste time in idle meditation; he put his thoughts on paper, analyzed their potential, and then moved on them.

Don't be the perfectionist who won't take action until everything is in order. Don't let it be said of you, "He (or she) had such potential. What a shame nothing came of it."

Jimmy Carter dreamed the impossible dream—and then he got up and achieved it.

16

THE GREAT COMMUNICATOR

RONALD REAGAN

President: 1981–1989
Personality: Popular
Principle to Learn: Personalize the problems with a story.

Do you remember the Carter-Reagan debate during the 1980 campaign? Perfect President Carter had been laboring through his national "crisis of confidence" for four years. He'd planned and charted out all his presidential aspirations, but somehow they had never come together at one time. He'd lured Israeli Prime Minister Menachem Begin and Egyptian president Anwar el-Sadat to Camp David and had gotten them on speaking terms, but he couldn't get the hostages home from Teheran. He'd become increasingly depressed and even changed the part in his hair to cheer himself up.

He had seriously approached the presidency, had only begun on his list of goals, and sincerely wanted another four years to work the whole thing through.

Carter considered his opponent, Ronald Reagan, a lightweight. But Reagan proved otherwise.

147

Carter prepared for the debate with an obvious edge. He was the incumbent, and he hadn't made what he felt were any serious mistakes. He was an honest and moral man; no one doubted that, even though many felt his religion got in the way of his good sense. He had worn the presidential mantle with humility, and he was one of the ordinary people—just plain folks from Plains. He wore sweaters, put his feet up with the boys, and most down-home of all, he grew peanuts. Everyone assumed that as long as Carter could keep Reagan groping for the facts that he as president already knew, he would come out ahead. It all seemed so logical.

Opposing President Perfect was Candidate Popular. It was assumed that because Carter as president had access to many facts that Reagan didn't, he would have the edge. On the other hand, Reagan was charming, sincere, and had down-to-earth anecdotes of a past we all remembered with nostalgia. He stood up for traditional values, the family, and the church. Even though he was far older than his Perfect opponent, Reagan appeared far younger than his years and had the vigor of youth.

Both candidates had prepared and practiced. Just before they went out, Reagan was handed his instructions from James Baker. It was a small piece of paper with one word of advice: "Chuckle."

Carter answered his questions Perfectly while throwing negative innuendoes toward Reagan, who appeared to be the underdog. The result was that people who were watching perceived Carter to be picking on his opponent, and at one point he pushed too far. Reagan looked up, tilted his head like a little boy, and with a slight, youthful grin and a shrug he said, "There he goes again."

With that one masterful stroke of his media brush, Reagan painted himself a winner. The next day reporters quoted that one sentence as the turning point in the debate. "There he goes again" will not go down in history with the Gettysburg Address, but it did provide a Popular man with a push toward his presidential goal.

President Popular

Ronald Reagan appeared on the national stage as if we'd called him up specifically. We had tried Powerful Nixon, Peaceful Ford, and Perfect Carter, and when they failed, we reached for President Popular to star in *Good Morning, America.*

We had been viewing the *Tragedy of Watergate* with the Shakespearian hero, King Richard, a brilliant brooding man with a tragic flaw, and we had been placated by the plotless pantomime of the Ford Theater. We had become depressed over the deep drama of Mr. Everyman, carrying his own suitcase and retreating to Camp David, and we were sick of those bags of peanuts at intermission. We were ready for a star who knew he could lead us. We wanted a Popular president to take charge and help us smile again.

As columnist George Will put it in his book *The New Season,* "The nation needed what he delivered—confidence and a sense that government could act decisively."

Ronald Reagan, a Popular president, had many of the obvious leadership strengths that people wanted, but leaders of both parties put impossible expectations upon him and then were stunned when he faltered.

In the beginning, no one expected his show to run for eight years, but in spite of conflicts inserted to heighten suspense, Ronald Reagan played to an exhilarated audience and sustained applause. Recession turned into recovery, and the federal deficit roamed around like a toothless dragon never quite scaring the public psyche. Iran and Nicaragua seemed too distant to be real, and if there was a problem, a new actor, Colonel Oliver North, with his courage and engaging smile, would surely get it all under control. Even perennial Soviet villains laid aside their cloaks and daggers in the face of Reagan's policies of peace through strength. The national media didn't believe it would work, but it did. The Soviets finally sent gregarious Gorbachev and his well-costumed wife, Raisa, to play the role of International Man of Peace and *Time's* Man of the Year, but it was Reagan who brought it about.

Not only did the plot progress according to Reagan's plan, but he and Nancy wore their costumes well and moved in Hollywood glitter and glamour to brighten the gray stages of Washington. They placed themselves against a variety of sparkling backdrops and kept fireworks blazing, flags waving, and balloons bobbing in the breeze. They marched to colorfully costumed bands, cried to the tune of funeral dirges, and waltzed to Lester Lanin and his high-society orchestra.

Francis X. Clives, writing for the *New York Times,* commended Reagan's ability to place himself in attractive settings. "He has used his Oval Office desk and the world beyond, such dramatic sites as the invasion beaches of Normandy, as a stage for presentations of a presidential image that is carefully groomed by his managers but instinctively acted by Mr. Reagan himself."

Winning Hearts and Building Hope

Like FDR, Reagan was Popular enough to win our hearts and give us hope for the future. And, added Clives, "Now, Mr. Reagan is again playing from his patented strength; his ability to appeal to the nation's idealism and simplicity in the face of the government's complexities."[1]

William Rusher, publisher of *The National Review,* commenting on Reagan's ability, said, "Like a skillful club boxer, Reagan moved into the attack, landed his punches, backed off, shifted his weight, parried, and attacked again. I came to feel that I was watching a protagonist who knew precisely what he wanted, enjoyed battling for it, and firmly intended to get it in the long run. Conservatism, it seemed to me, not only had never had a finer champion in the White House but, in the light of the odds in politics, could rarely if ever expect to be quite so lucky again."[2]

As a military leader, our president marched soldiers into a mystical little country named Grenada, slew evil men, and emerged a hero.

As with all Populars, President Reagan loved the spotlight and could take even an ordinary script and sanctify it into a moving soliloquy. After sitting through the "Perils of Presidents Powerful, Peaceful, and Perfect," the public was ready for the Marlboro man to come in on his horse, tell a few tall tales, and turn into President Popular right before our eyes. As we sat happily in the audience, our president played a wide variety of roles. In tribute to his leadership ability, our oldest president came across as the "all-American boy." *Newsweek* wrote, "There is a good deal of crinkly-eyed, apple-cheeked, next-door-neighborly warmth as well, a quality of likability that typecast Reagan as a nice guy in 53 of his 54 movies, and has disarmed his enemies ever since. His public persona is less Superman than Clark Kent, a decent, down-to-earth and occasionally tangle-footed mortal. Even his advanced age seems to work for him, placing him somehow beyond ambition. 'He has a high Q-factor,' one of his managers says. 'People like and trust him, and everything else is irrelevant. Clint Eastwood and Walter Cronkite have it, and John Wayne had it. So does Ronald Reagan.'"[3]

The article also called him "an unabashed period piece—an American-hurrah throwback to the can-do spirit and the black-and-white simplicities of the past, a revival of 'Mr. Smith Goes to Washington. . . .'"

President Popular turned his American-boy image into the aura of a hero and made everyone feel "tall in the saddle." As writer Lance Morrow said, "He gives America heroes—heroes in the gallery when he delivers a State of the Union address, heroes from the Olympics, heroes from old movies, John Wayne and Gary Cooper quotations in the middle of political speeches. His amiable being—the sheer niceness and normality of the man—seems to transcend his policies, to immunize him from the poisonous implications of some of his own opinions. Americans respond to the strength and clarity of his character, the predictability of his resolve. . . .

"He has made a brilliant career out of being underestimated. Critics have rather superciliously thought that an actor coming into politics was somehow getting in over his head, working in deeper professional waters than he should try. To a politician, an actor was a lightweight, which may say something about the limited self-awareness of politicians. If they had thought more carefully, or taken Reagan more seriously, they might have recognized that the actor's gift, applied to politics, has profound implications. . . .

"But then Reagan has always been attended by an aura of amiable averageness."[4]

The Reagan Magic

Our Popular President was not only the all-American boy of "amiable averageness" floating above the mundane problems of life, he was also a magician. "The Reagan magic" became a familiar term, used from the beginning of his administration to mean two things. One, he had such charisma that he drew people to him like a magnet, and two, he could get involved in sticky situations, face adverse circumstances that would have overwhelmed Ford and put Carter on Valium, and seem to wave his magic wand and come out smelling like the proverbial rose.

Morrow wrote, "The business of magic is sleight of hand; now you see it, now you don't. Ronald Reagan is a sort of masterpiece of American magic—apparently one of the simplest, most uncomplicated creatures alive, and yet a character of rich meanings, of complexities that connect him with the myths and powers of his country in an unprecedented way."[5]

Even when critics proclaimed Reagan to be down and on his way out, his magic touch could transform his public image. Hugh Sidey called him "the great Houdini of American politics . . . looking for the rainbow just beyond the thunderheads that always threaten but have not yet driven him down."[6]

After *Time* had raised the question of whether Reagan could recover from a particular crisis, a Bombay man said, in a letter to the editor, "In spite of his grave folly, President Reagan is well on his way to regaining public confidence. He is a survivor par excellence. A head of state can have all the requisites for leadership, but without charisma he will not make a dent. Even Reagan's worst critics must concede that it does not matter what attributes he has or lacks; he has that essential magnetic spell."[7]

With his magnetic spell, his magic touch, Reagan was able to create an aura of leadership, a combination of the best of FDR and JFK without the negatively aggressive traits that sometimes tainted their charm.

In addition to being Popular, Reagan had a touch of the Peaceful that kept him from appearing too eager or too tense. Writer Pat Buchanan, a former White House communications director, wrote in his book, *Right from the Beginning*, "Ronald Reagan was, and is, among the most decent and gracious human beings ever to serve in high office, a delight to work for and with, a genuinely lovable man."

Another commentator said, "He's the least neurotic president we've ever had." Some even saw Reagan as being so laid back and relaxed that he appeared to be "disengaged."

Lucky Irishman

Because the media have apparently spent no time learning the concepts of Hippocrates' four basic temperaments, they never seem to grasp why a political leader succeeds or fails in any certain direction. For those of us who do understand the different personalities, we don't have to grope for explanations. We know the Popular will have charm, style, and humor and be weak on details, memory, and facts. The Peaceful exudes an unruffled calm and amiability detracted by a stubborn streak and remote attitude when the subject is dull and dreary. Those characteristics defined Ronald Reagan.

Because we know the strengths and weaknesses of each personality, we are not as surprised by Reagan's magnetism as others seemed to be. *Newsweek* praised, "Although it may be too much to say that Ronald Reagan has reinvented the presidency during his first 45 months in office, he has unquestionably revitalized it.

"The aura of leadership may be the most significant accomplishment of Reagan's first term. . . . He has demonstrated a master of the bully pulpit that is equaled only by FDR in modern times."[8]

Yes, Reagan was the all-American boy, the hero, the balloon floating serenely overhead, the magician, the leader with unexplained appeal. Even though he made mistakes, the people loved him enough to forgive him. "That immunity from all the usual laws of politics—the teflon factor—is the ultimate mystery of Ronald Reagan's success."[9]

Another role Reagan played with ease was the lucky Irishman. Writing in *Newsweek,* Tom Morganthau attributed part of Reagan's luck to being in the right place at the right time and catching the sense of "the nation's deep-seated need to believe in itself again. Reagan was fortunate to take office after four failed presidencies and 16 years of national humiliation—Vietnam, Watergate, the Arab oil embargo, Iran."[10]

Reagan's Irish luck played well with his audience, who so desperately wanted a leader they could admire.

King Ronald

And there was something else. Even though we had won the Revolutionary War and emerged from the yoke of royal rule, for two centuries we've missed the pomp and circumstance of a monarchy and that settled feeling of a destiny determined by some divine appointment. I've always wanted to be a queen myself, and in my years of studying presidential personalities, aside from the brief spot of Camelot, no one else managed to lift our democratically elected leaders to the rank of royalty as well as the Reagans. At the time of Reagan's second nomination, Richard Moose, who had served as secretary of state for African affairs in the Carter administration, wrote from London that the Republicans should nominate Ronald Reagan to be king of the United States.

"Mr. Reagan obviously possesses many of the attributes of the modern constitutional monarch. He can play virtually any role. . . .

"Think, too, of the kingly duties that Mr. Reagan already handles so well. There could be no more appropriate figure in our United States to open the Olympics, to congratulate the Astronaut of the Week or to perform other non-controversial but meaningful national rituals. In sum, Mr. Reagan is a genuinely unifying figure."[11]

The most obvious strength of the Populars is their sense of humor and their ability to turn any trivial happening of life into a comedy routine, and that kind of humor served Reagan well.

In his book *Hold On, Mr. President*, Sam Donaldson gave Reagan credit for being funny. "In 1984 I told him, '[Walter Mondale] says you're intellectually lazy and you're forgetful. He says you're providing leadership by amnesia.' Reagan rose to the moment. 'I'm surprised he knew what the word meant.'"

Donaldson's favorite Reagan line on Mondale came when NBC's Andrea Mitchell yelled, "What about Mondale's charges?"

"'He ought to pay them,' said the president."[12]

Columnist James Reston, in writing about the 1984 election, said of Reagan, "He's the only guy in this presidential race with a sense of humor. He turns all his defects to advantage, and even laughs at his old age.

"The other day, addressing a convention of old geezers, he told them he had been around for quite awhile himself—now the oldest president in the history of the republic—but he insisted that he was still so active that he proposed this year 'to campaign in all 13 states.'"[13]

Let Reagan Be Reagan

When Reagan was running for reelection against Walter Mondale, a meticulous Perfect whose hair never blew in the wind, Ronnie played the engaging prince to Walter's pauper.

Murray Kempton, a columnist for *Newsweek*, wrote of these two: "Mondale's candle emits a faint glow, to be sure, but even if it took flame, the blaze of Ronald Reagan's light would still obscure it. For Reagan is an artist and Mondale is no more than the rest of us."

Although Kempton's assessment seemed to be quite prevalent during the 1984 campaign, many people were involved who, as all of us have sometimes felt, had an urge to make the candidates over into what the "experts" thought they ought to be. Of course, those of us who use the personalities in our everyday life have learned that everyone functions better when he or she is being natural. We know that when we play God with other people's personalities, we may change the original person's behavior, but then what do we have on our hands? We have a mongrel, a phony personality, one that is forced to function in weaknesses and not in strengths. It's like breeding a schnauzer with a poodle. It's a cute little thing, but what is it?

But in the political theater "handlers" don't always accept this fact, and they are often guilty of trying to make their candidates fit the image they have in mind. What they should remember is that each personality has strengths and weaknesses and the ideal situation is to keep our leaders functioning in their strengths and not in their weaknesses.

By the time Reagan was to debate Walter Mondale in 1984, the president's popularity was high, he'd learned some facts through daily experience, and his confidence level was at its peak. Mondale, who had been a Perfect vice president under Carter, had cataloged dates, figures, and places, but he had little charm or appeal. I tuned in that night, assured that Reagan would tell a few stories, answer the questions adequately, and come out a clear winner. But considering Nixon's 1960 loss on looks and Reagan's 1980 win on "There he goes again," I knew anything could happen. And it did.

We all expected Mondale to attack Reagan and run with his "lawn-mower approach," which he had used to cut up Democratic candidate Gary Hart during the primaries. Instead, Mondale came on kindly and even tried to tell a joke. He gave uncharacteristic smiles and looked strangely at ease. He didn't yell, accuse, or fight; he wasn't himself.

And what about the Great Communicator, the one who was a natural before the cameras, who had been on the stage forever, who never failed to answer difficult questions with an appropriate anecdote? He came on without his usual confidence, he floundered around for answers, and he seemed to have left his omnipresent mental joke book at home. *Newsweek* later called Reagan's sounds of silence "those painful spaces in which Reagan appeared to be searching in his mind and coming up empty." He was "groping for words and numbers, struggling to order his syntax and his thoughts, showing—or seeming to show—every last one of his 73 years." Overnight comments went from, "Isn't he adorable?" to "Is he senile?"

How quickly one view on television can shift opinion! What went wrong? Why did neither candidate seem to be himself that night? My personal assumption was that by some fluke each one of them had been trained to be like the other. I thought to myself that someone must have

said to Mondale, "You come across too heavy. You've got those dark circles, your neck tenses up, and you have no sense of humor. Why don't
you act cute like Ronnie, tell a few stories, smile a lot, and relax? Don't
be yourself, be like him."

Conversely, I assumed someone told the president, "The media say you
come across like a lightweight. You've been president now almost four
years, and they expect you to know everything to the most intricate detail.
We've prepared briefing books for you. In them is every fact you need to
know from the days of Eisenhower on to the present. The ones printed in
black are all-purpose information, the ones in red are hot issues. Don't
discuss these topics under any provocation. The blue printing means cool
issues. Take credit for them, look down in humility, and tilt your head.
You should not be yourself; you should be like Mondale."

I pictured Mondale practicing jokes and trying to change his personality while Reagan was locked alone in a closet memorizing details. The
Perfect presidential candidate was trying to put on a Popular mask that
didn't fit him and made him artificial while the Popular president was
being told to throw away what had made him popular and put on a Perfect mask of mastery.

If my picture were anywhere close, no wonder neither one looked natural. Reagan hadn't suddenly gone senile; he was a man who was over-
loaded with facts and figures. When a question was asked he couldn't
just answer it in his anecdotal, adorable style. He had to think about it
and grope for it. He wasn't being the Ronald Reagan America loved.

I used this little scenario that week in my seminars as a humorous
example of how phony we appear to others when we are masquerading
as someone we weren't meant to be. And within a week, my suppositions
had been verified. The news magazines told of the intensive training each
man had been put through, and as I hungrily devoured each article, I
was delighted to see how close to the facts my guesses had been. It wasn't
that I had inside information but that I knew their basic personalities and
could tell they were not themselves that night.

The facts were that Mondale's coaches had blocked out eight full days
for preparation and had presented him with two large, three-ring binders.
One had summaries of forty-five major issues, and the other gave answers
to twenty-two questions that might be posed. His writers had put in what
Reagan would probably say and what he should say that would, of course,
be better.

When adviser Patrick Caddell read the material, he felt that Reagan's hypothetical weak responses as written by the Mondale men sounded better than the right answers from Mondale. So he developed a new procedure for a different Mondale; he plotted a sneak attack along the lines of least expectation. Caddell devised the "gold-watch approach." Instead of beating Reagan down with his abundance of facts and risking a backlash in Reagan's favor, Mondale was to treat him like a kindly old gentleman who had served the nation well and who, for his own good, ought to retire—"sort of embracing a grandfather and gently pushing him aside."

Newsweek summarized the plan: "The President would be scripted to respond to Fighting Fritz and would find himself face to face with Gentleman Fritz instead—a deferential soul who praised him for his sincerity, credited him with honorable intentions and stipulated his achievements in reviving the economy and the national spirit."

Lacking a better approach, the trainers went along with Caddell's suggestions. Mondale was to look strong and masculine and hope Reagan would look elderly and confused. A reflective piece of white paper was to be placed on the podium, brightening Mondale's countenance and lightening his circles. One other tactic Caddell created was for Mondale to speak softly and turn his head away from Reagan so people would be aware of how deaf the president had become. Mondale, a decent man, refused to play this game.

No one was to know of the new Fritz, for the element of surprise was what would make it work. Caddell suggested, "a pantomime of deception . . . the strategy must be protected by a bodyguard of lies."

The same thing was happening in the Reagan camp, where the handlers were unwilling to let well enough alone; they weren't going to let the president go in there and wing it. One melancholy aide wrote a message creating a hypothetical scenario on how Mondale could win if Reagan didn't shape up and get serious about this whole debate. Obviously, this person had no understanding of the Popular personality that gets devastated by defeating facts. Even as children, the Popular, fun-loving, lighthearted nature is the one that cannot be disciplined by negative threats. While others may respond, the Popular at any age is motivated by positives—"Won't it be fun if we . . . ?" and "You will win when . . ." and "You look younger than you did four years ago if you. . . ."

Compliments are food for the Populars; confidence from their troops makes them great leaders and the roar of the crowds exhilarates them.

Remember how Roosevelt, sick and actually not far from death, revived and improved when he went out to the hustings on his fourth presidential campaign? Populars and Powerfuls receive strength from people while the Peacefuls and Perfects are drained by the crowds.

Conversely, being looked down upon as a dummy, being told the worst that could possibly happen, and being instructed to become something he wasn't discouraged Reagan and made him dread the debate that he had looked forward to with optimism in light of his past success and his innate feel for the camera.

William Buckley, the quintessential debater, had this to say about Reagan's ability. "Those who doubt that Ronald Reagan is an effective debater should try debating with him. I once did—subject: The Panama Canal Treaty. He was resourceful, humorous, cunning and eloquent." Left to his own ability Reagan could be a masterful debater. His aides almost made a fatal mistake.

Naturally, the men trying to train him to be perfect were Perfects. *Newsweek* called them "high-IQ sorts and unbashful about it." It said Reagan, as with all Popular personalities, was "uncomfortable in the company of intellectuals—those, in any case, whom he felt to be flaunting their own qualities of mind or belittling his. . . . They had intimidated Reagan by their bearing alone."

This group felt Reagan had gone soft and had no killer instinct, so they set up mock debates where David Stockman was Mondale. *Newsweek* said, "Stockman totaled him—pummeled him with facts, figures and accusations to a point where the president lost his patience, his temper and finally, some thought, his confidence in himself."

His trainers, not understanding the differences in personalities, tried to make a Popular into a Perfect like themselves. By doing this, they stripped him of his natural strengths, made him put on a foreign mask, and sent him out to function in his weaknesses.

How many of us are doing that to others? How many of us expect everyone else to function as we do, and when they don't, try to make them over? We force them to put on a mask and to tread water in a sea of weaknesses.

When we saw that debate, we viewed a Mondale trying to be funny and we saw a truly humorous man groping for facts. Neither one was natural. We were all uneasy as viewers, and now we know why.

As Senator Paul Laxalt said, they should have "let Reagan be Reagan."

Tell Stories and Personalize Problems

Despite the debate fiasco, Reagan won reelection, and his victory seemed to energize him—and us, as we settled in for four more years of Reagan's sterling, humor-filled performance on the political stage. On his seventy-sixth birthday he was heard to say, "I've been around for a while. I can remember when a hot story broke and the reporters would run in yelling, 'Stop the chisels!'"

At the 150th birthday party for the state of Texas, he quipped, "I'm always happy to be any place that's twice as old as I am."

When speaking in Florida, he opened with, "Ponce de Leon looked for the fountain of youth. And just in case he found it, I've got a Thermos jug."

Reagan used his humor to entertain, to defuse tension, and to help himself relax. Once he had the first laughing response in a speech, he was at ease. He often strayed from the text of a speech to insert a story. Speaking on the shores of Lake Michigan, he ad-libbed, "Being here along the lake reminds me of a story—when you're my age, everything reminds you of a story."

He told stories even at serious meetings. Some felt he rambled on to avoid confrontations and to distract the opposition.

He made a hobby out of collecting and telling Russian jokes. One favorite was, "A man goes to the official agency, puts down his money, and is told he can take delivery of his automobile in exactly ten years.

"'Morning or afternoon?' the purchaser asks. 'Ten years from now, what difference does it make?' replies the clerk.

"'Well,' says the car-buyer, 'the plumber's coming in the morning.'"[14]

Along with Reagan's sense of humor was his unique ability to personalize politics. He could take a complex issue and bring it into focus by making a personal analogy that the public could understand. Roger Rosenblatt, writing in *Time,* explained it this way: "In forests of complex issues, Reagan likes to point to the trees, to individuals. . . .

"Think back to all you know of Ronald Reagan, and there is almost always some other person in the picture. Originally, that person was you, the individual tree he addressed with startling success when he posed the question in the 1980 presidential debates, 'Are you better off than you were four years ago?' In the six years since, you have remained preeminent in the President's view. It still is you he addresses in weekly radio broadcasts and in television appearances, establishing an intimacy by look and voice that television, for all its domestic directness, usually denies. . . .

"Britain is America's ally, but that abstract agreement is brought to life by personification, by the friendship and ideological comradeship of Reagan and Margaret Thatcher. Libya is America's enemy, but that enmity glowers as a private hostility between Reagan and Muammar Gaddafi. If the values of American initiative need commending, Reagan will shed his spotlight on a Mother Hale of Harlem, as he did in the 1985 State of the Union message, and elevate one woman to emblemize an entire economic and social theory. If heroism in war is to be honored, a single veteran will stand beside the President on the White House steps, creating a tableau that speaks, if imprecisely, for itself. . . .

"Reagan wholeheartedly seems to believe that individuals and stories about individuals are the keys to general truths."[15]

Because he had been an actor, whatever Reagan said and did the press looked upon it as part of a play. I assume if he'd been a doctor the writers would have described him in medical terms, or, had he been a general like Ike, they'd have used military expressions. But Reagan was an actor, and the media loved to write reviews of his roles.

When Reagan performed well with Gorbachev at the Geneva Summit, Thomas Griffith wrote, "The press has long treated Reagan's acting career as a poor qualification for office, but one valuable lesson Reagan surely learned in Hollywood: how to fit himself into a role and stay consistent in the part, even when a film is being shot over a period of weeks."[16]

In March 1987, the President "put on a performance" for the press at a news conference and gave "well-rehearsed answers." George Church wrote in *Time*, "As theatre it was an effective show, calculated to convey the impression of a President physically and mentally recovered from his Iranscam doldrums and back in charge."[17]

When he was accused of political improprieties, in typical keeping with his personality type, Reagan remained "stubborn and unbowed and believing and upbeat; he refuses to hold a grudge. . . . Reagan is calling for the nation to forget and move into the future. Details be damned; unanswered questions be hanged. The great congressional inquisition is finished. Does that mean it is all over? Yes, says Reagan, 'as far as the audience is concerned.' And Reagan has read the American audience better than any other politician of this decade."[18]

The Great Communicator

Much to the dismay of his opponents, Reagan's years of acting experience, his natural humor and quick wit, and his sincere confidence in his ability all added up to his designation as the Great Communicator. He was able to bring people over to his side in such a charming way that they didn't realize they'd moved until they heard themselves saying "I do." Suddenly, they were married to an idea they didn't even like because the walk up the aisle had been so convincing.

In a September 1987 Times-Mirror report, the electorate was divided into eleven categories with colorful names such as moralists, upbeats, disaffecteds, and passive poor. One of the report's major conclusions was that Ronald Reagan cut across all previous segments of society to unite people behind him, but not necessarily to the Republican party. His personal magnetism was the attraction. In conclusion, the report stated, "Reagan surely earned his 'Great Communicator' fame by conquering four distinct appeals to four distinct groups without turning one against the other. It will be a difficult feat to match."[19]

And so it was!

Newsweek called Reagan "the Master of the Media," and told of his trip to Ireland, where he "played his part like a pro, hoisting a glass with the villagers in John and Mary O'Farrell's pub in Ballyporeen and noting his authentically humble origins in the authentically Irish town. Landing earlier at Shannon airport, he said he came to find not only his own roots, but America's roots as well—a bit of hyperbole that must have rung true to at least some of the 40 million Irish-Americans at home. It was boffo, solid gold at the political box office, and it left his aides wishing for more."[20]

And there was more. In his book Right from the Beginning, Patrick Buchanan summarized the successes: "In November of 1985, we had gone to Geneva for the president's first encounter with Secretary Gorbachev, with the press warning the summit would blow up if we refused to compromise on SDI [strategic defense initiative]. The president refused, and we came home in triumph.

"In October of 1986, we had gone to Reykjavik, where the president played that wild Sunday afternoon poker game on nuclear weapons; and when the president angrily walked out of the first-floor room at Hofdi House, rather than yield up SDI to Mikhail Gorbachev, he escaped the Russian bear trap and returned home to another triumphant welcome—

to the puzzlement, again, of a press corps that had already laid at Ronald Reagan's feet blame for the summit's collapse.

"From an approval rating in the mid-50s in February of 1985, Ronald Reagan, by the fall of 1986, was in the mid-70s—an unprecedented register of national esteem for a second-term president."

Accepting Weaknesses

As with every set of strengths, there are accompanying weaknesses. For the Powerfuls, the assets are strong and loud, and the weaknesses are equally noticeable. Peacefuls have quiet, low-key strengths and weaknesses that aren't obvious. The Perfects have deep, intellectual, analytical strengths that, when thwarted, turn into depression. Populars, like Reagan, have appealing, obviously optimistic strengths that show. They feel it's what's up front that counts. The Populars, claim their critics, have no depth, no goals, no concern for facts, and an utter disregard for the harsh realities of life. But Reagan minimized his weaknesses and if you asked him how he did it, he'd tell you a story to prove it.

His Popular charm enabled him to force his policies through a hostile Congress, an accomplishment that resulted in the great reduction in interest rates and eventually in unemployment. In foreign policy we saw him free Grenada and punish Libya for its terrorist acts against Americans.

However, because of his Peaceful tendencies Reagan often delegated responsibilities to others and was not as aware as he should have been of what they actually were doing. Throughout the Iranscam investigations, there were numerous explanations of Reagan's involvement in and detachment from the arms-for-hostages negotiations. Parodying a crucial phrase from the Watergate era, wags asked, "What did the president forget, and when did he choose to forget it?"

The thinking public was shocked at Reagan's lack of knowledge about what was going on and former Nixon aide Chuck Colson, who certainly had experience in cover-up operations, said, "In the Nixon White House, you couldn't make any foreign-policy decision, I don't care how insignificant, without the president. The fact that foreign policy could be conducted out of the basement of the White House without the president knowing about it—I slept less well at night."[21]

In all the different political perspectives I read about Reagan, no one connected Reagan's supposed failures with his inborn personality, especially as it fit so perfectly into a typical Popular pattern.

Brent Scowcroft explained that the president's concept of what was going on "was not accurately reflected in the reality of the operation." This is a diplomatic language for "he lied." And even after Reagan had the truth laid out clearly before him, he couldn't see that he'd done anything wrong. His classic explanation could well go down in a history book written for Populars. "A few months ago, I told the American people I didn't trade arms for hostages. My heart and my best intentions still tell me that is true, but the facts and the evidence tell me it is not."

Despite the fact that for months the press tried to present President Reagan as a liar to the American people, three major investigations of the Iran-Contra affair found him innocent of wrongdoing and as a typical Popular, he once again landed on his feet.

As the press wondered why the president often left details to subordinates, no one came up with a better rationale than "that's his management style." No one seemed to realize that he was born optimistic and his "happy days" approach put him in the presidency. He was not a peculiar, one-of-a-kind person, as the press made him appear. He was not "out to lunch." As a Popular he was out to win. He had known since childhood that each one of us wants to live happily ever after, and he kept that little flickering flame alive in the hearts of the American people for eight years.

Reagan knew that we, the public, like silver linings better than dark clouds and he correctly estimated that the majority of Americans wouldn't know Iran from Iraq and would think Oliver North's lying was patriotic. He sensed we weren't up to another Watergate investigated by sanctimonious senators and puritanical prosecutors, many of whom wouldn't have made it to the top if they hadn't compromised a few standards along the way.

Reagan had a sixth sense of what the public wanted, something that is typical of the Popular. He wasn't acting; for him, "all the world" was a stage.

In Washington, the Perfect pundits assumed the president was plotting all night, coming up with carefully phrased excuses, but he was sleeping soundly, full of confidence that when he opened his mouth creative reasons would flow forth effortlessly. After all, they always had.

But when the stock market crash produced Black Monday, when Reagan's Supreme Court nominees seemed to be chosen by some loony lottery, and when Nancy had breast-cancer surgery, even the ebullient Ronnie had difficulty bouncing back. As a Popular, he couldn't face life when it wasn't fun, and his Peaceful touch refused to deal with confrontation. While the people waited for a sign from him that all was well with the world, he stayed in his room. Suddenly the Great Communicator was refusing to communicate.

The Perfect Partner

Populars usually marry Perfects who prepare a way for them and pick up the pieces behind them. This arrangement worked well for the Reagans. He smiled; she worried. When he had surgery, she cared for him. Then the scene changed; Nancy was in the hospital. The steady one was unsteady. The roles were reversed. President Popular had his props pulled out from under him, and the press attacked.

Nancy said, "We've hit bottom. It can't get any lower than this." But after reviewing reality, Reagan packed up his troubles in his old kit bag and regained his usual optimism. He turned his back on his critics and invited Gorbachev to a summit. The king's not dead; he was just napping.

Seeing a Sunrise Instead of Twilight

Reagan's reign will not be remembered for the depth of its characters or the intricacies of its plot, but for the brilliance of its setting, the humor of its script, the resiliency of its cast, the charisma of its leading man, and the conclusion we all wanted to see: "They lived happily ever after."

No one can be all things to all people, but Ronald Reagan used his strengths to their fullest and did not let his weaknesses slow him down.

President Reagan, a legend in his own time, received the standing ovation of his life at the 1988 Republican National Convention in the Superdome in New Orleans. I had the exciting privilege to be among the chanting and foot-stomping thousands at the Republican convention, so I was able to personally experience the magnetic attraction that Reagan's appearance created by his merely standing at the podium without saying a word. Here was the all-American boy with his winning smile looking down from the huge TV monitors high above the convention floor. Here was the hero we all desperately wanted, tall in the saddle, an average person who had fulfilled the American dream of becoming president. Here was the magician who took words that appeared ordinary on paper and turned them into a moving message so full of conviction, so rich in rosy images, so touching as to bring tears to thousands. Here was the master showman who, with a sweep of his hand or a catch in his throat, would cause chanting and applause to interrupt his forty-four-minute message sixty times. Here was the king with the passionate desire to please his subjects, waving to the beat of "Hail to the Chief," as the delegates erupted into screams and cheers while holding placards saying "Ron for King." Here was the eternal optimist, lifting the hopes of his people.

"When I pack up my bags in Washington, don't expect me to be happy to hear all this talk about the twilight of my life," he said. "Twilight? Not in America. Here it's a sunrise every day. Fresh new opportunities. Dreams to build."

Here was the movie star encouraging his cast, telling candidate George Bush, "So George, I'm in your corner. I'm ready to volunteer a little advice now and then, and offer a pointer or two on strategy if asked. I'll help keep the facts straight or just stand back and cheer. But George, just one personal request: Go out there and win one for the Gipper."

By that time I was in tears and couldn't imagine our country without the Popular personality of this president. No matter what anyone might think of his credentials, his creeds, or his accomplishments, one could hardly resist feeling moved by his magnetic presence and wondering who could possibly fill his shoes. As the convention crowd exploded in cheers and tears that night, thousands of red, white, and blue balloons dropped from the Superdome ceiling, confetti floated through the air, and a costumed marching band played "The Stars and Stripes Forever."

We watched the last act of an eight-part play as Ronnie kissed Nancy tenderly, took her hand in his, waved a last good-bye, and walked off the stage to the lyrics of "I'm Proud to be an American."

This was the swan song, a classic moment, the last hurrah of a Popular president.

Reagan will remain forever as a true representative of the Popular personality. No matter what criticism he received he could turn it into humor, gently making fun of himself. No matter how serious his mistakes or how forgetful his mind, he could shrug his shoulders and smile and we'd be on his side. No matter how difficult the problem, he could always bring it down to a simple story that made a point.

Ronald Reagan knew how to win friends and influence people; he could keep the public's eye focusing on his strengths and quickly forgiving his weaknesses. The teflon president closed his era of peace and prosperity with the extraordinary approval rating of 60 percent. The Great Communicator came in on his strengths and, with minor dips in his ratings, maintained his popularity at a remarkable level.

Even people who hadn't voted for him had a genuine affection for him, and we all were saddened in November 1994 when he bravely announced that he was in the beginning stages of Alzheimer's disease. In his own handwriting, Reagan told the nation, "I now begin the journey that will lead me into the sunset of my life. I know that for America there will always be a bright dawn ahead."

Ronald Reagan
Popular Personality

The following lists of strengths and weaknesses include words and phrases used in newspaper articles, magazines, books, television, and radio to describe President Reagan's Popular personality. Check the characteristics that also apply to you.

Strengths
___ Able to personalize problems
___ Master of the media
___ Magnetic storyteller
___ Totes a magic wand
___ Has that essential magic spell
___ Refuses to hold a grudge
___ Fairy tale of American power
___ Makes reality conform with his desires
___ Looks through lens of best intentions
___ Afternoon family-theater performer
___ People like him and trust him
___ The old master
___ The great communicator
___ Looking for the rainbow
___ Accentuates the positive

Weaknesses
___ Sometimes disengaged
___ Drifts into oft-repeated anecdotes
___ Unfounded optimism
___ Erratic and selective memory
___ Gives salesmen speeches
___ Slides around the question
___ Tends to delegate too much authority
___ Too impetuous
___ Unduly confident

___ Waxes eloquent
___ Able to stage the news
___ Inspires loyalty
___ Evokes praise
___ Discerning nature
___ Stands tall in the saddle
___ Upbeat spirit
___ Patriotic vitality
___ The great disarmer
___ Persuasive
___ **TOTAL**   ___ **TOTAL**

Total of your presidential profile of Popular strengths and weaknesses: _____

Are You a Leader Like Reagan?

Reagan was called the Great Communicator but not because he was a gifted orator like Winston Churchill or a studied politician like Richard Nixon. It was because he knew how to reach the hearts of the people. He knew how to take complex problems and boil them down to a simple story that would relate to his listeners. He annoyed his critics who said he was superficial and without knowledge on the subjects on which he spoke. They were baffled by his ability to pull out a story to make a point they had written position papers on that no one seemed to understand. They couldn't see that while he might not have been an intellectual he had a mind full of file drawers stuffed with stories. He had anecdotes on poverty and heartache, on patriotism and the military, on Democrats and doubters.

Even though he'd not bothered to alphabetize his mental files, he knew how to pull out the right example for any occasion. And if he pulled out the wrong one, he'd somehow make it fit and by the time he'd told the story the people would have forgotten the original question.

This ability to charm with words and humor seems to be a talent open only to the Popular personality, those who don't take themselves too seriously and who don't try to be something they really aren't. Phonies aren't relaxed enough to be spontaneous.

Peggy Noonan, presidential speech writer, said that Reagan was the easiest person she'd ever worked with. She would put the text on the

TelePrompTer and at the end of each point she would leave a space and print "tell story here." When Reagan saw that, he would smile, look up, and tell a story. It didn't always fit the point, but people loved his humor and they didn't care.

If you have a Popular, fun-loving nature, capitalize on your sense of humor and learn to use it as a positive. Discipline yourself to listen so you can play off of other people's lines and don't talk just to fill space. The biggest problem for people who can tell stories with humor and panache is that they tend to ramble on and not make a point. Reagan had a sense of timing that he honed over the years, and he knew when to stop. He never milked too much out of a good story.

Reagan also taught us that you don't have to tell dirty jokes to be funny. You only have to make sure what you're saying relates to the people and the occasion and that it has some moral value. Learn from Reagan, discipline yourself, listen to those around you, don't use humor to knock down but to build up, use stories that make a point. You may not become president, but you'll make life for yourself and others a lot more fun!

17

THE COMICAL CAMPAIGN
OF 1988

Principle to Learn: The people want a leader with all strengths
and no weaknesses.

History has shown that every campaign has its own brand of humor, but
the presidential race of 1988—especially the primaries leading up to the
presidential election—seemed exceptional, not only in its moments of
genuine hilarity but also in its candidates' shocking lapses of what seemed
like common sense. As we consider presidential personalities, it will be
insightful to us to study the dynamics of the more recent elections because
most of the candidates who played important roles in those campaigns
are still in the public eye. And, of course, a couple of them have ended
up in the White House!

In 1988 the American people were searching for a superman, someone who could perform with the charm of Reagan without any of his
weaknesses. We wanted a Shakespearian hero without the tragic flaw.
But does such a person ever exist?

When people don't understand the basic personality patterns, they
assume there really is a leader who has all strengths and no weaknesses.

The week before the 1988 election *Newsweek* wrote, "The dream persists of a candidate who will one day cast off the handlers, ignore the polls and focus groups, sound genuine notes of leadership and rouse the country to a new sense of purpose."[1]

When we're realistic (and we understand the personality types) we want to find out what's behind the public appearance of candidates as well as potential partners or employees. Often persons in those positions try to hide their feelings and opinions until they can get a sense of which way the wind is blowing. Doris Kearns Goodwin wrote that all politicians are "skilled at concealing those aspects of character and belief that might antagonize or intimidate the observer."[2]

Because of human beings' ability to hide their real feelings in order to be all things to all people, we have often assumed flawed candidates were virtuous and then we've been surprised later when their true colors began to bleed through. In the campaign before the 1988 election, however, morality became a focal point, and we opened up every Pandora's box we could find, looking for dirt. Not since we chose Jimmy Carter for his obvious morality and spiritual values had we been so concerned with finding a virtuous man whose price was far above rubies. Old Diogenes, the Greek philosopher, had been so desperate to find one honest man that he carried his lantern with him night and day, but in the years preceding the campaign of 1988 Diogenes would have worn himself out and burned his candles to the nub while seeking truth.

Leading up to this point we had abandoned morals as old-fashioned and restrictive; we had poured black and white, right and wrong, into the same container and produced a comfortable gray. We'd not been concerned with a little deception as long as it was packaged attractively.

But in 1987 things finally got bad enough to jar our jaded sensibilities so that we appreciated the merit of truth. All around us, candidates vying for election—as well as other public figures—were philandering and lying, plagiarizing and lying, tattling and lying, making illegal trades and lying, and one, Oliver North, even became a hero through lying. Martin E. Marty, University of Chicago professor, named 1987 the "Year of the Lie" and asked where we could look for truth.

"Politics, however, offered the most flagrant examples of lying in recent seasons. A bipartisan assault on truth reached the highest officers and office-seekers of the land who were not quite convincing when they 'could not remember' hundreds of details that would have spread truth but would have hurt them. Television images of those who admitted that they lied—and proud of it for a noble cause—disqualify government officials as tour guides in the search for truth."[3]

Once lying became a recognized sin again, the press began to make demands on the candidates' morality that had never been required before. Snooping and reporting by avid newspeople brought true confessions into the open, and when some candidates were asked in public the A (adultery) question as well as the M (marijuana) question, those who kissed felt led to tell all.

Democratic candidates Al Gore and Bruce Babbitt quickly admitted to having smoked marijuana way back in their youth and even Gore's wife, Tipper, known for her purity and pursuit of producers of records with lurid lyrics, confessed to a smoke or two in the past. Massachusetts Governor Michael Dukakis, another Democratic candidate, said he was glad his wife had licked her addiction to diet pills, and Jesse Jackson's wife cut off reporters' questions by saying that if Jesse had been fooling around, she didn't want to know it.

For those candidates who had faltered but were running anyway, there was still hope—*if* they had produced a proper and contrite confession. The public was a forgiving lot if only the sinner would say he or she was sorry. Columnist Cal Thomas told me in November 1987 when we were both speaking at the same forum, "If I were running for office I'd put out a press release on every known sin I'd ever committed and then there'd be nothing left for the press to discover."

Many of the candidates seemed to do just that. To prevent the press from blasting them with surprise exposés, they began confessing sins they'd committed in third grade and asking for forgiveness. And for those who learned how to play the game, the ploy seemed to work. In contrast, those who refused to play the game paid the price in the polls. A *Time* survey showed that only 7 percent of the public was bothered by Democratic candidate Gary Hart's affair with Donna Rice but 69 percent were upset that he lied about it.[4]

Let's take a closer look at some of the key players in this extraordinary campaign and examine how their personality types helped determine the outcome of the race. Perhaps by studying the personalities of some of these characters of the past we will be better able to judge them should they aspire to the presidency in the future.

Joseph Biden Jr.
Popular Personality

Whether or not you remember Joseph R. Biden Jr.'s appearance in the 1988 campaign, he is worthy of reading about for his pure representation of the Popular strengths and weaknesses. Even though he was born in 1942, Biden talked of himself as a "baby boomer," waxing eloquent on "my generation" and boasting that he was the second youngest person ever to be elected to the U.S. Senate.

Wherever he went, Biden talked about youth and vigor, apparently in hopes of distracting the viewer from focusing on his funny, fuzzy see-through hair. He touted himself as an orator and told touching tales about what the American family used to be like in the good old baby-boom days when Mother stayed home where she belonged, kissed you good-bye in the morning, and met you at the school bus with warm cookies in her hand. By the time he had painted this pretty picture, all of us who ever had mothers who baked cookies were wiping away tears of nostalgia.

But that never lasted long, for as soon as he pulled on our heartstrings he would jerk them up sharply and cry out, "The world has changed! Only 19 percent of the children in America today live in a family, the so-called nuclear family, with Mom and Dad, Mom at home and no divorce." Now all those who've been divorced are gasping in guilt.

And so it went with Biden's oratory, a veritable roller-coaster of emotion. Popular, talkative Biden only regretted he couldn't run against the Great Communicator because, Biden assured us, Reagan would have met his match.

The *New York Times,* reviewing Biden's New Hampshire campaign, said when Biden connected with an audience, "he can moisten eyes and set heads to nodding . . . He is buoyed by such moments, by those who show up to hear the 'hot' candidate, who come ready to be transported. Even in a living room at a modest house party, Mr. Biden seems incapable of giving a low-key speech."[5]

Senator Shoot-from-the-Lip, as he was sometimes called, had a Popular personality with a few attributes of the Powerful—driven, high-powered, hot, confident, impulsive—but not Powerful enough to get himself under control.

Biden was also a clear example of the principle "strengths carried to extremes become weaknesses." As a Popular he had the ability to talk flu-

ently, speak passionately, and use colorful examples. But he carried those
strengths to the extreme, monopolizing any conversation, exaggerating,
unconcerned with the facts, making careless remarks, and thinking with
his mouth. He obviously loved people and wanted them to love him, but
if they faulted him, he jumped on the defensive.

The Populars frequently have a problem with the truth because they
exaggerate so consistently that after a while they don't have any idea what
the facts might once have been. They have little concept of statistics, frequently make up their own to fit their need, and will innately top whatever story has just been told.

Biden's mouth was "both his greatest asset and his greatest liability,"
according to a *Time* campaign portrait asking "Does Joe Biden talk too
much?"[6]

In retrospect, Joe did not follow the easy path or the difficult path; he
followed the wrong path, a path strewn with misstatements, exaggeration, anger, and worst of all, plagiarism.

Biden was riding happily down that wrong path until the *New York
Times* printed a story exposing the fact that Biden had not only dupli-
cated a touching tale originating with British Labor Party leader Neil Kinnock, but he had even copied the same gestures. The *Times* cited paral-
lel videos to prove its charge. Suddenly people were calling in to say Biden
had used also Robert Kennedy's and Hubert Humphrey's words as if they
were his own, and the nightly news showed Biden and tapes of his selected
mentors side by side, giving clear evidence to any doubters.

Next came the report that Biden had plagiarized parts of a *Law Review*
article while at Syracuse University in 1965. This news alone would not
have been enough to derail him, but added to the other quotes, it was
indicting. As Biden and his staff were trying to dig out from under the
damaging details, news was phoned in that *Newsweek* was publishing a
story that C-SPAN had a film of Biden lashing out at a man who had dared
to ask about his academic credentials.

"I think I probably have a much higher IQ than you do, I suspect,"
Biden told the man as he began a rapid-fire account of his credentials. "I
went to law school on a full academic scholarship, the only one in my
class to have a full academic scholarship. I decided I didn't want to be in
law school and ended up in the bottom two-thirds of my class and then
decided I wanted to stay, went back to law school and, in fact, ended up
in the top half of my class. I won the international moot-court competi-

tion. I was the outstanding student in the political science department at the end of my year. I graduated with three degrees from undergraduate school and 165 credits—only needed 123 credits. And I would be delighted to sit down and compare my IQ to yours if you'd like."[7]

The angry, defensive way in which Biden attacked the poor questioner reflected his touchy nature and his suppressed, hair-trigger anger. Had Biden been secure in the fact that he had followed his own principle of "uncompromising candor," he would have had no reason to react so strongly. But in examining the tape, the reporters had found that Biden actually had "attended law school on a half-time scholarship based on financial need and . . . he graduated 76th out of a class of 85. His undergraduate academic records show he graduated from Delaware 506th in a class of 688 with a 'C' average and that he got his undergraduate degree with a dual major in history and political science, two majors, not three."[8]

In a year when character and honesty were considered key virtues and Gary Hart had already self-destructed, Biden's collection of misstatements and plagiarism were more than the public could bear. The great orator had overspoken.

Joe Biden's Popular strengths were carried to extremes, and they caught up with him.

Robert Dole
Powerful Personality

The presidential candidate of 1988 with the most Powerful personality was Robert Dole. As a born leader with driving ambition, Dole spent a lifetime projecting an image of power and strength. Even though he didn't make it to the campaign finals, he, like Roosevelt, is a clear example of the born leader who rose above crippling circumstances, and his Powerful profile showed both the strengths and weaknesses of the born leader.

From the time he was a child, Bob Dole knew he was going to make something of himself. Living in the dust bowl of Kansas during the depression, he learned, as many of us did, that hard work was the only hope for success. Bob got up at 5:30, did his chores, exercised, lifted weights, and delivered papers. He studied hard enough to be a member of the National Honor Society, was captain of the basketball team, played end on the football squad, and was a winner on the track team. In his spare time, he was a soda jerk for the local drugstore in Russell, Kansas, where he frequently stayed to close up at 11:00 P.M.

Right from the beginning, he had the Powerful traits of wanting to be in control of his life, to be independent, and not owe anything to anybody. He kept himself in physical and mental shape, he had natural good looks, and even as a teenager he had an air of authority.

With three hundred dollars he had reluctantly borrowed from George J. Deines, a banker and drugstore customer, Bob headed off to the University of Kansas. He wanted to become a doctor and show those hometown people what he could make of himself, but instead, World War II roared onto the scene and any real American man just had to join up. Those who copped out for any reason or were rejected when they applied were designated "4-F," a label equal to wimp or nerd today.

Dole enlisted in the army, was commissioned a second lieutenant, and was sent to Italy. In typical army style, the young man from the plains of Kansas was assigned to the mountain division. Three weeks before the end of the war in Europe, Dole was hit by a mortar while helping a buddy on Hill 913, forty miles south of Bologna.

Although he received two Bronze Stars for his heroism, the awards did little to cheer him as he lay paralyzed for thirty-nine months, enduring eight operations. Anyone would be depressed over such a devastating disruption of his life's plans, but a Powerful personality can't handle being dependent upon someone else for survival. When we understand the basic personalities and their desires, we can see what causes depression in each type of person. Take away what we want in life, make us feel helpless to achieve our goals, and we will become discouraged.

The Populars get depressed when life is no longer fun and no one is giving them complimentary attention.

The Perfects get depressed when things aren't lining up properly and people aren't sensitive to their inner feelings.

The Peacefuls get depressed when they have to face conflict personally (they can always mediate other people's problems with a cool detachment) and no one is appreciating their worth.

The Powerfuls, like Bob Dole, become depressed when any part of their life is out of control, whether it is work, family, finances, health, or body.

In our awareness of the four basic temperament patterns, we can understand that the Powerful must be in control and that his greatest fear is appearing weak. Dole was born with a personality that wanted to be in charge and be strong, so his incapacitating tragedy hit straight across his major desires, crippling him physically and draining him emotionally.

As a determined winner, Dole, like Roosevelt, underwent painful rehabilitation and tried to bury his handicap from view, carrying a pen in his useless right hand to give the appearance that he could write momentarily, if he chose to. It also kept unknowing people from reaching out to shake hands with him. He trained himself to write with his left hand, which still had no feeling in it, and to button his shirt.

The one word most frequently used about Dole by columnists and critics was "contradictory." In Dole's case, his contradictions confused the public. He resented any help and yet he needed support to win. He didn't seek suggestions and yet he couldn't succeed without the input of others. He had strong opinions and yet he held back until he saw which way the wind was blowing.

Dole was described as a hatchet man, acid-tongued, an opportunist, friendless, a slasher and cutter, tactless and obsessive. On the other hand, he was said to have compassion for those with disabilities, and he quietly visited their homes, pushed for legislation supporting them, and set up a foundation to train them.

People who knew him avoided doing anything to cross him up; no one wanted to be on his "black list." He seemed to be perpetually looking down on dummies. In the 1988 primary contest Dole made strong, bold statements against his peaceful opponent, George Bush. "Bush says [he's] been standing by the president for 7 years. Well I've been out there working for him," he said.[9]

Dole used terms like "hard choices," "sacrifice," and "an end to self-indulgence" to predict what needed to be done to get the country's economy on the move again. While Bush smiled and talked of "continued prosperity" and "peace through strength," Dole latched heavily onto the stock-market crash as a precursor of gloom and doom.

Newsweek said, "Dole is tough, combative, and decisive." His dry wit, the magazine stated, "can curdle into bitterness and anger. While he is compassionate toward the infirm and ailing, his patience is often wafer-thin with the shortcomings of people who are—as he puts it—'whole'. When he ran for vice president with Gerald Ford in 1976 and in his abortive 1980 bid for the presidency, Dole sank armadas of advisers, occasionally flinging briefing papers at them."[10]

With Bob Dole, now majority leader in the U.S. Senate, there will always be contradictions. He will never be predictable, but he has, at some point in the last few years, taken time to assess his weaknesses and set out to overcome them. He has realized that his strengths, when carried to extremes, have become weaknesses and with the help of his talented wife, Elizabeth, he seems to be making progress. If he can temper his driven combative nature, quit straddling fences for security, and trade in his sword for a plowshare, he could become the leader he was born to be. If he never becomes president, he may be the perpetual opposition leader, the thorn in the side of each Democratic president.

Michael Dukakis
Peaceful-Perfect Personality

Massachusetts Governor Michael Dukakis, a Peaceful-Perfect, was known for his rock-solid integrity and his hands-on management style.

A lackluster campaigner, Dukakis, nicknamed "the Duke," had originally drawn attention not because of his personality but his ability to raise money, a constant necessity for presidential candidates. In his first three months of fund-raising, Dukakis collected $4.2 million, two-thirds of it coming from Massachusetts.

The staff Dukakis put together had seasoned political veterans John Sasso and Paul Tully in charge. Sasso was so close to Dukakis as to be considered by insiders as his alter ego or his brother. With this unified relationship and reputation for strong business ethics, it seemed unlikely that the Dukakis team would be involved in trying to shoot down fellow Democratic candidate Joe Biden. So when Sasso reported to Dukakis that *Time* was printing a story saying the videos showing that Biden had "borrowed" a speech by British Labor Party leader Neil Kinnock had come from the Dukakis camp, the Duke didn't even *ask* Sasso if it were true. Instead he went directly into a press conference to deny any involvement and righteously reported, "Anybody who knows me and knows the kind of campaigns I run knows how strongly I feel about negative campaigning." That should have been the end of the matter except that the press kept after the team until Tuesday afternoon when John Sasso confessed to Dukakis that he was, in fact, the person who had sent the tapes to the *New York Times*, the *Des Moines Register,* and NBC News.

Had Dukakis been a Powerful personality, he would have fired Sasso on the spot. But being Peaceful, he had the typical reaction: Don't make hasty decisions and avoid conflict as long as possible. The governor eventually had to admit publicly that his men had sent the video, but he claimed he'd known nothing about what they were doing. This admission was a hard one for a man to make who'd boasted about his hands-on management and who had ridiculed Ronald Reagan for being out of touch with his administration. Again, because of his Peaceful nature, Dukakis, even with such hot evidence in hand, couldn't bear to fire his alter ego; instead he gave Sasso a two-week leave in which to reform his strategy. But the public, in a state of disbelief, caused enough of an uproar within the next four hours that the beleaguered governor had to reconsider and dismiss both Sasso and Tully, who had been aware of what was going on and hadn't told Dukakis. With his two campaign strategists gone, Dukakis, the hands-on CEO, had no close aides to keep his hands on.

Newsweek called it the "Dukakis fiasco."

While some of the press assumed loss of the Dukakis top strategists might derail his campaign, they did not count on his underlying will of iron, a hidden Peaceful trait, or his Perfect ability to regroup efficiently with or without his staff. The Duke kept his peace throughout the difficult days following the disclosure and didn't resort to name-calling or blame-shifting.

In contrast to Biden's contrived coal-mining ancestors, Dukakis's father really was a Greek immigrant to this country when he was fifteen, and within eight years he was in Harvard Medical School. His mother was the first Greek girl to go to college after graduating from Haverhill High School—my alma mater and the school where I taught for four years.

As the Kennedy family had a driving desire to lift themselves from low-class Boston Irish to the highest position in the land, so the Dukakis family had a need to continue demonstrating that immigrants from Greece could become doctors, governors, and even the president. The family had a strict moral code and high standards, and Mike became president of the student council and lettered in three sports. His high school yearbook labeled him "Big Chief Brain in the Face." He became a lawyer and entered politics, but he never was the Popular, hail-fellow-well-met, typical politician.

"The third-term governor of Massachusetts has the oratorical skills of the fellow who has been announcing the arrival and departure of the trains from the depots of America for the past hundred years, and he faced Vice President George Bush, a man rendered faceless in the comic strips."[11]

The Duke's Peaceful, bland nature kept him consistently quiet, reserved, and well-liked. In his campaigning, he didn't seem to have any obvious weaknesses, a trait known only among the Peacefuls, and he was always able to keep his feelings hidden. In fact, many people found his lack of emotional response in the campaign to be too cold and aloof.

His Perfect side made him appear organized, disciplined, and detail-conscious, and his bushy eyebrows helped him look deep, thoughtful, even brooding.

His friends described him as both sensitive and frugal, noting that Dukakis bought his suits in Filene's bargain basement, drove a Dodge Aspen, and the family still lived in a modest duplex. Some acquaintances went so far as to call him stingy.

Dukakis was called "Meticulous Mike," a Perfect name. He liked to cook, following the recipe exactly, and he cleaned up as he went along. His daughter Kara was heard to say, "He's very careful in the kitchen, never spills or dribbles anything. You don't even know he's been cooking."

This Peaceful-Perfect combination gave Michael Dukakis a cool, laid-back look. *U.S. News and World Report* said he had an "icy calm." The magazine compared him with Perfect President Jimmy Carter and asked if he would be "another technocrat governor given to picking nits and focusing his considerable intellect on the most sparrow-small aspects of public policy."[12]

Knowing that opposites usually attract, it was no surprise that Peaceful-Perfect Dukakis married a strong, dynamic, active Powerful personality with some Popular traits. Kitty's ambitious and persistent personality helped push her low-key, somewhat reticent husband along in his career, and the Boston papers referred to him as "henpecked," a term frequently used to describe Peaceful husbands married to Powerful wives whether or not it happens to be true.

While Mike was cautious, Kitty charged forth without caring what anyone thought about her. This forthright attitude was not always an asset to her husband, and she was sometimes described as the proverbial loose cannon.

As the *Dallas Morning News* revealed, "she is the antithesis of her husband. He is mechanical and technical; she is emotional and dramatic. Shopping for clothes is a chore for him; to her it's a birthright."[13] When asked if Kitty would borrow clothes if she became first lady, Dukakis replied, "No, she'll buy them in Filene's basement."

You could expect the unexpected with Kitty. She was independent, strong-willed, unorthodox, volatile, and impulsive. The Dukakis staff assigned a "Kitty litter patrol" to clean up behind her. She didn't let public opinion sway her and when asked, "How would you describe yourself?" Kitty replied, "I'm intense, impatient to get things done. I always think everything should have happened yesterday."[14]

This typical description of a Powerful woman shows why she was able to accomplish so much and also why she came across a little too strong for some.

The apparent lack of Popular traits in Michael Dukakis and the presence of only a few in his wife indicated a strong serious family pattern with little time for fooling around or playing trivial pursuits. Friends verified this supposition, saying Michael Dukakis had almost no sense of humor and was only a fair joke teller.

Gary Hart
Perfect Personality

Senator Gary Hart, with his Perfect personality, had hardly given up to Walter Mondale in the 1984 primaries when he announced he would run again in 1988. Because of his name identification and a ready organization, he got an early start and was labeled the front-runner before there really was a pack to be in front of.

Hart had never been a typical candidate; there was something strange and mysterious about him. He was apparently intellectual and focused on idealistic issues, but Washington worried about why he'd changed his name from Gary Hartpence and why, when asked about it, he seemed to be uncertain about his own age.

He grew up in Ottawa, Kansas, with a Peaceful father, Carl, who delivered heating oil and spent the rest of his time fishing. His mother was a Perfect: neat, orderly, fastidious, religious, moralistic, and directive. She believed that to be a good church member you couldn't do anything that might be considered fun. Frivolity was a sin. Nina wore no makeup or jewelry and forbade Gary from smoking, drinking, dancing, and going to the movies.

This didn't leave him many options but studying and going to church. He stayed by himself and read books. In the fifth grade he set a goal to read a hundred books, and he did. He was obviously looked upon as a bookworm and seemed a little remote, somewhat out of the mainstream of life, small though the social stream was in Ottawa, Kansas.

At Bethany Nazarene College he fell in love with the most popular girl on campus, Lee Ludwig, whose father was a Nazarene pastor. While at Yale Divinity School, he began to question his faith, his marriage, and his purpose in life. He transferred from Yale Divinity School to Yale Law School, dropped the idea of ministry, and changed his name.

No one would have cared that he changed it except for the fact that he hid the transfer and when pressed on it denied it was his idea. Later he recanted, causing us to wonder why he would be deceptive on such a minor matter.

He always had organizational skills, he carefully outlined his messages, and he wrote spy novels; yet he found it difficult to be real with people and to show warmth and affection. He seemed to be playing a part, rehearsing for the lead.

In April 1987 after he had announced he would try a second time for the presidency, *Time's* Walter Shapiro wrote about the $1.3 million still owed from the last campaign and the raids made by U.S. Marshals on two of Hart's Los Angeles fund-raisers. Then Shapiro added, "In 1984 underlying doubts about Hart's personality took the form of an over-heated discussion of his name change and his frequent misstatements of his age. This time around Hart is plagued by rumors of womanizing, all advanced without a shred of credible evidence . . . Inevitably, Hart himself will become the issue."[15]

Little did the author know when he wrote these words that within a matter of days there would be more than a shred of evidence as *Miami Herald* reporters took Hart at his word when he had dared some *New York Times* staffers, "If anyone wants to put a tail on me, go ahead. They'd be very bored." But no one was bored, and Hart himself did become the issue.

The big weekend started with an anonymous tip to the *Herald* that Hart was having an affair, had been on a yacht trip with his mistress, and was about to meet her at his townhouse in Washington. On Friday, reporter Jim McGee hopped on a plane from Miami. Ironically, Donna Rice was on that plane also and McGee, when he saw her enter the town-house with Hart, remembered having seen her on the plane. On Satur-day evening the pair came out of the townhouse, sensed the reporter's presence, and went back in. Then Hart came out alone, and the ques-tioning began. Although he denied any wrongdoing, Hart was obviously nervous and refused to let the reporter talk to "the woman." The next day the scoop was in the *Herald's* Sunday edition, followed by confirmation of the yacht trip.

Within a few days the *Washington Post* got proof of another relationship. Then CBS paid five thousand dollars for a videotape taken by an insurance salesman from Iowa while vacationing in Florida that showed Hart relaxing on a yacht with a young woman in a white bikini. She wasn't Donna Rice. After the trip she entered a dockside beauty contest for the title of "Miss Hot Bod." Hart's campaign was over.

The third problem that Hart demonstrated after the dalliance and the dishonesty was the apparent denial that he had done anything wrong or that it was his fault. Lance Morrow wrote, "One sensed in him a territory of ignorance about himself. On the evidence of recent weeks, Hart has moments when he's overtaken by a denial of reality, a trait that might be dangerous in the Oval Office."[16] In the same issue, *Time* reported, "Hart challenged the moralistic conventions of political behavior and ultimately paid the price for his apostasy. Until the very end Hart seemed oblivious to the reality that his actions had consequences."[17]

He was not quite able to come out with a statement of Hart-felt repentance, and his weak apologies reflected his inability to look the facts in the eye, accept the truth, and put his introspective talents to work on examining the "why" of his mistakes.

The Preachers: Pat Robertson and Jesse Jackson
Popular-Powerful Personalities

During the long battle of the 1988 primaries, the question of religion and politics was brought to the fore. With morals at an all-time low, people began to look for candidates who didn't lie about their age or credentials, who were faithful to their mates, and who believed in something.

Attempting to answer the call were two charismatic preachers: Jesse Jackson, a Democrat, and Pat Robertson, a Republican, both with personal magnetism, evangelistic fervor, missionary zeal, and patriotic preaching. Although the press gave neither one a chance of becoming president, reporters followed the two closely for their colorful personalities and for the "nuisance value" they added to the campaign. Because of the dedication of their diverse supporters and their emotional drive to succeed, each one was expected to arrive at the conventions with committed blocs of delegates they could use as bargaining tools to chisel away at the platforms and as influence in the selection of the party nominee.

No one seemed to know what to do with these two master showmen. Each party quietly wished they would go away like a bad dream, but neither side dared to attack them. It was as if there were a secret belief that there might be divine consequences if anyone dared touch one of God's anointed.

Although Jackson and Robertson are both similar in their Popular-Powerful personalities, their differences are as obvious Democrat and Republican, liberal and conservative, civil-rights and moral-rights, rejected minority and Moral Majority; yet they both had a touch of martyrdom about them.

Time's Walter Shapiro said criticism only consolidated their supporters. Negative press coverage "may have enhanced the image of candidate as martyr; some African-Americans may see Jackson as besieged by the 'white' media; Evangelicals could view Robertson as crucified by 'secular humanist' reporters."[18]

How unusual it was that we had two preacher-politicians, two Popular-Powerfuls, who fervently led opposite groups of "dispossessed and resentful" people who felt they'd never had a real voice in politics in the past.

In a field of bland candidates, Jackson and Robertson stood out and stood up for something. They presented clear-cut choices, black and white decisions, for those who complained of a dull gray slate in 1988.

Jesse Jackson, who has become an icon to African-Americans and an inspiration to many disaffected whites, was noted for his passionate oratory, his magnetic charm, and his ability to bring even a skeptical crowd to its feet. He could address a pot-smoking auditorium of teens and have them walking the aisles in repentance. He could go to the Mideast and negotiate the freedom of a navy flier, and he could visit Cuba and take Castro to church. Jesse, with his Popular personality with a touch of the Powerful, was daring, dynamic, and adorable.

But with his formidable campaign skills and his obvious platform strengths came accompanying weaknesses. As is typical of his personality, his ability to organize was missing, he was often functioning in chaos, and he did little advance planning. He was a charmer on the stage receiving applause but his temper flared when someone questioned his loose facts or his fidelity. He was a song-and-dance man creating his own music, but he was also a loose cannon on deck rolling wildly from one idea to another. He operated his finances out of an offering plate, yet his ability to pull money out of people who didn't have any was without compare.

Born of a statuesque black beauty who wanted to be a singer and fathered by the man next door, a mulatto with some Cherokee and Irish blood, Jesse was, in his own terms, "a bastard and rejected." He determined from childhood that he would show his people he could defy all odds and make it in the big white world.

His father, Noah Robinson Sr., had five preachers in his previous generation, and Jesse declared he would be one also. As Gail Sheehy said, "Jesse believed he was set aside by God for a purpose—one of the hallmarks of the victorious personality . . . Those who suffer shame as children often cover it up with a false superiority. A sense of shame drives some people to build an inflated self-image through the pursuit of fame or excessive amounts of money, hoping to convince themselves of their lovability. The emotion, ignored by psychology until very recently, is now seen as a 'master emotion'. If it is carved in early, it is father to all the other emotions. For Jesse, its child was envy."[19]

Spurred on by envy and not held back by humility, Jesse stated triumphantly, "I'm a man on a mission. I was born to lead . . . Jesus was never anybody's patsy. Nobody pushed him around." Popular-Powerful Jesse Jackson electrified the crowds and inspired indifferent people to action. The Democratic Convention, the least-watched convention in history, had its most exciting and emotional moment when Jesse Jackson came to the platform and cried out, "Keep hope alive!" With his electric personality sparkling, Jesse turned on the crowds. He seemed to be the fulfillment of Martin Luther King's "I have a dream." Yet everyone seemed to agree he was unelectable.

In contrast to Jackson's climb from humble beginnings to a place in the political spotlight, Pat Robertson started out with a political background and base. His father, A. Willis Robertson, was a congressman for fourteen years and a U.S. senator for twenty. A typical southern gentleman, Willis Robertson paved the way for his son's classical education at Washington and Lee University and his military discipline at Virginia Military Institute. Pat went to Yale Law School with an idealistic mind and was disillusioned to the point he didn't study for his bar exam and flunked it. He was always in search of some crusade, and when a minister named Cornelius Vauderbregger shared his faith with Pat, he accepted Jesus Christ into his life and found his new direction.

A Popular-Powerful like Jesse Jackson, Robertson had been a "gregarious party animal" who supposedly pinched the Korean maid who cleaned the barracks while he was in the marines; yet when he dedicated his life to the Lord he, like the prodigal son, gave up wasting his life on riotous living and had a complete change of attitude and desire.

Pat went to New York Theological Seminary, and after his graduation he felt called to minister to the poor. He moved his wife, Dede, the granddaughter of an Ohio state senator, into a one-room ghetto apartment, gave away their possessions, and subsisted on a soybean diet.

In his autobiography *Shout it from the House Tops,* Robertson tells about his friend George Lauderdale, who had "a vision . . . , one of God's coincidences." In his vision, Lauderdale found a defunct television station in Portsworth, Virginia, for sale and brought it to Robertson's attention. Pat raised thirty-seven thousand dollars and bought the station.

When questioned later by Kevin Menida at the *Dallas Morning News,* Lauderdale admitted that there was no vision, but it made a good story. "In other words, it wasn't all that mystical an experience as it comes out in the book," Lauderdale said.[20]

As with each type of personality, Robertson has both strengths and weaknesses. One of the key weaknesses the Popular personality has is a lack of concern over details. The Populars sometimes remember incorrectly and colorfully, and after they've told about an event a certain way for a while they really believe that's how it happened.

One of their key strengths is their ability to charm those around them, inspire others to join their movement and donate to it, and to attract volunteers who will lay down their lives for their leader. Using his Popular appeal and his Powerful drive in the next twenty-five years, Robertson built the Christian Broadcasting Network and set up broadcast operations in twenty-four countries and also established an accredited university.

The *Dallas Morning News* said Robertson had "a magnetic public persona that helped attract viewers and fueled the growth of his electronic ministry. On the campaign trail, the man who lists his heroes as George Washington and Abraham Lincoln is an engaging figure who spins a good yarn and keeps a broad smile . . . In private, he can be ever the commander in chief, displaying his temper and rejecting challenges to his way of thinking."[21]

Robertson's Popular side made him appealing and refreshing. He said whatever came to his mind, knowing from experience that most of it would be well received; he didn't worry about possible inaccuracies.

He assumed everyone would love him, and most did; he hoped they wouldn't know the facts anyway, and most didn't. One day on TV he confessed that he occasionally "misspeaks and forgets," but in spite of his creative history, Robertson was the only Republican candidate who could generate wild enthusiasm and revival-meeting rapture upon entering a room. His beaming countenance and electric charm transmit power on an equal voltage with Jackson.

At the 1988 Republican Convention, Popular Ronald Reagan was the obvious master of the medium, but coming in a close second was Pat Robertson. As he was introduced, the crowds went wild for this charismatic leader who stood there beaming proudly and nodding affirmations to his screaming supporters. He hadn't won the prize—George Bush came away with the nomination—but he'd run a good race, and everyone knew it. He stood with the stature of a statesman and dispelled the myth that he was only a country preacher.

It was Robertson's Powerful side that was able to create the grand plan, that dared to dream so ambitiously, that organized so efficiently, that traveled with such energy while keeping the standards high and the supporters motivated to work and maintain intense loyalty.

Because I know Pat Robertson personally and have appeared on the *700 Club* show many times, I can speak from experience as to his gracious manner, his magnetic appeal, and his control over his empire. He is highly respected by his coworkers, and two that I interviewed gave me reports of a man who has all strengths and no weaknesses. He can inspire people to work for him for little or no pay and be grateful for the opportunity. He has motivated people who never voted before to register, people who never got involved in politics to run for office. He is the first leader of the Christian conservatives to have the ability and the power to organize a serious political machine and the Popular personality to keep the people motivated and enthusiastic.

Both Jackson and Robertson have the Popular charismatic magnetism laced with some throw-away lines, and both, for different background reasons, have the Powerful drive to succeed and the supreme self-confidence to keep them going in spite of adverse circumstances.

18

A KINDER AND GENTLER NATION

GEORGE BUSH

President: 1989–1993
Personality: Peaceful
Principle to Learn: Face tough issues quickly.

One week before the 1988 election the *New York Times* summed up the two candidates, Michael Dukakis and George Bush, as bland and colorless. The writer did not analyze the Peaceful personalities of Bush and Dukakis that kept them from exhibiting the Popular presidential personality we had come to expect after eight years of Ronald Reagan, but Professor Larry Sabato's quote in the article summed up that explanation: "Could it be that it's been a passive campaign and that fits television perfectly? The candidates are not emotional. They don't arouse passion. It's a campaign that's well suited to spectatorship. It's the ideal couch potato campaign."[1]

What better way to describe a duel between two Peacefuls than as a "couch potato campaign"? We all know by now that a Peaceful blends in anywhere, adapts to differing circumstances, and avoids conflict at all costs. The Peaceful does not have a flashy personality like the Popular, obvious skills like the Powerful, or deep strengths like the Perfect. The Peaceful's greatest strength is invisible: It is that he or she has no obvious weaknesses. A Peaceful will always try to do the right thing and avoid problem situations. As George Bush said at the Republican convention, "I am that man."

James David Barber, author of the book *Presidential Character,* wrote of George Bush, "He wants to do the right thing, and above all, not do the wrong thing. He defines his virtue by what he does not do. By restriction."[2]

Both Presidents Eisenhower and Ford were chosen not for their outstanding political strengths or innovative programs, but for the fact that they had no obvious weaknesses. Ike won on a grin and his ability to tread water for two terms; Ford kept everybody happy and healed the wounds of Watergate without getting into trouble. They were men for their hour; they gave us Peace when we were tired of conflict.

In the 1988 campaign, the "wimp factor" was a new measuring stick for candidates, and it was focused primarily on George Bush, our Peaceful vice president. Because he had been put in the awkward position of supporting President Reagan and being loyal while at the same time trying to establish a strong identity of his own, the press pictured him as weak and vacillating, a view not backed up by the facts.

While other candidates had to scrounge for credentials and exaggerate their abilities, Bush had quietly lived an exemplary life. As a Peaceful, he was willing, from childhood, to put the other person first and not insist on his own way. He was generous, well-mannered, and gracious. As a child, he was nicknamed by his mother "Have Half" because whenever she gave him a cookie, he would turn to the person beside him and say "have half."

His family background was similar to that of Franklin Roosevelt in that he grew up with solid financial footing, patrician social standing, classical education, and a desire to serve those less fortunate. As it had been for FDR, Bush's mother was the dominating influence in the children's lives.

Dorothy Walker Bush, daughter of George Herbert Walker, champion polo player, founder of golf's Walker Cup, and head of the New York State Racing Commission, was herself a Powerful-Popular personality who disciplined the children firmly while making the whole experience fun. She was a warm, religious woman who read Bible verses at breakfast and then challenged the family to a seasonal variety of athletic pursuits: tennis, boating, football, hunting, golf, baseball, backgammon, and charades.

Where FDR spent much of his sheltered childhood alone, reading books on history and recreating naval battles with toy ships, George Bush engaged in athletic events proving him the opposite of a wimp.

A Team Player

In contrast to the Kennedy clan who also emphasized sports but were taught to win for the sake of always being first, the Bushes were encouraged to be the very best they possibly could be without gloating over the victory. As the Kennedys collected trophies, the Bushes were trained to say, "I was lucky." When George would tell his mother he had won, she would ask, "How did the team do?" Individual pride was discouraged, and being a team player was essential.

The word *good,* a typical Peaceful adjective, had been used to describe George from childhood on. His teachers remembered him as a *good* boy, and his siblings called him a *good* brother. As a teenager, he stayed out of trouble without being a sissy or being preachy about being good. Everyone enjoyed his company, and while he liked a good joke or a good prank, he was never mean or vulgar. He was never a goody-goody, and he was always strong enough and concerned enough to protect those who were weak.

As the *Los Angeles Times* described him, "George Bush always had about him a sense of bearing. It kept him from going astray. He was a good boy from a good family, headed for good things."[3]

I remember Prescott Bush, George's father, our U. S. senator from Connecticut when Fred and I lived there in the late fifties and sixties. Senator Bush was a Perfect patrician, a person of pedigree, and the press had to push to find anything wrong with him. He was tall, dignified, refined, and gracious, and there was never much point in anyone running against him. He was a Perfect prototype of the Eastern Establishment, an investment broker, and a civic leader. While he made money, he never talked about it as a path to power, as Joseph Kennedy did. He was not dying to climb hastily to the top; he was already there. He was never trying to "show them"; they could already see his genuine character and quiet success.

Senator Bush considered lust for money a sin, and he instilled in his children the idea that financial substance required civic service. With privilege come obligations, he taught them; give generously with no desire for credit.

From this family background, George Bush grew up as a fair and decent person with the desire to serve his fellow man and his country. At Phillips Andover Academy, he was the all-purpose person and was president of almost everything he joined. Not because he craved position, as a Pow-erful would, but because he was so likable, inoffensive, and willing to work for the benefit of others.

Even though he could have escaped military service in World War II by going to college or using his father's influence, he chose to enlist on the day of his eighteenth birthday, June 12, 1942. He worked diligently to learn to fly and was the youngest pilot in the navy to receive his wings. Bush never held back or looked for favored treatment; he plunged into the war with dedication to duty, piloting TBM Avengers.

While flying into enemy territory and daringly dodging the flak, Bush was twice thrown into the sea and narrowly escaped death. On the sec-ond crisis, as he bailed out of a plane about to explode, the Japanese sent gunboats after him and he swam desperately for ninety minutes before an American submarine emerged and swept him to safety. George Bush's wartime record was hardly that of a wimp! But with customary modesty, he never pointed out his patriotic deeds. He just considered them part of his obligation to serve.

After his time in the navy, Bush entered Yale in 1945. As an econom-ics major, he sped through his requirements in two and a half years, made Phi Beta Kappa, and graduated with the necessary credentials to enter the blue-blooded financial fields so readily open to the son of Prescott Bush.

Heading for Texas

But once again, George didn't opt for the easy life. He didn't want to be pulled along on his father's coattails, and he didn't want to settle into the safety of the status quo. He and his wife, Barbara, daughter of the pres-ident of the McCall's publishing empire, drove off to Texas, where he learned the oil business from below ground up. Before he was forty, Bush had become an oil-millionaire, an established Texan, and an accepted leader in the Republican party.

In 1966, when he was forty-two, he was elected to Congress, one of only two Republicans from Texas. Because of his easygoing nature and friendly attitude, he fit in quickly with the establishment, and with some influence from his father he was soon assigned to the Ways and Means Committee.

"He made friends as fast as a small boy collects baseball cards. Sunday afternoons at the Bushes drew a crowd: congressmen, ambassadors, a Supreme Court justice. He seemed to know the whole town."[4]

During the Nixon-Ford era, Bush served as ambassador to the United Nations for twenty-two months, as chairman of the Republican National Committee for twenty months, as chief of the liaison office in Beijing for sixteen months, and as director of the CIA for twelve months.

Nixon admired Bush's humility, good nature, and willingness to be a team player. Bush never had the smell of mutiny about him, and Nixon was drawn to obvious loyalty.

In all of George Bush's diverse areas of public service, he was considered a kind, encouraging, soothing, understanding, amiable, witty person who listened politely to all opinions, tried to take the middle road and didn't need to get the credit. He personified the old adage, "There's no limit to what you can accomplish when you don't care who gets the credit."

All of these Peaceful strengths are quiet low-key attributes that don't make headlines. When Bush took over the CIA, the agency was trying to recover from exposés and excesses. His don't-rock-the-boat attitude calmed the troubled waters and steadied the reeling spy-ship. He testified in Congress without drawing attention to himself, and he quietly healed the hurts of the agency.

Like President Ford, another Peaceful, had done, Bush worked to bring harmony to the government, but because of his low-key nature, Bush, like Ford, did not come across as a powerful leader. Neither of them was credited with any life-changing ideas or legislation, and both proved the principle that the Peacefuls' greatest strength is their lack of obvious weaknesses. This often unseen and unaccepted strength doesn't carry the excitement and glamour that the public envisions as leadership, so Ford (Mr. Clean) lost to Carter (Mr. Perfect), and Bush (Mr. Nice) won over Dukakis (Mr. Dull) in 1988 but lost in 1992 to Clinton (Mr. Charm).

A Willingness to Play Second Fiddle

In 1980, after Bush lost the nomination to Ronald Reagan, Reagan offered Bush the vice president's position and he accepted, even though, politically, the two men were poles apart. But because of George's Peaceful personality, his willingness to moderate his positions, and his ability to play second fiddle in a new symphony, he was able to become a loyal Reaganite. Had Bush been a Popular, he might have tried to steal a spot in the sun during his eight years as vice president, but instead he stayed quietly in the background. Had he been a Powerful, he might have tried to exert control and get his personal points across to the president; instead he supported positions he had formerly opposed and didn't propose any policy shifts. Had he been a Perfect, he might have held grudges against Reagan for the divisive comments he'd made about Bush in the primary campaign and subtly sought revenge, but instead he accepted the negative as part of politics and was able to put the past behind him without rancor.

Only the Peaceful is naturally able to play the role of the bridesmaid when he or she wanted to be the bride. Only the Peaceful can sit in meeting after meeting and not need to make a comment. Only a Peaceful can support other people's ideas continually without insisting they adopt a few of the Peaceful's.

These Peaceful attributes were appealing to President Reagan, who loved center stage and didn't like conflict. Bush's soft sense of humor appealed to Reagan, and he would often ask Bush to repeat a joke he'd particularly enjoyed.

Writer Gail Sheehy, commenting on Bush's personality, said, "Some of the world's unfunniest people suddenly feel, in Bush's presence, like true wits. The secret to his sense of humor is that he plants the punch line in someone else's mouth. . . . George Bush has made a career out of nicing people to death."[5]

The Reward for Loyalty

In 1988 Bush was rewarded for his years of loyalty and selflessness when, at the Republican Convention in New Orleans, he received the party's nomination for president. My publisher had brought me to the convention, and on the afternoon when Bush was to make his entrance to New Orleans on the riverboat *Natchez,* I received two formal, engraved invitations that would allow me to enter the VIP viewing area. I immediately imagined I would be seated in some restricted section with important people. As I followed the crowds through the French Quarter toward the waterfront, I wondered what dignitaries would be in the VIP lounge and whether there would be refreshments. Surely with the engraved invitation would come some special treatment!

As I moved along I looked over the crowd to spot some lady of a similar age and style who might enjoy accompanying me into this prestigious position of prominence. Spotting a solitary soul, I spoke to her and offered her my extra ticket. We had much in common, and my excitement grew when I found someone to share it with.

By the time we got to the dockside, this woman and I were firm friends. We followed the signs for "VIP Viewing" and found ourselves in a long line standing still in the hot August sun. After a half-hour of hardly moving we got inside a flat, roped-off area and found that the tall people in front of us were all VIPs. Like a child behind adults stretching to watch the Rose Bowl Parade, I tried to stand on tiptoes and focus on finding the river. I knew it was there but I couldn't see it. I began to apologize to my new friend for my failure to get her up front with the Bush family as I had inferred we might be. Surely I had not imagined that everyone in New Orleans was a VIP with an engraved ticket!

As I stretched my neck up I spotted the corner windows of Abercrombie and Fitch jutting out over the crowds. Since we had nothing to lose in leaving this far-from-intimate gathering, I suggested we push our way out of the throng and go into Abercrombie and Fitch.

We weren't the first to think of standing in the store windows somewhat like a pair of plaster dummies, but we managed to get our faces up to the glass with our backs against a table of polo shirts in assorted colors. During those two hours we stood in the Abercrombie and Fitch shirt department we became well-acquainted with the others who had chosen that spot, and I even picked out a few shirts for Christmas presents. Finally the *Natchez* came down the river preceded by a barge shooting up fountains of red, white, and blue water. Our clear, unobstructed view through the store window let us see the Bush family as they stood waving on deck and gave us almost a front-row position.

A Surprising Choice

It was on that afternoon of August 16, 1988, that George Bush stood before cheering crowds on the Spanish Plaza under impending thunder clouds and announced his choice for the Republican vice-presidential nominee. The announcement had not been anticipated until later in the convention, so it took us all by surprise when Bush proclaimed the name Dan Quayle. Many of us had no idea what Bush had said or who Quayle was. Murmurs grew to shouts: "What did he say?" "Dan who?" "Who's a quail?" "Let's see him!"

Suddenly a handsome young man, seeming to smile in wild disbelief, emerged from the crowds and bounded toward the vice president. He whipped off his jacket and joked, "Actually, I was just in the area and stopped by."

With his boyish charm and Robert Redford looks, Danny brought out maternal instincts in many of us and gasps of admiration in others. When he turned to give George Bush an appreciative hug, he almost knocked him over with enthusiasm and eagerness to get on with the campaign.

At the end of the arrival festivities, George Bush walked off the stage toward our window and a limousine drove in between us and the river to pick him up. We couldn't believe we were in the only spot to see him closely. As he and his sons came in our direction, he noticed us waving and jumping as animated mannequins in the Abercrombie and Fitch window. He laughed at the sight, pausing to call out, "Thanks for coming!" As the Secret Service agents walked beside the limo, George Bush waved good-bye to our special group of front-row fans.

I paid for my selection of shirts and sweaters and felt grateful that I had been at the right place at the right time to see the relaxed and natural personality of the future president of the United States and the surprise selection of the unknown and pleasantly bland Dan Quayle.

Stunned by the Fallout

Bush, a Peaceful with few emotional juices, surprised the Republican Convention with his dramatic choice of Peaceful-Popular Dan Quayle of Indiana. Instead of selecting Powerful Bob Dole or any of the other well-known and available Republicans, Bush chose a relatively unknown senator who was inoffensive, young, and attractive.

Typical of the Peaceful personality, Bush had delegated the research of the candidates to underlings, had taken their recommendation, and then was stunned when Quayle's dutiful service in the National Guard became an instant hot potato. Bush, whose nature kept him from facing controversy, suddenly found himself defending his choice of what appeared to be a draft dodger who had used his wealthy family's influence to keep him out of Vietnam. No credible evidence was ever produced and the furor died down when polls showed that around 80 percent of the American people thought the media were out of line in its attacks on Quayle. Few people seemed to care about what Quayle had done twenty years ago as more than half the people surveyed said they would have done the same thing if given the opportunity.

As with every personality, Dan Quayle came equipped with both strengths and weaknesses. The media did instant studies on Quayle and found him to have the accommodating attributes of the Peaceful plus the strengths of the Popular: He was relaxed, easygoing, affable, sunny, well-balanced, talkative, charming, eager to please, exuberant, naive, and had a dry sense of humor.

Within twenty-four hours of his selection, some of Quayle's Peaceful weaknesses also began to appear: He seemed too bland, too square, too middle-of-the-road. At times when he opened his mouth he seemed to immediately put his foot in it. When faced by probing and aggressive media, he looked confused and upset.

Time gave both his positive and negatives in one paragraph: "Quayle radiates the same bumptious enthusiasm, the same uncritical loyalty, the same palpable gratitude and the same malleable mindset that Bush brought to the GOP ticket in 1980. But by appointing Quayle, Bush also stepped into deep doo-doo. Within 24 hours of his selection, Quayle became a political bumper car careening from one public relations crack up to another."[6]

The Bush team had not expected the news media to make such a mountainous storm out of so little a mole hill; thus Bush's aides had not prepared Quayle for what he was about to face.

Even though Quayle was pushed into keeping a low profile toward the end of the campaign, he certainly added color to the gray months of 1988.

Comedians said Bush chose Quayle as "impeachment insurance," and in the fall of 1988, while Dan Quayle was trying to find his political soul, Democratic vice-presidential candidate Lloyd Bentsen was looking presidential; in the televised debate he appeared to sneer down at "Danny boy." When Quayle stated that he had just as much experience as Jack Kennedy did when he ran for president, Bentsen pulled himself up to an imposing height and uttered the most-quoted line of the night: "Senator, you're no Jack Kennedy."

Immortal though the line became, some of its brilliance faded when Ohio Representative Dennis Eckart admitted that during the debate preparation he played Quayle and threw out the Kennedy line as a possible Quayle comment. This triggered the retort in Bentsen's thinking, so when Quayle made the hoped-for comparison, Bentsen was ready.

Patrick Thomas, political writer in Washington, happily stated that Quayle passed the "sidekick test" in that he would certainly not overshadow Bush.

Dan Quayle got an unlikely boost toward the end of the campaign from Democratic Senator Ted Kennedy, who said the press had not been fair to Dan who is much better at the "give and take of the Senate" than he appeared to be on the political stump.

Barbara the Powerful

At the time of the 1988 election, the Bushes had been married for forty-three years and had five living children out of six and ten grandchildren. The family members obviously enjoyed each other's company, and they exemplified the values they wanted for America.

Barbara's Powerful personality balanced and completed George's Peaceful nature. She was open, candid, and expressive and wasn't worried about what people thought of her. She had been the disciplinarian of the family and the caretaker of the home while her husband had been traveling and working long hours. Before moving into the White House they had lived in twenty-eight houses in seventeen cities, and it was Barbara who had found each new home and moved the family into it.

Her son Marvin called her "the enforcer," and she agreed she was the one who carried out the family rules. *USA Today* said of her, "Barbara Bush is down-to-earth and outspoken, always lets you know what she thinks and where you stand, is confident enough to know there are more important things in life than being a perfect size 6 or dying your hair."[7]

Many of us women were glad to have a first lady who was a size fourteen and didn't look like a Dresden doll. Perhaps, we thought, the 1988 to 1992 years would be the era of the average woman. Perhaps we finally could stop starving ourselves and be proud of the natural look God gave us.

Barbara had the strengths of the Powerful Personality without the abrasiveness that often accompanies these characteristics. Her son George said of her, "I predict that my mother will be the most loved first lady this country has ever had. Everyone who knows her, loves her."

Of his father he admiringly stated, "If my father died tomorrow, as his soul ascended to heaven, he would be content, knowing he'd never done anything he wasn't proud of, to accomplish his aims."[8]

George Bush was the political model of a Peaceful leader. He was able to mediate between contentious people and moderate hot tempers while staying calmly above the fray.

Time cited Bush adviser and secretary of the treasury Nicholas Brady as saying he marveled "at how Bush has kept the potentially combustible group of strong-minded aides from blowing up." As a prediction for how this Peaceful talent would help Bush in the future Brady said about the campaign, "It's a peek behind the veil. You'd have many strong personalities, but they'd work as a team."[9]

In the major positions Bush had held, he always came in at a time of trouble, calmed everyone down, brought harmony out of chaos, made differing opinions into unity, and built an effective team, all without drawing attention to himself. These might not be flashy traits, but they were what we needed in the post-Reagan era.

In typical Peaceful fashion, Bush has also been known for skirting conflict as well as for his stabilizing influence. Like Gerald Ford, he arrived at the White House with few enemies. His affable nature, expressing no extremes of opinion, adjusted according to each situation and kept him from offending anyone.

Dan Quayle showed an understanding of the different personalities when he said in a *Time* magazine interview, "People are swayed by Reagan's personal charm. That's part of the greatness of Reagan. George Bush will achieve greatness, but it's not going to be the same as it was with Reagan. He doesn't have that engaging speaking manner, and there is no use trying to project it if it's not there."[10]

"A Decent Man"

During the 1988 campaign Bush became a master of his personality strengths, and even the Democrats were not able to find anything of significance wrong with him. Bush didn't try to be something he wasn't but kept his middle-of-the-road, easygoing, pleasant personality before the public, who finally accepted him as an honest person, a decent and moral man, who might not ever be exciting but who would wear well. Even though his managers tried to turn him into a Powerful to enhance his leadership image, he held true to his nature and came through as sincere and genuine.

New Jersey Governor Tom Kean, in his keynote address at the Republican Convention, summed it up this way, "George Bush is a decent man—and he shouldn't have to defend his being one. If defending values such as loyalty, family, or belief in God is no longer fashionable, then I fear for our country."[11]

Just prior to the election, the *Wall Street Journal* summed up what I believe to be the reason George Bush won in a landslide. "Mr. Bush has built his lead through his success at painting Mr. Dukakis as out-of-step with mainstream America, and through rising voter satisfaction with Mr. Reagan and with staying on the path of his policies.

"The poll suggests that Republicans' attacks on the Massachusetts prison-furlough system, Mr. Dukakis' membership in the American Civil Liberties Union and his veto of a pledge-of-allegiance bill appear to have taken hold with the voters. Seventy-one percent of likely voters believe that Mr. Bush represents traditional American values."[12]

Once George Bush had been overwhelmingly elected, winning forty states with 426 electoral votes to Dukakis's ten states with 112 electoral votes, the press began to view him through new eyes. They used descriptive words and phrases typical of the Peaceful personality: Extending the peace pipe, minimizing problems, bipartisan person, reaches out to all, heals wounds, slow-starter, too neutral, lacking depth, obstinate, opaque, and elusive.

George Bush certainly had the Peaceful personality needed to be a president of consolidation. After years of being number two and winning the election because he tried harder, George Bush became number one, was put in the driver's seat and headed over bumpy roads in hopes of consolidating the electorate and making the United States "a kinder and gentler nation."

George Bush
Peaceful Personality

The following lists of strengths and weaknesses include words and phrases used in newspaper articles, magazines, books, television, and radio to describe George Bush's Peaceful personality. Check the characteristics that also apply to you.

Strengths

___ A sweetheart of a human
    being
___ Relaxed and funny
___ Uncommonly nice man
___ Looks for the best in others
___ Courtly demeanor
___ Ultimate team player
___ Crisis manager
___ Unpretentious
___ Unfailingly courteous
___ Thoughtful to a fault
___ Never challenges others
___ Keeps a low profile
___ No meanness about him
___ Defuses tense situations
    by being funny
___ Not interested in getting even
___ Not a bitter bone in his body
___ At peace with himself
___ Emotionally self-controlled
___ Makes witty asides
___ Astonishingly resilient
    and persevering
___ A blue-chip individual
___ Unquenchable loyalty
___ Vastly self-assured
___ Squeaky-clean image
___ Good in crises
___ Steady-handed and tempered
___ Comfortable and consistent
___ Passes the peace pipe
___ Heals wounds
___ Brilliant in mediation
___ Mr. Status Quo
___ **TOTAL**

Weaknesses

___ Lackluster
___ Acts insecure
___ Makes few bold statements
___ Uses if's and maybe's
___ Lacks emotional juices
___ Mr. Boring
___ Not at ease in spotlight
___ Numbs audiences
___ Difficulty expressing deep
    feelings
___ No independent identity
___ Vaguely admirable
___ Verbal dyslexia
___ Obstinate
___ Opaque and illusive
___ Dithering
___ Paralyzed leader
___ Bored by domestic policy
___ Looks the other way

___ **TOTAL**

Total of your presidential profile of Peaceful strengths and weaknesses: _____

Are You a Leader Like Bush?

If you checked off many of these items, your personality is Peaceful. You don't wish to cause trouble, you are inoffensive, and you are able to mediate smoothly between contentious people. Your leadership style is one of quiet confidence, you look for the best in others, and you are a team player. You are polite and gracious and would rather please the people than have your own way. You don't have a mean bone in your body, and you don't have to get even with those who have hurt you.

You would be happy to be a follower or even get out of the way, but it would be a waste for you not to take a leadership role. There are too many arrogant and bossy people trying to push others around, and the world needs pleasant likable leaders who have a relaxed attitude and a dry sense of humor as you do. You have a high believability factor, others feel they can trust you, and you are a genuinely nice person.

Your biggest weakness is your lack of motivation and your desire to stay home versus getting out of the chair and moving on. You will do best in a job where your day is programmed for you, but if you wish to develop your leadership potential you will have to stretch and force yourself to take some risks.

As with George Bush, you may have a reticence to face issues that are unpleasant. You would rather look the other way and hope the problems will go off on their own. Or you may have learned that if you procrastinate long enough, someone else will do the work. If you wish to develop your leadership potential, you must confront questionable situations quickly. You are not impulsive like the Powerful personality, so you don't have to worry about jumping to conclusions. Look at the problem squarely and force yourself to make decisions instead of hoping someone else will do it. If you do not train yourself to face issues and make decisions, you will have little chance of becoming a leader others will follow, but if you do, you can glory in your strengths of spreading peace among all those you meet. Sometimes being nice isn't quite enough.

19

PERSONALITIES AT WORK: THE AMAZING 1992 CAMPAIGN

Principle to Learn: In some situations, charisma wins over
integrity.

By the spring of 1992 the Gulf War was over, the Soviets were busy cutting up their own country, and America's upcoming presidential election seemed to be the most exciting thing going on in the world.

Bush was expected to be the winner, and the Democrats, who hadn't sat in the big chair in the Oval Office since Jimmy Carter's reign, were searching for a sacrificial candidate. No Democrat of stature and stability wanted to take on an incumbent president with an 80 percent approval rating.

This leadership vacuum allowed some "lesser lights" to start flashing, among them a relatively unknown governor from the politically insignificant state of Arkansas. But Bill Clinton knew how to twinkle. As a Popular personality, he could bite his lower lip like a little boy, bringing a rush of maternal voters to his side. He could tilt his pelvis like Elvis and make playing the saxophone a seductive experience, drawing votes from both the younger women and the men who wished they had his romantic appeal.

The public, already fascinated by soap operas, scandal, and sleaze, seemed ready for a provocative presidential candidate. People began to wonder if there was a possibility that Clinton's charisma could replace proper George and frumpy Barbara the same way the magnetic Kennedy personality had overshadowed old-soldier Ike and tipsy Mamie.

We were exposed to pictures of young Clinton meeting Kennedy, and those with fertile minds could begin to sense a reincarnation. Clinton's combination of the Popular personality that seemed to charm those around him and a touch of the Powerful personality that made him determined to win gave excitement to a candidate who didn't seem at that moment destined to become president. His youth, vigor, and libidinous appeal, however, so captured yuppie hearts that when Gennifer Flowers, appearing on TV as a pricey prostitute, burst onto the scene with supposed evidence of a lengthy liaison with Governor Clinton, the story actually seemed to enhance his image. What had brought Gary Hart to defeat somehow elevated Bill Clinton, causing conservatives to bewail the decade's decline in moral values.

No Tammy Wynette

Bill and his wife, Hillary Clinton—she had not yet insisted the press insert her maiden name, Rodham—appeared on *60 Minutes* as a loving and devoted couple, and when pushed about her passive acceptance of Bill's supposed philandering, she responded, "I ain't no Tammy Wynette," referring to Tammy's song, "Stand By Your Man." The remark brought a public protest from Tammy herself as well as a few old English teachers.

Hillary soon proved she was no passive pushover, either, but the driving force behind Bill's life. While he played to the audience and worked the room, she checked on the details backstage. Her personality combination soon became obvious: Powerful (I know where I'm going) and Perfect (I know exactly how to get there).

Political Charisma

People began to talk about Hillary's brilliance and power and about Bill's bubbling optimism and seductive charm. Once he found that women on a national level liked his hair and were fascinated with the little-boy way he worked his lower lip and jutted out his jaw, he made sure his head rotated in the spotlight, showing his well-coiffed silver locks. He paused occasionally to bite his lip as he appeared to be searching for hidden depth, somewhat in the style of an elusive mystic. He had practiced the art of political charisma since he was in high school where, in his own words, he "yearned to be voted most popular." He was so eager to be a Powerful leader at Hot Springs High that the school had to change the rules and limit the number of times any one person could be president of the various organizations just to give someone else a chance.

As more of Clinton's background became known, the public realized he had been in politics forever. Running for congressman as an unknown at twenty-eight, he almost unseated a popular opponent, and at thirty-two he became the youngest governor of Arkansas, receiving national attention.

He had been influenced and encouraged from youth by his Powerful mother, who had strong opinions and a love for politics, Las Vegas, and the racetrack. Her first husband, William Blythe III, was killed in an auto accident four months before Bill was born. Not one to be defeated easily, Mother placed Bill with her parents in Hope, Arkansas, and went to nursing school in New Orleans.

When Bill was seven, she and her new husband, Roger Clinton, moved to Hot Springs. The stepfather was quiet and pleasant when sober but turned into a madman when drinking. Bill found himself not only abused but defending his mother and young brother, Roger. The tale is told that one day after the father had been violent to the point of shooting a gun inside the house, teenage Bill faced him bravely and said, "You will never hit either of them again. If you want them you'll have to go through me!" The abuse stopped.

Compulsive Ambition

In principle, when a child has been brought up in a dysfunctional family due to drugs or alcohol, physical or sexual abuse, his or her natural personality tendencies seem to be accentuated and often driven to extremes. Clinton's Popular personality longed for attention, love, and praise. Carried to an extreme, he seemed to demand center stage, was willing to compromise his positions to keep people loving him, and was obsessed with his public image. His Powerful portion apparently went from desiring control, excitement, and power to a compulsion to be in charge of everything, to refuse to delegate authority, and to take risks with women.

Clinton looked back on the counseling sessions the whole family had when brother Roger was caught selling drugs. "For the first time I saw how much my ambitions had gotten out of control. I finally realized how my compulsive and obsessive ambition got in the way. I think that dealing with that helped me to achieve some better balance."[1]

Clinton worked to bring his compulsions under control, but the pattern of youthful lust continued to reappear.

Seductive Power

"It's not that Clinton seduces women" an observer told the *New York Times Magazine*. "It's that he seduces everyone."[2]

"Shaking hands with Bill Clinton is, in and of itself, a full-body sexual experience, I promise you," said novelist Judith Krantz on *Lifetime Magazine,* broadcast on June 8, 1994. "He has the sexiest handshake of any man that I have ever experienced in my entire life."

I've already described how my experience in meeting Clinton on the south lawn of the White House verified Krantz's description. Such natural seductive powers in a politician can be a plus if they are channeled to win votes and influence constituents positively, but they can easily presage a downfall if these powers become a thread stringing together a series of sexual liaisons. Clinton's nickname, Slick Willie, was not dropped upon him only because he was able to wiggle out of political problems but because he could charm those who knew too much into knowing nothing.

Clinton's initial appeal over his uninspiring primary opponents was his charisma, his touchy-feely approach, his mesmerizing look into the eyes of the beholder.

Sydney Blumenthal of the *New Yorker* wrote, "Bill Clinton is like the old-style politician who is the student of human nature and focuses on the voter in front of him. The premium is on the personal encounter. But unlike the old-style politician, Clinton can perform this seduction before cameras."[3]

In this era of extreme self-disclosure by every dysfunctional victim that Oprah and Geraldo can exhume, is it any wonder that the public fell in love with Clinton's "I feel your pain" therapy? Later, when Clinton was sued by Paula Jones for supposed sexual harassment in a Little Rock hotel room, cartoonist Darcy pictured him in his underpants, holding the page of accusations and saying with an innocent look, "I felt her pain! And that's it!!"[4] Clinton had the same ability as Reagan to tell personal stories that touch people's emotions and show the public that he did feel their pain.

A Call for Change

Seduction without substance isn't enough to win the presidency. Feeling pain without focusing on what to do about it is too vague. Clinton needed a plan. Contrary to Franklin D. Roosevelt telling us as he ran for his fourth term that we should not change horses midstream, Clinton decided to be the new horse, urging us to clean out the stable and let the stallion charge forth.

A candidate in search of an issue can always call for *change*. Especially when the public knows the budget can't possibly be balanced and when pictures of sad, homeless people are flashed onto the TV news and workers who expected to stay with IBM forever are laid off in droves.

Tip O'Neill often said, "All politics is local," meaning what hits me in my pocketbook will sway my vote more than the threat of Castro invading Miami or the questionable morals of a candidate. With this premise in mind, underdog Clinton began to bark loudly about the economy. Even though he had no plan for fiscal freedom, he began to call for change. Signs went up backstage in order to focus Clinton's wandering attention onto the issue at hand. When he headed for a platform to rouse up the people, the last words he saw were, "It's the ECONOMY stupid!"

Peaceful President Bush treated Clinton and his economy ideas as an annoying disease that, if left untreated, would ultimately go away. During the campaign Bush ignored the fiscal problems and concentrated on looking presidential. He came up with no fresh ideas to catch anyone's fancy, and in interviews seemed content to say nothing at great length. James Carville, Clinton's strategist, told the *New York Times,* "George Bush wouldn't know change if it ran over him."[5]

Carville's statement represented the truth for the Peaceful personalities. They love the status quo, and they see no need for change. If it's not broken, don't fix it. If it was good enough for last term, why should we change now? Similar to Gerald Ford's assumptions in his reelection campaign, Bush thought that being a nice, honest person with no scandals should be enough to keep him in office, especially when the opponent carried the baggage of scandals everywhere he went. And in most cases it *would* have been enough. The people knew that Bush was always a gentleman and that he never tried to manipulate the media. The press hadn't forgotten that in his early months in office Bush had invited them to movie screenings in the White House, showed them around his private quarters, and answered personal questions. This friendship on an equal basis was highly unusual for a president.

"George Bush was a nice man who always treated us (the press) with respect as human beings," says Karen Hosler, correspondent for the *Baltimore Sun*. "How can you dislike someone like that?"[6]

Bush probably asked himself, *How could anyone really dislike me and Barbara and our all-American family?* And he had a point. Who knew the job better? Who had more impeccable credentials? Hadn't he just won a war?

How could Bush possibly go from an 80 percent approval rating to losing the election? He took his position for granted and allowed his personality strengths to get carried to extremes until they became weaknesses. His desire for stability and peace came across to the public as a lack of vision; his passive approach to domestic issues seemed to be indifference to the economic problems of the country.

Bush appeared to have little empathy for the little people—he didn't really know any—and when his handlers took him shopping to buy his own white socks and show the nation he was one of us, he looked as ill-at-ease at a blue-light special as Dukakis had looked when his campaign managers had posed him driving a tank. He showed genuine surprise at the electronic price-scanning system the rest of us have been using for years, causing people to wonder where he'd been. This apparent detachment from reality and this ivory-tower living made the people think it was time for someone of a baser nature, someone who had walked in our shoes. Bush showed his vagueness—some called it his out-to-lunch attitude or approaching senility—during the debates on TV when he looked at his watch as if to ask himself, *When is this thing going to be over?*

Not only did the apparent lack of vision and sense of detachment present obvious problems that Bush didn't seem to notice, but his single-minded focus on foreign policy kept him from looking at other issues that were beginning to concern the public.

As a general principle, people with Peaceful personalities like Bush and Ford are born with single focus and the lowest level of motivational desire. Popular personalities get excited over everything that sounds like fun, Powerfuls over whatever they can control, and Perfects over a few projects that can be done properly. Because the Peacefuls have the lowest motivation and are single-minded, they tend to choose one area of interest to the exclusion or neglect of others.

For George Bush, it was the subject of foreign affairs. He was raised in a home where politics was second nature, and his love was peaceful diplomacy.

While this skill was brilliant during the Gulf War, it turned sour in the search for a presidential victory. Bush liked governing but was ill at ease in the rough and tumble of campaigning. No one was sure how Clinton would govern, but he sure seemed to love campaigning.

20

ROSS FOR BOSS

ROSS PEROT

Presidential Candidate: 1992
Personality: Powerful
Principle to Learn: Keep it simple.

Before the party conventions had officially chosen Bush and Clinton as the candidates in the 1992 election, a surprise third candidate arose. The American public was disgusted with conventional politics, depressed over the economy, and angry with government abuses and excesses, so when outsider billionaire Ross Perot came riding forth into the political arena, he was looked upon as a bright new entrant to the old process.

Newsweek put his picture on the April 27, 1992, cover and asked "Who is Ross Perot?" Everyone wanted to know. They called him a "wild card—rich, outspoken, unpretentious, even messianic." He defied all odds with confidence, and we could tell no one would ever be able to push him around or buy his support.

He fascinated us on TV talk shows, stating, "People are looking for a leader, not a detail man." He inferred both Bush and Clinton weren't even up to being detail men and certainly couldn't be counted on for any form of leadership. He had simplistic answers for all problems: "If it's broken, fix it." The whole country seemed broken, and he offered us a tool kit with a high-class repairman. He took complex issues and made them simple and understandable. He showed us charts that were clear. He seemed to make sense.

Suddenly pictures of Perot were everywhere. We saw a short, feisty, jug-eared capitalist who always looked as if he'd just gotten a too-short haircut and was waiting for it to grow out. But he didn't care what we thought about his looks. "What you see is what you get," he said simply. There was to be no makeup or image-doctoring with Perot. We liked that about him, his straightforward honesty with no guile or pretense. What a change from created candidates dressed for success!

Newsweek noted, "With his fortune, his twang and his endless supply of zingers, Ross Perot is launching his latest crusade. This is not the navy, IBM, or General Motors: this is, he believes, a crusade for America itself. As he has many times before, Perot is now casting himself as the under-dog—as a folksy, self-deprecating David, the only guy around with the guts and the smarts to take on the entire United States political system and beat it."[1]

We began to cheer for the underdog and pasted "Ross for Boss" stick-ers on our bumpers. *USA Today* praised Perot's "Leadership ability to rally people" and said he was "in the right place at the right time."[2] The *New Yorker* added, "Perot is playing on a potent force—the public's disgust with conventional politics and sense that government doesn't work any more." It concluded, "He is benefiting from the weaknesses of both major parties' probable candidates. The government is in gridlock and the frus-trated public may take a chance on something utterly new and different. But it's a very big gamble!"[3]

In the beginning the descriptive words about Ross Perot were posi-tive. His obviously Powerful personality was affirmed by words of achieve-ment such as engaging, hardworking, fascinating, heroic, confident, chal-lenging, unconventional, determined, energetic. It was not until his opponents attacked him that people began to call him "slippery as an eel" as well as manipulative, deceptive, impatient, egotistical, testy, and autocratic.

Perot's rise from unknown to cover material was called meteoric. Before he'd officially declared his candidacy, he was moving up the charts. A *Newsweek* poll of April 15–16, 1992, showed Bush at 44 percent, Clin-ton at 25 percent, and Perot at 24 percent.

It was at this point that I attended a luncheon in Dallas where Perot was the speaker. My brother, Ron Chapman, the number-one radio dee-jay in Dallas for twenty-five years, invited me to the charity event to honor volunteers for their selfless service to the community. The program was chaired by Ron's wife, Nance. As Nance formally introduced Ross Perot, who stood up behind a large lectern that dwarfed him, all the photographers swarmed forth to get pictures. We all settled in for his message and had barely gotten comfortable when he concluded his folksy talk. It was only five minutes long!

We were collectively shocked as he sat down after those few minutes of dubious inspiration. When the awards were given out and the program finished early, TV and press cameras were sprouting up everywhere. My brother took me up front to meet Perot, and as we were chatting I sensed a camera nearby; I turned and smiled, then we went back to conversing. He was charming, witty, and relaxed and promised to make me an ambassador if he won. That night as I tuned in to CNN and heard the announcer say, "Ross Perot spoke in Dallas today . . ." I looked up, and there I was! Ross and I filled the screen and looked like old friends. The next morning the same picture was in *USA Today*. From then on, I naturally followed his campaign even more closely.

Politics Is Dirty Tricks

Once Perot officially declared his candidacy, both sides went on the attack. With the dirty-tricks squads of both parties after him, his strengths turned to weaknesses before our TV eyes. His intriguing Texas accent became "an annoying nasal twang." His unconventional thinking became conspiratorial, his devout patriotism became flag-waving hysteria, his ability to enter where angels fear to tread became irrational showmanship, and his straight talk became narrow-minded bigotry. Private investigators found he was guilty of private investigating. Questions came up that most of us hadn't thought about before.

Did Perot secretly bankroll Oliver North to ransom hostages in Beirut?

Did he give President Carter money to free hostages in Iran?

Was it right for him to charter a plane and fly food and medicine to POWs in Vietnam?

When he said his solutions to the drug problem "will not be pretty" did he mean he intended to line up all pushers in the village square and shoot them?

In spite of both parties' looking under Texas-size rocks for Perot's hidden perversions, money-laundering, and playboy dalliances, they couldn't find a genuine scandal.

The magazine covers that started in April with "Who is Ross Perot?" moved on in May to "Waiting for Perot—He's leading in the polls but can he lead the nation?"[4] *Newsweek* pictured him with the headline "President Perot?"[5] but later *Time* had misgivings. "Nobody's Perfect" the cover proclaimed, "The Doubts about Ross Perot."[6] The June 1992 issue of *Texas Monthly* had a cartoon of Ross on the cover looking like Alfred E. Neumann of *Mad Magazine*. At the same time *D*, the magazine of Dallas, pictured a somber Perot and headlined "Perot's Gamble—will he change the system or will it change him?" and *Fortune* put him on the cover with the line "What business thinks of Ross Perot." *U.S. News* in June 1992 did the same with "Ross Perot's America—His boyhood, his career, his values—in his own words." *TV Guide* proclaimed him "Man of the Year (so far)," and a quick book on Perot's life was produced by Crossway, asking, "Is he the problem or solution?"

June 1992 was indeed Perot's hot month. His face was not only on every magazine in the Dallas airport, but he kept appearing on TV. Little Perot faces peered at us wherever we looked; it seemed we couldn't get enough of Ross Perot.

To show he was serious about this challenge, Perot hired two top political operatives: Ed Rollins, who had directed Reagan's 1984 campaign, and Hamilton Jordan, Jimmy Carter's campaign manager in both 1976 and 1980. The first was a Republican and the latter a Democrat. Ross had covered all the bases. The two advisers were to build this one-man operation into a viable political campaign.

If these two men had understood the personalities, they would have been more prepared for what happened. Along with Perot, they were both Powerful personalities, Rollins with a touch of the Perfect and Jordan with a bit of Popular humor that didn't last very long. Anytime you get three Powerfuls with different ideas in charge of the same project, trouble is imminent.

Rollins jumped in quickly with a plan for a $150 million publicity campaign. Perot, not wanting anyone to tell him how much of his own money to spend, cut the amount in half, eliminating the direct-mail program. "Spend money on the kind of junk I throw away? No way!" Nor could he see any use in buying TV time when he was already the darling of the talk shows for free. He didn't like paying money for polls, either, especially when they seemed to show him slipping. From June 1 to July 1, 1992, he went from a 37 percent rating, leading Bush and Clinton, to a 26 percent following.

Obviously he had done better without the handlers, and he told them so. He didn't want to be taught the lessons of campaigning, he didn't like to share authority, he had never been a team player, and suddenly the whole thing seemed out of his control. When a Powerful is out of control he gets depressed. "When is it going to be fun again?" he asked, meaning, "When can I be in charge again?"

As Perot wrestled with these two men he had hired to make his case a legitimate one, he lost his zeal for the whole operation. When he added up the cost on top of the effort, he fired Jordan and Rollins—and then quit himself. In typical Powerful form he implied, If I can't win, I won't play the game. He had not learned to be a good sport. He wasn't used to people investigating him, even though he'd done his share of it himself, and he wasn't about to have his children criticized. He hadn't learned that politics is dirty tricks. He wasn't ready to take direction from anyone, he hated criticism, and he didn't understand that the public tests candidates to gauge their stamina and persistence under attack. The testy Texan didn't want to be tested. The campaign officially lasted from June 3 until July 16, 1992. Ross the boss didn't want a loss!

"In the aftermath, it is easy to see the Perot-for-president boom as a strange, short-lived phenomenon," wrote Eleanor Clift in Newsweek. "Perot became a blank screen on which millions of American voters could project their discontents, an empty vessel into which they could pour their hopes for a government that is free from partisan conflict and brokered compromise."[7] Perot's followers were devastated. Those who had put in volunteer hours and raised money for the campaign didn't know what to do with themselves or the money. The July 27, 1992, Newsweek cover pictured Perot looking small with a huge black headline over him that said, "THE QUITTER."

August and September went by with the usual partisan attacks on each side. Then, just when Clinton was trying to put his questionable past behind him and appear presidential and Bush was fighting boredom with the whole process, suddenly Powerful Perot galloped back into the arena. With a surprise announcement on October 1, 1992, he reentered the race with no handlers to try to rein him in.

"He has always been a driven man—a boat rocker and a maverick who is determined to prove that he is smarter and more nobly motivated than anyone around him. . . . For a few brief weeks in early summer Perot looked like the answer to a disgruntled voter's prayer—the gritty, homely personification of the Horatio Alger myth come to politics, a megabucks Mr. Fixit with a Boy Scout sense of ethics and a penchant for putting things right," *Newsweek* reported.[8]

Trust or Change?

But was this enough? By October it was too late. Perot's followers didn't want to be duped again, and Clinton had already charmed the disaffected. Bush was looking tired and visionless. The greatest contribution Perot made in his October outing was to give some excitement to the debates and make simple folksy comments like, "It's time to pick up a shovel and clean out the barn," and "Lift the hood of the car and see what's wrong and fix it." He also stated, "I wouldn't hire Bill Clinton for a middle management position in one of my companies." And he quipped, "Taking action in Washington is an unnatural event." He frequently inserted his motto, "It's just that simple."

His pithy comments gave us all a few amusing moments. But toward the end Perot's efforts seemed to be only a small part of a political sideshow. Ultimately, the campaign boiled down to two words: *change* and *trust*. *Simple* lost out.

Clinton called for change, but people didn't trust him. Bush said "trust me," but he couldn't seem to find a plan for change. "Clinton may be able to handle trust better than Bush can handle change," wrote Jonathan Alter in *Newsweek*. "But trust me, that can all still change—a dozen times—between now and the election. The guy who can also wear the other guy's hat for a few autumn weeks will win."[9]

Finally the people spoke: They would rather have the hope of change with someone they couldn't quite trust than trust the same status quo with a person too steeped in tradition to change. When the votes were counted, simple Perot and trustworthy Bush both lost, and William Jefferson Clinton, the candidate of change, was the only one left smiling. We had seen not only an unusual campaign but a display of personalities. We had observed Bush reaching out the hand of peace and avoiding a fight but lacking an apparent vision, Clinton displaying the seductive charm of his Popular personality, and Powerful Perot wanting to be in charge of the country and fix it his simple way. In this three-way race, charm and change came out on top!

Ross Perot
Powerful Personality

The following lists of strengths and weaknesses include words and phrases used in newspaper articles, magazines, books, television, and radio to describe Ross Perot's Powerful personality. Check the characteristics that could also have been written about you if the press had been following you through your life.

Strengths
___ Tough, outspoken
    entrepreneur
___ Unconventional approach
___ Defies labels
___ Folk hero
___ Clear vision
___ Grandiose
___ Cuts his losses
___ Counsels himself
___ Avoids pain
___ Verbal machismo
___ Amazing salesmanship
___ Determination and energy
___ Ability to rally people
___ Action-oriented
___ Right place at right time
___ 20 hour work days
___ Engaging and interesting
___ Made-to-order
___ Unconventional thinking
___ Refreshing/heroic image
___ Down-home folksy
___ Can cut through
    impediments
___ Gets things done

Weaknesses
___ Shoots from the lip
___ Cranky independence
___ Deserts the little people
___ Betrays supporters
___ Messianic vision of himself
___ Feisty guerrilla operator
___ Volcanic reaction
___ Hyperactive mouth
___ Wily and quirky
___ Testy Texan
___ Can't take the heat
___ Recoiled at reality
___ Petulant autocrat
___ Bizarre behavior
___ Inspector Perot
___ Delusions of grandeur
___ Obnoxiously arrogant
___ Ruthless and petty
___ Devious
___ Slippery as an eel
___ Brutal, unfeeling
___ Petulant
___ Blowing his cool
___ Manipulative
___ Impatient

    ___ Can-do answers   ___ Pain to work with
    ___ Confidence he's right   ___ Thin-skinned
    ___ Self-assured appeal   ___ Answers question before
    ___ Smart and clever   hearing it
    ___ Loves challenges   ___ Annoyed and irritated
                                  when questioned
                              ___ Edgy, testy
                              ___ Conspiratorial bent
___ TOTAL   ___ TOTAL

Total of your presidential profile of Powerful strengths and weaknesses: _____

Are You a Leader Like Perot?

If you have checked off many of these Powerful personality items, you are a born leader. You are in control of your circumstances, you set goals and achieve them, you are confident in your ability, and you are able to get others to follow you. You love to work and you can't understand why other people seem lazy. You have learned to present deep truth in simple terms. You can organize any project quickly in your head and get it done while others are thinking about it. You don't need to listen to other opinions because you already know what you're going to do, you know it's right, and you don't need any superfluous suggestions from uninformed people. You have the greatest chance of success of all the different personalities; however, you have some fatal flaws that if not eliminated will slow down your progress and curtail the leadership heights you were created to achieve.

Because you don't like to consider other people's opinions, you jump in where angels fear to tread, and your impulsive decisions and love of taking risks may cause you to lose in a big way. Your family may live in fear of what you are going to get involved in next. Your need to be on top may cause you to manipulate others and treat them as dummies. When you win you may appear arrogant and when you lose you find a way to blame the consequences on others.

Before you can be the leader others will follow, you need to gain a respect for the people you live and work with and learn to weigh their opinions even when you don't believe you need them. You must develop patience with those who don't move at your pace and integrity in all your actions. If people can't trust you they won't dare to join your crusade.

Perot offered simple, exciting, unconventional leadership, but the people lost heart when they saw it was his way or the highway. If you wish to make the most of your life, turn down the volume, move in from your extremes, be a good sport, and don't quit!

21

ALL THINGS FOR ALL PEOPLE

WILLIAM JEFFERSON CLINTON

President: 1993–?
Personality: Popular-Powerful
Principle to Learn: Bounce back!

When Clinton won the election my friends called and asked, "What's he going to be like as a president?"

"He's going to love it—the fun, the spotlight, the pageantry," I predicted. "He's going to dress up and go to the big city and have eternal party time!"

Friendly and Bubbling Over

Clinton entered the White House seemingly expecting four years of party time. The stories of inaugural balls showed him at his best: dressed in a tuxedo, movie-star handsome, smiling and charming the people and the press. His warm, emotional, and friendly nature has been his most engaging trait and has helped him with European leaders who have been accustomed to the diplomatic skills and dignity of both Ronald Reagan and George Bush.

Clinton thrives in social occasions, and he has taken a special liking to his German counterpart, Helmut Kohl. Look at the uncontainable joy that spilled out of the president as he hugged the hefty Kohl and announced they had a new relationship. He must have been secure in this budding friendship as he dared to tell Kohl in front of an audience at the NATO summit, "I was watching sumo wrestling last night, and it made me think of you."

Personally, I would not have been thrilled to be compared with a sumo wrestler, but Chancellor Kohl kept smiling, at least until he saw the cartoons the next day with his head on the body of an overstuffed sumo!

Clinton must have made the comment in such an engaging manner that Kohl thought it was funny—of course it could have changed meaning in the translation—because at the G-7 meetings in July 1994, they were back together again a "huggin' and a chalkin'." The headline of the *International Herald Tribune* on July 12, 1994, stated cheerfully, "Clinton and Kohl Chemistry Bubbles Over." Writer Ruth Marcus pointed out that the two leaders have a few things in common: "Their common working class origins, their mutual passion for politics, and their equally impressive appetites. The chunky president looks positively svelte next to his portly German counterpart."

If we have such a friendly, fun-loving, bubbling-over president, could he possibly have some weaknesses? "Where will he have trouble?" friends asked me.

Right from the beginning we could see he would probably falter with a lack of organization and discipline, with doing things impulsively without thinking them through, and by trying too hard to make everyone love him. The Popular personality wins on friendship and loses on discipline. It's always more fun to talk than get down to the work at hand.

Suspecting this scenario would soon unfold, I have been very interested in reading analyses and comments that describe how President Clinton's Popular-Powerful personality has revealed itself since he lay claim to the Oval Office. Former Chrysler CEO Lee Iacocca gave one of the most succinct descriptions. Iacocca, a Powerful personality himself, spent sixty days in 1993 working for the passage of North American Free Trade Agreement (NAFTA), and during that time he visited often with the president. Later he said, "I got to know Clinton pretty well. He's got a good sense of humor, and he's pretty loose. He's pretty outspoken, and so am I."[1]

Without realizing it, Iacocca described the president's Popular-Powerful personality accurately in just a few words. Popular: "good sense of humor" and "pretty loose"—and Powerful: "pretty outspoken."

Master of the Bounce-Back

In interviewing people in Arkansas I found two extremes. They either considered Clinton the most charming, delightful, seductive, mesmerizing individual they ever met, or they felt he was an opportunistic, low-class, slick, philandering phony. Some saw only his strengths, some only his weaknesses. There seemed to be no middle road through Arkansas. One lovely lady who proudly told me she had been one of his "very close friends" said she could tell plenty—but "wouldn't do a thing to hurt Bill." Another who knew him in church felt he was a deeply spiritual man— "at least on Sunday when I saw him."

The one thing they all agreed on was Clinton's amazing staying power. He could look as if he's going to lose and then smile his way through to victory. "You could throw him out a window like you would a Cheshire cat," one man said, "and he'll land on his feet and have a big grin."

Republican Bay Buchanan, sister of Pat Buchanan and president of the American Cause, stated on a TV talk show, "Clinton has an uncanny ability to take a disastrous situation and turn it into a plus."

This ability to bounce back from scandal and negative publicity is a strength of the Popular-Powerful combination. Those who have observed Bill Clinton agree that he is a master of the bounce-back. His Popular personality has a convincing, wide-eyed look of innocence, and his Powerful personality knows he hasn't done anything that any other red-blooded American male hasn't tried with less success. One aide, referring to some new attacks on Clinton, sighed and said, "He needs to go out on 'charm patrol' again."

One of Bill's friends told me, "When trouble comes, his pattern is denial as a first course of action followed by charm. If that combination doesn't work, he counterattacks." Another said, "He 'has something' on just about everybody in Arkansas, so he rarely has to resort to attacks." This technique has not been so successful in Washington, where he hasn't been there long enough to store up negative ammunition to use on the enemy.

Because of his lifetime ability to make good out of bad and to charm potential opponents, Clinton rode optimistically into Washington assuming it would be no more than a big Little Rock. He brought many of his Arkansas buddies with him and was confident he could take on the system.

His ability to always end up on the right side of things, to compromise or capitulate, and to explain his way out of controversies, had earned Clinton the moniker "Slick Willie" while he was governor of Arkansas.

Memory Gap

Another way he has turned negatives into positives is by forgetting what he said in the first place, assuming the public would also forget, or by changing the wording so that what was originally said doesn't mean that anymore. Clinton has used memory gaps effectively. Since most people didn't listen carefully in the first place, a lapse or a distortion is hardly noticeable. Thus a campaign promise of "No discrimination against homosexuals in the armed forces" turned into "Don't ask; don't tell," and we were all happy.

One of the most clever twists of words came with the highly touted healthcare package created by Hillary Clinton and her friends. The president shook his black pen at us on TV and affirmed he would veto any bill that came short of total healthcare for all Americans, but when the realistic hope faded into committee land and the bus tour didn't generate enough response, Clinton could see the word *failure* flaming on the horizon. He couldn't change the facts, but he could vary his vocabulary; the result was a headline on the July 18, 1994, issue of *Time* that declared, "*Failure* turns into *Pathway*." Healthcare hadn't failed, no; instead, we had created a *pathway* toward future reform. We had made the first step. We had parted the Red Sea of red tape so that someday President Moses could march through, followed by his healthy troops.

Why did healthcare fail? In the beginning there was tacit agreement among unlikely allies. The American Medical Association, insurance lobbies, major corporations, the U.S. Chamber of Commerce, and even Senate minority leader Bob Dole all believed in the principle of universal health coverage. The president was told from the beginning that he needed to build on this consensus potential, find middle-of-the-road answers, and come up with a plan that could be passed by Congress. With Clinton's charm and position he could have been persuasive, but Hillary didn't want compromise. She wanted a bold and dramatic plan created in secret. As one who worked on the committee said, "It was as if she was the first person to ever think of healthcare."

When, in October 1993, it was time to brief the economic advisers, Hillary was "articulate and in command as she walked through the massive and detailed blueprint."[2] By the time she had finished, the group was in quiet shock. Those who had experience with what Congress might consider expressed concern. Where would the money come from to finance this plan? In retrospect, the handwriting was on the wall, but Hillary wouldn't listen. "With a wave of her hand, she simply said everybody was wrong."[3]

Clinton could have achieved a compromise plan, but because of Hillary's insistence that she was right and her husband's willingness to go along with her opinion, the Perfect plan was doomed to failure.

Wiggling and Waffling

As president, Clinton has had to wiggle out of many other unexpected controversies. He underestimated the country's resistance to gays in the military and had no idea anyone would care a whit about attorney general nominee Zoe Baird's baby-sitter. He had to water down his repayment to the gays for supporting him and come up with a middle-of-the-road plan. Zoe had to be sent back home only to be replaced by Kimba Wood, who also had not paid proper taxes on her hired help. Who would have thought homosexual sailors and imported baby-sitters would have put the president to the test so quickly in his administration?

As with most political issues, these stumbling blocks faded in the brilliance of new problems: the DOA appointment of Lani Guinier as chief of the civil rights division in the Justice Department, the two-hundred-dollar haircut aboard Air Force One that shut down much of Los Angeles International Airport, scandals in the House post office, and troubles in the White House travel office as well as in Somalia. Then there was also Clinton's troubling indecision and daily waffling regarding the festering situations in Bosnia, Haiti, and North Korea, new sexual-misconduct allegations, and nagging questions about his and Hillary's investments in the Whitewater Development Corporation. That's quite a list of problems for one year, 1993, along with the political demise of some Arkansas cronies and the questionable death of one close friend!

The president reached for a new woman for attorney general: Janet Reno, a six-foot-tall single woman, hardly a sex symbol, who had no babies who needed sitting. Born of a mother who was an alligator wrestler, Reno needed her Powerful personality just to stay alive. Even though she is short on style, she is tall in stature and can easily intimidate those around her. In a city where placing blame on the other person or party is as natural as breathing, Attorney General Reno won applause when she actually took responsibility for a debacle in Waco, Texas, where cult members and children were burned to death following a raid on their compound by federal law-enforcement officers. Her willingness to shoulder the blame when she could have "wiggled" out of it made her a star, and it has been said that the president is fearful of her popularity and has ordered her spotlight turned down a few watts.

Through this plethora of problems, Clinton not only smiles through one trouble after another but he has the strength to bounce back, put the problems behind him, exude confidence, and go on. His staff members wish he would level out and keep them from constant crisis management, but the joke continues to be, if Clinton has a good week, can crisis be far behind?

Facility for Convenient Evasion

The pattern of denial, charm, attack, and bounce-back can only be repeated a few times before the American public begins to wonder. By March 1994, according to a USA Today survey, "More than half the people think Clinton is hiding something. He suffered his biggest hit in personal qualities—values, leadership and ability to inspire confidence—all of which are under 50 percent."[4]

Among other first-year problems Clinton faced was the report by certain Arkansas State Highway Patrol troopers that they knew personally about some of the governor's philandering. When asked directly about these charges by a reporter, Clinton couldn't say no but he didn't dare say yes either. Instead he stammered, "We . . . we did, if, the, the, I, I, the stories are just as they have been said. They're outrageous, and they're not so."[5] The amazing miracle for Clinton was that no one pursued this allegation, and the troopers were "reassigned."

According to *Newsweek*, the least attractive aspect of Clinton's political personality is "his facility for convenient evasion."[6] Even though they didn't bring up his Popular personality, they hit on one of the major weaknesses, a poor memory, especially when remembering would be embarrassing. (Reagan, also a Popular personality, was often fuzzy on the details, not having a clear picture of Irangate, the Contras, or Oliver North. However, when North ran for U.S. senator from Virginia, Reagan's mind cleared up and he remembered that he had never liked him and wouldn't support him.)

When Clinton was pressed to explain his financial losses in the Whitewater Corporation, he had a sudden revelation while reading his deceased mother's autobiography. It came to him in a flash that he had given her twenty thousand dollars to buy a log cabin in the woods. Few of us would forget a twenty-thousand-dollar gift to our mothers, especially when it represented 50 percent of our year's income, but Clinton has a "facility for convenient evasion."

Charm Your Socks Off!

Each year when the Malcolm Baldridge Award is given out, the president of the United States is invited, and he usually attends. A friend who was present at the 1994 awards ceremony told me that after Clinton's part of the program was over, he spent an hour going from table to table and personally greeting the people. This was the first time at these awards that a president had come down and mingled with the people, and they loved it. Clinton's charisma pulled in those who didn't think they even liked him.

Opponents have learned that they never want those who vote on any measure to meet with Clinton for fear he'll change their minds. "He can charm your socks off!" one reported.

Typical of the Popular personality, Bill Clinton uses his charm in order to be liked. He loves to be loved. He tries to make everybody happy and offend no one. When Arkansas journalist Paul Greenberg was asked about Clinton before the election he wrote, "Who is Bill Clinton? He is whatever you want him to be at the moment—and he will be it with remarkable energy, savvy, intelligence and everything else except constancy. He's got lots of smooth but no traction. He waffles and waits to see which course is popular before saying he'll support it."[7]

Peggy Noonan, speech writer for both Reagan and Bush, captured Clinton's need for approval when she said, "Clinton's charm and warmth and intelligence are obviously real. His friends whisper the famous flaw: he wants too much to be liked. All presidents manipulate. Franklin Delano Roosevelt did, and so did Ronald Reagan. But with them, people perceived that beneath the overlay was a core of hardness and toughness. Clinton has survived a great deal this year. But one wonders: at the core, where it counts, what is there?"[8]

This charm is the strength that keeps all the Populars on top, but when carried to extreme this need to please all ends up pleasing no one.

Clinton's acceptance speech at the Democratic National Convention included promises to every imaginable constituency. When he was done, *Newsweek* summed it up, "The result was a weak cup of coffee, somewhat stimulating but essentially insubstantial."[9]

From the moment Clinton took office he had to face his need to have everyone like him. When he would make a statement today that displeased one group, he'd change it by tomorrow. He seemed to be rushing from policy to new policy with the speed of a juggler trying to keep all those plates spinning at one time. He sold himself as a "new Democrat," but he kept spinning the plate labeled "liberal agendas."

Suzanne Garment, author of *Scandal: the Culture of Mistrust in American Politics,* put it this way: "In a *Saturday Night Live* takeoff on TV advertising, the announcer held up his product and told the viewing audience triumphantly, 'It's a floor polish and a dessert topping!' President Bill Clinton should remember this line in the coming months. He sold himself to the country as a smooth political blend of views and characteristics that barely belong in the same universe. Now the people who wanted a floor polish are angry that they can't see their face in the linoleum, while the folks in search of a dessert topping feel a little queasy in the stomach."[10]

Whether Clinton will end up being floor polish or dessert topping no one knows, but whichever it is he will be smiling, bouncing back, and charming our socks off.

The Three Faces of Bill Clinton

Right from the beginning, Clinton couldn't articulate a clear position and stay with it. *Time* pictured him with one head looking left and one heading right and explained that he campaigned as a new Democrat trying to walk the middle line but in reality he was lurching to the left or right according to the circumstances and the audience.[11] Some see this lurching as trying to placate everyone, and some see it as duplicity and vacillation.

While he works toward liberal reform and help for the poor, he appoints white moderates to his cabinet, which includes more millionaires than either Reagan's or Bush's. "Maybe it's been so long that we've forgotten what 'left' is and how to tell it from right," concluded Barbara Ehrenreich in *Time.* "At the simplest, most ecumenical level, to be on the left means to take the side of the underdog, whoever that may be: the meek, the poor and, generally speaking, the 'least among us,' as a well-known representative of the left position put it a couple of millenniums ago. Thus it is not leftish to have a $200 haircut while planes full of $20 haircut people circle overhead; nor would a leftist contemplate selling the president's favors at $15,000 a plate fund raisers. Such behaviors belong way over on the right, along with supply-side economics, capital-gains tax reductions and other efforts to pamper the pâté-eating classes. . . . He felt for the underdog, as he never tired of telling us, but whenever the overdogs began to howl, he obediently rushed back toward the right."[12]

This running back and forth from left to right shows Clinton at his best and worst. The positive is his amazing ability to please whatever group he's with, and the negative is his unwillingness to state a position and stay with it. People aren't sure whether they're with him or against him because they're not sure what he really believes.

During the Democratic National Convention Lou Klein wrote in *Newsweek,* "If the idea was to introduce Clinton to the nation last week, his acceptance speech was a true portrait. For 53 minutes the three faces of Bill—person, politician, and policy wonk—struggled for ascendancy, with varied results."[13]

By 1994, Klein had amplified his opinion on Clinton's three faces into an article entitled "Bill Led Three Lives." Klein called Clinton's quick changes "the abiding mystery of the president's multiple-personality-disorder." He outlined in humor three separate personalities:

1. The Moderate Clinton—this one is the best, the one he campaigned with and the only one that hasn't brought him grief. Strange then that he has "stocked the administration from his other lives."

2. The Liberal Clinton—this personality is not so engaging as the first one. This one had to pay off supporters, put the right ethnic mix in cab-

inet positions. This personality jumped into the "gays in the military" issue quickly without enough analysis. This Clinton courted Senate Democrats, hung out with the Hollywood crowd and reminisced on his Yale and Oxford days.

3. The Political Clinton—this one is grasping for power and will do whatever it takes to stay in the White House. In the past this personality gave out government grants and low-interest loans to "the not-so-needy who in turn contributed generously to his political campaigns." This one brought his friends to Washington to run the country and has found what worked in Arkansas is naive in D.C.

Klein concluded, "The president's ability to swim so effortlessly in different waters would be an admirable trait—if it weren't carried so often to excess."[14]

How true it is that our strengths, no matter what they are, when carried to extremes become weaknesses!

As Lou Klein saw three faces of Bill Clinton, Newsweek's Howard Fineman came up with "The Four Faces of Bill Clinton," saying, "Like the genie in Aladdin, the president morphed himself into a series of familiar figures—each created to appeal to a different coalition in Congress and the electorate." Going on about the State of the Union address, Fineman continued, "At the rostrum of the House of Representatives, Clinton was, by turns: a Perot-ista on the deficit; a conservative Republican (or New Democrat) on crime and welfare; a liberal on education, training and health care, and a cross between a Baptist preacher and Dan Quayle on family and traditional values."[15]

Not only did some see Clinton as duplicitous as having three or four faces, but the New York Times suggested in a front-page article entitled "The Faces Behind the Face that Clinton's Smile Masks" that he was wearing a series of masks. The Times said that when he is on television, Clinton "radiates earnestness, empathy and polite deference, coming across as an odd hybrid of television evangelist and think-tank analyst. But in person, it is possible to see more; his commanding attitude and his supple political shape-shifting, his fascination with and yearning for the adulation he is getting, and his surliness and finger-wagging upbraidings when something does not go exactly as he likes." It went on to share his burst of anger when a fan got too near and he snapped at the security agent only to turn toward the crowd and smile. "He transformed his face back into the political mask of the easy-going country boy and resumed his loose, unhurried gait."[16]

Ronald Reagan was considered an actor, but at least he was consistent. He played the part of president with style and grace and never seemed to step out of his role. The difference with Clinton is that he hasn't thoroughly read the script and he moves in and out of character. He pleases some of us some of the time but none of us all of the time.

One reporter said, "Clinton has natural phoniness," and *Newsweek* labeled him a "Faux Kennedy with tin charisma." As analysts discussed whether the president's personality was genuine, most people agreed he was a natural on TV, was at his best when answering questions, and had a gift for dazzling little children into cute responses. In January 1994 when the Clintons went to Russia the president staged a town-hall performance where he gave a message of hope and challenge and then stood in the crowd with microphone in hand taking questions from ordinary people. He also visited groups of children who stared up at him, wide-eyed. When these events were shown on national television with millions watching, the *Auckland Sunday Star,* in an article headlined "Clinton Charms Russia," said, "Clinton's outgoing style appeared to go down well in a wintry Russian capital heavy with hardship as the country endures a chaotic transition from a communist to a market economy."[17]

In August 1993 the *New Yorker,* searching for hopeful phrases about the president, concluded he is charming, intelligent, well-informed, and well-spoken. But the magazine noted that he and Hillary don't have the needed "aura" to capture and keep the people's loyalty. "They impress you while they're on the air, but they don't stay in the room after you've changed the channel."

Faraway Places with Strange-Sounding Names

As each new president comes into office, he is faced with two major areas of activity: the home front and foreign affairs. While running Arkansas Clinton didn't have an embassy in London or a hot line to Moscow. His form of governing was local. Because Clinton's experience had been domestic rather than global, some of his problems have been in his waffling and waiting for the world to change since he didn't have much interest in faraway places with strange-sounding names.

In contrast to Bush's single-minded focus on foreign policy, Clinton wishes these remote countries would tidy up their own houses and stop shooting at every American that comes in to help. Clinton sorely "feels their pain," but he frankly doesn't know what to do with them. Foreign policy is to Clinton what the economy was to Bush, a mosquito annoyance that swatting doesn't seem to kill.

In 1993 Clinton charged some of his brightest cerebral associates with creating some kind of a foreign policy. They struggled for months trying to come up with a plan that would sound good without any real commitment. No one wanted to get involved, and yet the official statement had to sound as if we cared which side occupied Gorazde.

During the campaign, Clinton made George Bush sound mean and heartless. Clinton showed pictures of what were assumed to be our troops under the president's command intercepting boatloads of pitiful Haitians hanging off the side of boats with splitting hulls while starving babies clung to their emaciated mothers. Could any decent man send these people home to certain execution? Once Clinton became president the responsibilities for those pitiful Haitians became his; they didn't disappear on inauguration day.

To keep the most people happy, Clinton came up with a compromise. Intercept boats from Haiti out in the ocean away from TV cameras, process their requests, and then send them back. To facilitate this keep-them-out-of-sight ruse, the Pentagon chartered two Ukrainian vessels to sit in the sea as sudden office buildings staffed with government employees who reached out the hands of the law and pulled the confused refugees on board to check their asylum applications. Could anyone doubt the government came up with this plan? Would it take a president, desperate to please, to dream up and even find two leftover steamers from the Ukraine? Where does one find such things? At some international flea market?

Ironically, now that he is president, Clinton has quietly appropriated the Bush policy and not only pushed all the pathetic people back home but even sent in American troops to occupy the country and reestablish the questionable Jean-Bertrand Aristide as its president.

George Bush must be laughing over Clinton's solution to the Haiti problem and also over his compromise with China over its Most Favored Nation status, another bone of contention during the campaign. Since the 1989 Tiananmen Square massacre, the United States has felt we needed to punish China like a bad child, but nothing has been done of any significance.

During the campaign Clinton accused Bush of "coddling tyrants" in Beijing, and in tough tones he scolded the Chinese government and told it to behave. Now that he's president and needing to deal with these people in a practical way, he has had to modify his threats.

As *Time* said, this is "yet another campaign pledge he now seems to find it wiser not to keep."[18] Clinton sent Peaceful Warren Christopher to China to sort things out and tour state-owned factories supposedly full of slave labor. The press labeled the trip "a disaster of gigantic proportions," and Clinton has desperately tried to find a solution to make everybody happy. According to the head of Malaysia's Institute of Strategic and International Studies, partial sanctions are "a compromise which will satisfy no one and will merely strengthen Clinton's image as a wishy-washy leader. It's a crazy idea, and it won't work."[19]

George Bush has reason to both laugh and cry as he sees his passion for foreign policy become a nontransferable commodity. Bush lost the election because he was preoccupied with foreign affairs and not concerned enough with the economy. Clinton won the election on his concern for the economy and seems to be losing his grip because of his amateur status on foreign policy. The American public doesn't like to think much about foreign problems on a daily basis, but we do expect our country to be the leader of the free world. How proud we all were when Reagan stood tall, regal, and impressive among the European heads of state. How excited we were when Bush won us a war. How shaky we all feel now as Clinton wavers and waffles.

A senior Clinton administration official, quoted in *Time,* said, "All the polls show it. Real people are getting real nervous. The perception of ineptitude is growing. The public doesn't like foreigners thinking the president is out of his depth. Americans don't like being embarrassed. It's hurting the President's overall job-approval ratings, and it'll continue hurting unless something's done about it."[20]

Only time will tell how Clinton, a hands-on performer, will deal with distant people his charisma can't seem to control. According to the old theory promoted by historians Arthur Schlesinger Sr. and Arthur Schlesinger Jr., the nation does an about-face every thirty years. After a time of "conservative retrenchment" we seem to opt for liberal action, purpose, and idealism. The New Deal of Franklin Roosevelt in 1932 and the New Frontier of John Kennedy in 1960 represent this type of activism, and Clinton expects this new hour of hope and human desire will be his to foster and fan into a flame of liberal progress. With this potential for greatness comes the necessity for seeing the truth and having the nerve to present hard facts to the American public, which seems to prefer to live in the castle of denial.

"But historical cycles are not inevitable," wrote Walter Isaacson in *Time*. "They depend on the strengths and frailties of those who become the repositories of the hope for change. In a democracy, successful reformers must have, above all, the backbone to convey brutal facts unflinchingly. Especially now, America's current plight has been aggravated by a willful refusal to inhale unpleasant truths."[21]

In contrast to Franklin D. Roosevelt, who laid it on the line on day one, shut the banks down to show his grasp of the desperate financial situation the nation was in, and gave us the bad news pleasantly but firmly in his fireside chats, Clinton would rather avoid the truth. He has apparently lived in personal denial of negative truth for so long—and gotten away with it—that he doesn't want to be the bearer of bad news—the public might shoot down the messenger. "Clinton's tendency to waffle on tough issues is worrisome," suggested *Time*.[22]

For those of us who understand we are born with a set of personality strengths and weaknesses, it is no surprise that Clinton's Popular nature of looking on the bright side, avoiding problems, and saying what will cause people to love him did not change because he became president. He's still the same bouncing, optimistic, emotionally needy person he's always been. "Please love me," he seems to be saying, "and I'll protect you, the common people, by giving you all I can and getting the money from the rich people who can afford it." Doesn't that sound appealing? But will it work? Clinton doesn't mention the bitter truth. It's not in his nature.

"His economic program," Isaacson added, "was a no-pain pastiche that involved taxing only the rich and foreign corporations. The resulting feelings about his trustworthiness produced enough near death experiences for his campaign to serve as a warning that being all things to all people will not work!"[23]

Confidence Becomes Confusion

In so many of Clinton's personality traits he seems to hover precariously above the center line so that a push in either direction turns a potential positive into a negative. A determination to be in charge shows strength and leadership in the eyes of a public desiring a confident president, but if your well-publicized way fails, you take the step of defeat as your own personal failure. Clinton's stand on healthcare, along with his stand on gays in the military, are examples of ideas that became impossible to implement.

Campaigning on a promise of universal healthcare—similar to Hoover's vow to put "a chicken in every pot"—was appealing to all voters. It pricked a fear resident in each person's mind that asked, *What if I get really sick? Who will take care of me?* Since most of us have never read the fine print in our health policies, we don't have any idea what they actually cover. Lack of knowledge instills fear. So when a champion comes riding in promising healthcare for everyone, it seems like the answer. No more worries.

When Clinton threatened to veto anything short of universal care during his State of the Union address in January 1994, he staked his political status on what appeared to be a good idea. But he never seemed able to convince those millions who already had health insurance that they would be better off. Soon the middle class had a new fear: We may have to pay for those others who can't afford it and end up with less for ourselves. People began to ask, Who will pay for all this? Small business was the answer, and it alienated everyone in that category. How about putting the cost onto the insurance companies? some proposed. But the insurance industry countered with a ten-million-dollar TV campaign starring "Harry and Louise." Then came an idea to require everyone to buy his or her own mandatory insurance, just like car insurance is required in most states. This frightened everybody and was the kiss of death on the whole program. Everyone wanted insurance, but no one wanted to pay for it.

In the midst of this, House Ways and Means Committee Chairman Dan Rostenkowski was indicted for seventeen counts of fraud, including paying salaries to phantom employees who never showed up. "We do things differently in Chicago," he explained innocently. His resignation from the committee took the fire out of the possibilities and hastened the defeat of the healthcare proposal. His slide from power ended with his defeat in the 1994 election.

Senate Finance Committee Chairman Daniel Moynihan, who had never cared much for Clinton anyway, let him know the end was near for Hillary's healthcare proposal. But to show that there was still a sense of humor in the Senate, Moynihan brought the ranking Republican on the Senate

Finance Committee to the White House to explain the imminent defeat to the president. Bob Packwood was an ironic choice, for while Clinton was trying to fight off charges of sexual harassment from Paula Jones, Packwood was facing sexual-misconduct charges from twenty-nine different women. The fact that Packwood held the key to healthcare reform and the success of Clinton's presidency was "terrifying," said a White House aide.

By making universal healthcare his top priority and staking his political life on it, Clinton made retreat more obvious and compromise the only choice. How easy it is for cocky confidence to take the step over to confusion.

Vaulting Ambition

All leaders soon learn that their initial strengths when carried to extremes can become weaknesses. Because the American public is so fickle and seems to enjoy knocking down today what it voted for yesterday, a president can see his assets become liabilities in a hurry.

George Bush, sitting on his 80 percent approval rating, couldn't believe his success in foreign policy would be perceived as a weakness on the home front. His steadiness became a lack of vision, and his Peaceful personality became boring and irrelevant. We wanted change, and we liked Bill Clinton's drama, style, excitement, and ambition.

Columnist William Schneider in his *Los Angeles Times* article headlined "When Your Strength Is Your Weakness" wrote, "What people like about Bill Clinton is his ambition. But that's what they don't like about Clinton. All his life he has been driven by ambition to conquer the world outside Hope, Arkansas. You can see Clinton's ambition in his relentless drive for self-improvement. The voracious reading, the tireless policy discussions, the jogging."[24]

Lady Macbeth to the Rescue

In Shakespeare's play *Macbeth*, the leading characters are an ambitious couple who are on the path to success. By tradition Macbeth will become king when the present monarch dies, and he is willing to wait his turn in pleasant anticipation. Macbeth is well liked and inoffensive, but his wife, Lady Macbeth, is a definite Powerful personality who wants to hurry the progression along. She knows she was made to be a queen, and she wants the position now! As she pushes her husband to kill the king and gain the throne, he mulls it over.

"I have no spur to prick the sides of my intent, but only vaulting ambition, which o'er leaps itself and falls on the other," he answers her. In other words, I have no reason to do something morally and legally wrong except for my vaulting ambition, which is jumping ahead of me. Lady Macbeth tells him he has no nerve and is less than a real man. When he ponders what would happen if they fail, she responds, "We fail! But screw your courage to the sticking-place, and we'll not fail."

In the light of the Clintons' problems with their questionable investments in Whitewater and Hillary's playing the commodities market in a doubtful manner, there could be a comparison to the Macbeth situation. Bill was on his way to more power, but it was reportedly Hillary who pushed to overstep the normal progression and make sure they did not fail. Together Bill and Hillary had spent several years getting Arkansas under control, and I'm sure they sincerely felt that Washington, D.C., was just a building with a bigger dome. This wishful thinking was on a par with taking Hillary out of her Little Rock kitchen and placing her in the factory that turns out Mrs. Field's cookies. Not that she couldn't put those chocolate chips in the right places and end up CEO within the year, but the circumstances would be more than just a larger kitchen.

The president has also found himself a larger kitchen, and one by one his cronies who held the spotlight on him have had their own lights dimmed by death, legal entanglements, or just plain incompetence. Now the president may be feeling that a party without his friends isn't so much fun anymore. But there are always new friends and more exciting places to go. . . .

By understanding Clinton's basic nature, we could have predicted what Bob Woodward wrote in his book *The Agenda,* that Clinton would soon be presiding over a White House staff in chaos and disarray, still disorganized and in need of reshuffling. Or that his healthcare and welfare plans couldn't find either votes or funding. Republican Senator Trent Lott from Florida said on CNN's *The Capitol Gang,* "Until the president is willing to become disciplined there will be no change."

This was nowhere more evident than at the Summit Meeting of Industrial Democracies, where even though Clinton enjoyed a special friendship with Kohl, a friendly stroll down the path with Boris Yeltsin, and jolly fun with John Major, he came to the meeting apparently unprepared and with shifting policies that confused the other leaders. His staff is "always on damage-control alert" the *New York Times* stated. "They never seem to get over putting out one fire before another bursts forth."

When you understand the personalities and are observant of people's behavior, you can predict where they will rise and where they will fall. Clinton has the charm but not the discipline to organize a staff and make it function as a team. He's had moments of excitement when he offered hope, but too often the party ends abruptly. There's only so long you can be excited by the cheerleader if the team doesn't win any games.

In July 1994, *Newsweek* headlined a presidential story with "How Reality Spoiled the President's Party." The writers explained his strengths and weaknesses paralleling his personality pattern and wondered when he would get down to serious business. They noted that the harsh realities of the problems in Haiti had forced him "to play a role for which neither interest nor experience has equipped him. Like a smelly camel the tiresome old world pushed its nose inside Clinton's tent once more."[25] In the first half of his term in office, Clinton has been faced with large doses of unwelcomed reality.

Bill Clinton
Popular-Powerful Personality

The following lists of strengths and weaknesses include words and phrases used in newspaper articles, magazines, books, television, and radio to describe President Bill Clinton's personality, a combination of Popular and Powerful traits. Check the characteristics that also apply to you.

Popular Personality

Strengths
___ Born pleaser
___ Winning smile
___ Enthusiastic schmoozer
___ Earnest friendliness
___ Makes instant acquaintance
___ Always talking
___ Shoulder patter

Weaknesses
___ Frat-house lounge lizard
___ Too smirky
___ Lust for the pinnacle
___ Too glib
___ Faux muscularity
___ Facility for convenient
        evasion

___ Glory boy
___ Enjoys human contact
___ Shoots the breeze
___ Connects with the people
___ Gregarious and ingratiating
___ Yearned to be "Most Popular"
___ Gets excited over
       everything
___ Great charisma and humor
___ Buoyancy and common
       touch
___ Teary-eyed and sensitive
___ Eternally fresh and youthful
___ Thrives on talk
___ Smiles through one trouble
       after another
___ Seductive glances
___ Joy in his work
___ Jokes with aides
___ Starry-eyed
___ Art of building coalitions
___ Graced with a touch of
       self-deprecating humor
___ Addicted to pressing the flesh
___ Dexterous accommodator
___ Schoolboy politician
___ Persuasive powers
___ **TOTAL**

___ Everywhere and nowhere
       stance
___ Denies unpleasant reality
___ Undisciplined and
       disorganized
___ Reputation for slickness
___ Too happy with himself
___ Hedges on issues
___ Prone to mistakes
___ Needs to be loved too
       much
___ Extreme efforts to please
___ Will do or say what
       you want
___ Tries to find middle ground
       where none exists
___ Waffles and waits
___ Devoid of inner truth
___ Overeager to please

___ **TOTAL**

Powerful Personality

Strengths
___ Born leader
___ Quick organizer
___ Automatic winner
___ Genial hustler
___ Collects contacts
___ Bull-session stamina

Weaknesses
___ Relentlessly striving
___ Needs to be number one
___ Must win
___ Defensive
___ Defiantly wonky
___ Fierce determination

____ Astonishingly well-
     informed
____ Emphatic
____ Driving ambition
____ Loves a crisis
____ A in candor
____ Eager to learn
____ Resilient, bounces back
____ Skilled
____ Persistent
____ Motivator
____ Fortitude
____ Super-responsible
____ Realist
____ Plows through charges of
     infidelity
____ Eyes glittering with ambition
____ Fire-in-the-belly
____ Bold planner
____ Rare talent for sniffing out
     issues
____ Remarkable energy
____ Single-minded in pursuit
     of power
____ Must get A's
____ Clean well-lighted mind
____ Eager to learn
____ **TOTAL**

____ Drive-obsessed
____ Oversubscribed
____ Policy addicted
____ Compulsive-obsessive
     ambition
____ Elements of macho excess
____ Too smug
____ Poor manager
____ Arrogant whiz-kid
____ Too brilliant
____ Passion for skating on thin
     issues
____ Angry flare-ups
____ Temper tantrums

____ **TOTAL**

Total of your presidential profile of Popular-Powerful strengths and weaknesses: _____

Are You a Leader Like Clinton?

One of the amazing traits of the Populars is their ability to make a negative seem positive. While Peaceful Bush allowed victory in the Gulf War to slip into electoral defeat, Clinton took a lack of Beltway experience seasoned with supposed adultery and, like a wide-eyed magician, turned it into victory.

This process reminds me of the large inflated toy my children had. It was taller than they were and had weights in its bottom and the grinning face of a clown at the top. No matter how hard the children hit the clown, punched it, or sat on it, the minute they relaxed control, the clown bounced back up with a perpetual smile on its face. This action is typical of the social Sanguine like Clinton, who has the proverbial nine lives.

Clinton has taken experiences that would have killed off any other political personality and has turned them into success. Part of this ability comes from the public perception that if you are wearing a happy face you must have won. Losers cry—or at least look depressed—so if you bounce up and smile, the situation must be under control.

If you checked off many of Clinton's traits, you probably have the ability to bounce back also and keep a smile on your face that denotes victory. This is a talent that other personalities do not possess. Looking like a winner will always put you a few steps ahead of those who appear doubtful or confused.

Clinton is a master of the bounce-back and sometimes redeems himself so quickly we hardly notice he was down. Whether he is fending off failed cabinet appointments, financial scandal, or bimbo eruptions, he can, at least in public appearances, slough them off as momentary attacks and move on.

We hear of temper tantrums in staff meetings and swearing at those who cross him up, but we see the smile and the shrug of his shoulders in public. He has the same little-boy look of innocence Reagan used so effectively that says to the people, "It was nothing. Please forget it."

Being able to bounce back is an amazing talent that the wide-eyed Populars use to their advantage. If you look happy, unruffled, and innocent, the people will believe you. It's surely worth a try. It's convincing often enough to keep playing the odds.

Are you one of these people? If so, you know why Populars need this ability to wave off problems more than the other personalities. If you have the Popular personality you know how easily you get into trouble. You don't take the time to analyze situations carefully so you make poor choices. You're not good with money except for spending it, so you run out of cash and bounce checks.

You have a natural magnetism about you that is a come-on to others, and that can get you into trouble. And you'll go just about anywhere at anytime if it sounds like fun. These little escapades don't seem like serious weaknesses to you—surely they're not as ominous as robbing banks or beating up your sister. They're cute little frolics that somehow went astray. Don't worry; you'll bounce back and, if need be, make colorful excuses cloaked in innocence. "How did I know Kimba Wood had an illegal baby-sitter?" "What do I know about cattle futures? Ask Hillary." "Who are these women anyway? Do you think I'd ever be interested in the likes of her?"

It is certainly a talent to bounce back quickly, but perhaps we should try harder to stay out of trouble in the first place! Perhaps we should cut down on our risk-taking adventurous spirit and become more responsible for our actions. Growing up is so hard to do, and the Popular personality doesn't really want to try.

But if we could come in from our extremes, look before we leap, count the cost, and resist attractive temptation, perhaps we wouldn't need to bounce so often or so high, and we could save our energy for good, clean fun. Realize that to become a leader others will follow you need more than charm, for charm without conscience and responsibility will not last. Be grateful for your ability to attract a supportive team, but discipline yourself to be reliable so others can count on you for the long haul and not just for an inspired moment here and there.

You have presidential potential!

22

TWO
FOR THE PRICE OF ONE

HILLARY RODHAM CLINTON

First Lady: 1993–?
Personality: Powerful-Perfect
Principle to Learn: Listen to other people.

After eight years of Popular Reagan telling stories while Perfect Nancy stared at the stars and four years of Peaceful Bush being kind and gentle while Powerful Barb reigned as the all-American grandmother, we now have a new personality combo in the White House. Both Bill and Hillary Clinton have a similar core of the Powerful personality, which means they both want to be in charge.

Clinton campaigned by offering two for the price of one: "You get me; you also get Hillary." And we did.

When two Powerful personalities marry, the potential for chaos is quickly evident. In the Clintons' case, they have similarities in several ways—they both have exceptionally high intelligence quotients, they both have Yale law degrees, they have been independently successful, and they are accustomed to being in control of whatever they touch.

241

They are also opposite in that Bill's other half is the Popular personality and Hillary's is Perfect. That means he wants to have fun while being in charge and she wants to be in charge and also have everything perfect. Can you see the potential for a double set of marriage problems in both their similarities and differences?

Anytime a couple overlaps personalities in the Powerful area one of four things happens:

1. They buck for control and fight constantly.
2. One or both play Peaceful and refuse to make decisions.
3. They find their positive traits and march toward the same goal.
4. They divide responsibilities according to their personality strengths and don't tread on each other's territory.

Although we've heard rumors of wild arguments in their private quarters, we see no evidence of that in public, where they appear to be impressed with each other's brilliance and supportive of each other's goals. We can assume they are probably functioning in number four.

My husband, Fred, and I are the same set of personality combinations except I am Bill and Fred is Hillary. We tried possibility number one and bucked each other for control. This pushed us apart and made us each angry—anger being one of the major weaknesses of the Powerful personality. Next we shifted into possibility number two: Both of us pulled back and insisted the other make the choices. This attempt of suppressing our true feelings made us angrier still. When we learned about the personalities, we were set free to be real, and we began looking for common goals. Ultimately, as we began to travel together night and day speaking, writing, and counseling, we sat down and made a list of the duties that needed to be covered and divided the responsibilities. Now I'm in charge of everything that is fun (the platform, the subject matter, the creativity, the social times), and Fred is in charge of everything that has to be perfect (schedules, contracts, airlines, and budgets). We have mutually agreed on our roles, and we don't cross over that line in the sand.

The Clintons seem to have a similar acceptance of each other but in reverse—(along with a large dose of forgiveness on Hillary's part). He's in charge of socializing, talking, and loving the people, and she's in charge of research, details, and logical conclusions. He is quick to talk about himself and personalize the issues with humorous stories. She gives organized speeches on deep subjects without notes, dispensing information without mentioning herself. He makes decisions emotionally, based on whether people will like him. She analyzes the facts and decides after calculating the probable consequences, not caring whether people like her.

The president's sentimental selections and his obsessive need to be popular are often seen as waffling, zigzag alternations, and muddling around when he is actually acutely aware of the right decision but is weighing the probable reactions and trying to please the largest amount of people at the least cost of votes. While Bill shmoozes, Hillary analyzes. She does quick studies of all she surveys, and she doesn't need to be liked as long as she's right. In this type of double-Powerful marriage, success depends on not crossing the line of responsibility and staying out of each other's way.

Hillary Handles Healthcare

When Bill took over the presidency he might have said to himself, *What can I assign Hillary to do that no one has ever been able to handle that will keep her busy and out of my way for four years?* The obvious answer was healthcare. No one had ever been able to control this burdensome issue. He knew Hillary's Perfect personality would make an exhaustive search for possible solutions that to him were like seeking needles in haystacks. Sure enough, Hillary's Powerful personality took control. She called in the top minds in the country, didn't tell anyone who they were, locked them in a room, and wouldn't let them out until they produced a plan. She motivated them to action, probably so they could go home to eat—and in nine months she produced what would have taken Congress four years to put together. Even though the final plan was too cumbersome and costly, she did the impossible in record-breaking time.

A Courageous Leader

An Arkansas friend of Hillary's told me it is not Hillary's nature to talk when there's work to be done. She can quietly produce without looking for credit. When I asked this friend what one word she would use to describe Hillary, she quickly chose *courageous*. "She has more courage than anyone I've ever met and she's willing to take a stand even if it is unpopular."

244

She went on to tell me how Hillary had tackled the education issue in Arkansas. The state was sitting at the bottom of the country's educational ratings and couldn't attract industry and investments. Executives who had the power to locate businesses and factories didn't want their children in "dummy schools." Because Bill as governor was trying to improve Arkansas's reputation and finances, she decided to lift up the standards of education. Hillary's friend said, "The schools all turned against her. The teachers didn't want competency testing, and the school boards didn't want any changes. When she entered a classroom the children would boo her. Only Hillary would have hung in there and had the courage to fix the problem, no matter what."

Ultimately, when her goals were achieved, the schools became proud of themselves, Hillary became a hero, and educators pretended they'd been with her right from the beginning. She didn't have the same results with healthcare, and critics have said it was her arrogance and refusal to look at compromise that brought failure to her months of planning and her presentation of 1,342 pages of overwhelming material.

Hillary has given of herself tirelessly to noble causes she didn't need to touch. She founded the Arkansas Advocates for Children to provide legal support for children in needy or abusive situations, and she gave six years to the Children's Defense Fund, which was run by her friend Marian Wright Edelman. People who know her say she thinks like a man; she sees the problem and heads for the solution.

Even when Hillary was a senior in college she was in charge. She was chosen by her peers as the first student to speak at the Wellesley College commencement. She challenged the other speaker, Senator Edward Brooke, and made international headlines because she seemed to make more sense than he did.

Despite Hillary's life of good works, her presence in Washington strikes fear in the hearts of many. Opponents of women's lib see her as an arch-feminist who admittedly won't stay home and bake cookies, a contrast to Barbara Bush, who always looked as if she'd just come from the kitchen. When criticized for doing too much too quickly Hillary snapped, "I'm not one of those Energizer bunnies." Yet many feel she is.

Typical of her Powerful personality, Hillary can appear dogmatic, self-righteous, intolerant, and controlling. She doesn't come across as the sweet submissive wife of the past, and her Perfect nature seems too deep and intellectual for some and too moody and sensitive for others.

After the defeat of healthcare, Hillary appeared to be, as *Newsweek* stated, "troubled, bitter, angry, chastened, and shellshocked." She has pulled back from her decisive "de facto chief of staff" role. She can hardly believe "how easily the historic moment of opportunity disintegrated. . . . She was once certain about her ability to judge people, confidants say, but the experience of the last year has shaken her faith in her own political skills."[1] As Hillary pulls back to re-create herself as the first lady, we might wonder what we want her to be.

Would we, the American public, be satisfied if we had the Virgin Mary as the president's wife? Mamie and Betty drank too much, and Rosalynn didn't drink at all. Jackie and Nancy had expensive taste in clothes while Eleanor and Bess were too plain. Will there ever be a balance? Will we ever have the perfect president's wife, a first lady with all strengths and no weaknesses?

Hillary Rodham Clinton
Powerful-Perfect Personality

The following lists of strengths and weaknesses include words and phrases used in newspaper articles, magazines, books, television, and radio to describe first lady Hillary Clinton's personality, a combination of Powerful and Perfect traits. Check the characteristics that also apply to you.

Powerful Personality

Strengths
- ____ Immerses herself in her work
- ____ High-profile policymaker
- ____ Strong, outspoken feminist
- ____ Can do it all
- ____ Up front and undaunted
- ____ Preoccupied with success
- ____ Single-minded and self-confident
- ____ Assertive
- ____ Vibrant
- ____ Spunk and fire

Weaknesses
- ____ Formidable
- ____ Intolerant
- ____ No small talk
- ____ Quick, sharp tongue
- ____ Hyper law-student mode
- ____ Overly ambitious
- ____ Radical
- ____ Blunt authenticity
- ____ Demanding
- ____ Goes ballistic
- ____ Insists on the last word
- ____ No apologies here

___ Ready to change the world
___ Focused
___ Unflappable
___ Stoic
___ Makes no mistakes
___ Pragmatic
___ Feminist pioneer
___ Thrives under pressure
___ Unprecedented power
___ Hard-line ideologue
___ Task-oriented
___ Crisply decisive
___ **TOTAL**

___ Picks fights with bullies
___ Hardboiled with answers
___ Too powerful a presence
___ Too assertive
___ Arrogant
___ Angry and fuming

___ **TOTAL**

Perfect Personality

Strengths

___ Perfectly punctuates
    paragraphs
___ Most organized
___ Logical and focused
___ Shrewd tactician
___ Always thinking
___ True to her deep faith
___ Pathbreaking theorist
___ Legal genius
___ Weighs in on even minor
    details
___ Sensitive to trends
___ Wins points for preparation
___ No fact she hasn't
    memorized
___ Nothing gets by her
___ Sensitive mother
___ **TOTAL**

Weaknesses

___ Moody and touchy
___ Too serious
___ Easily hurt
___ Withdraws from public
___ Stonewalls her feelings
___ Seldom smiles
___ Critical and judgmental
___ Freezes out enemies
___ Obsessed with secrecy
___ Bitter and holding grudges

___ **TOTAL**

Total of your leadership profile of Powerful-Perfect strengths and weaknesses: _____

Are You a Leader Like Hillary Clinton?

If you have a leadership personality similar to Hillary Clinton's, your biggest problem is dealing with people who just don't get it—people who don't see that what you've concluded is the only way. You have grown up with the ability to do everything faster and better than your peers and have risen to leadership positions because you were the obvious one to be in charge. You have not depended on charm as the Popular personality does but on your command of each situation.

Because of your impressive track record, you have been considered a sure winner, and people have always looked up to you. When something of major responsibility comes along, your friends immediately think of you. You never won the Miss Congeniality award, but you don't care as long as you know you are right.

Some of you go through life without ever experiencing defeat, but if it comes you are the most shocked of all, wondering, *What went wrong? Don't they understand?*

These persons can go from confidence to desperation in a short time if they find their plan has been defeated. This is what happened to Hillary. She had always been a winner, and she tackled healthcare with the confidence that she could produce what had never been done correctly before. She didn't look for other opinions or alternative methods. She wanted it her way and perfect.

If you are always right, realize that this attitude is often unpopular and may cause you grief in personal relationships. You can be right and say it wrong. Learn to moderate your statements, ask opinions, and listen, and don't make others feel stupid. If you wish to be a leader people will follow, you must lift others up and not push them down.

23

PLAY SECOND FIDDLE SOFTLY

ALBERT GORE

Vice President: 1993–?
Personality: Perfect-Powerful
Principle to Learn: Lighten up!

Vice president Albert Gore is opposite from Clinton in that he wants things done properly and perfectly and he has little interest in party time. As Clinton loves to mingle with the people and work the crowd, his vice president differs from him in every way but age and church membership.

In background, Clinton was tossed around from a widowed mother to the grandparents, then back to his mother and her new husband, who abused them all. In contrast, Albert Gore Jr. was raised in a similar manner to George Bush. His father was a U.S. senator, and Gore grew up in the Fairfax Hotel in Washington surrounded by government officials conversing on Senate bills and protocol. While other children sat in the playground sandboxes, Gore roamed the corridors of Congress. As one senator said, "He's been for quite a while a young man in an old man's game."[1]

Life has never been much fun for Albert. His father groomed him for government service much as Joe Kennedy poured himself into young Joe and then, after Joe's death, into Jack. When questioned about his son

249

being nominated for vice president, Gore Sr. replied with pride, "We raised him for it." According to *USA Today* "Gore seems half suburban high school principal and half preacher man; he'll be good on the stump and tough in debate."[2]

Gore understands Washington and knows how to deal with Congress. Clinton came in as an outsider and has been baffled by congressional complexities ever since. He thinks they should do what he says because he's president, but they all have minds of their own and a home base to satisfy. As Clinton has floundered and Gore has seemed more prepared and presidential, Gore's face has all but disappeared from view. The sweet, photogenic family that rode buses with the Clintons during the campaign seems to have been sent off to summer camp. Could this be because they looked too good and Gore seemed to know too much?

Clinton's Popular personality demands center stage; he has even pushed Hillary into the wings. Gore's advisers wondered if he could play second fiddle because he likes to be the smartest man in the room. He does his homework, knows both sides of every issue, is relentlessly disciplined, and faithfully follows his schedule, methodically ticking off each item on the list. He dresses perfectly in conservative Brooks Brothers suits and never seems to wrinkle.

In contrast, Clinton has a casual look and was pictured in *Fortune* magazine leaning back in a lounge chair wearing a bright tie embellished with big yellow "happy faces," smiling at the reporter.[3]

Gore has been scrupulously straight and moral, and his wife Tipper received national attention for trying to clean up the foul language in the lyrics of popular music for teens. Gore has occasionally dared to correct the president and has told him he's too defensive. In return Clinton does hilarious imitations of Gore, straight-faced, intense, nodding, with wooden gestures and a stiff walk.

Gore measures his words; Clinton lets it all hang out and has yet to learn *not* to mention what he did on the Astroturf in the back of a pickup truck as a teenager.

"The president's style is much more laid back," wrote Eleanor Clift in *Newsweek*. "Clinton runs a meeting like a grad-school seminar, throwing out ideas and endlessly circling the subject. Gore is linear. He has a fondness for tabbed binders and detailed talking points. Gore and Clinton have lunch together every Thursday. It is one of the few sure things on the president's calendar, because aides have learned that changing it offends Gore's sense of order."[4]

As we look at the personalities of this pair of presidential players we can first see the differences: Clinton with the Popular personality, fun-loving, loose and undisciplined; Perfect Al Gore with his starchy exterior and his desire for order and accuracy. They should be a complementary pair if they focus on each other's strengths, but the problem comes when they disagree and each one thinks he's right. Because they each have a secondary Powerful personality that says "I'm right and you're wrong," they can be in for a contentious relationship.

Clinton's obsessive need for power and control and Gore's lifelong climb to the top may prevent the possible unity that seemed so hopeful during the campaign. If Gore preaches one sermon too many, he may stay in summer camp for the rest of his term.

Al Gore
Perfect-Powerful Personality

The following lists of strengths and weaknesses include words and phrases used in newspaper articles, magazines, books, television, and radio to describe Vice President Albert Gore's personality, a combination of Powerful and Perfect traits. Check the characteristics that also apply to you.

Perfect Personality

Strengths	Weaknesses
___ Potent intellectual	___ Not backslapping
___ Cautious	___ Aloof
___ Mr. Straight	___ Fun-averse prig
___ Blue-suit sincere	___ Starchy exterior
___ Deep and thoughtful	___ Wooden, smug
___ Mastery of issues	___ Unctuous
___ Relentlessly disciplined	___ Boring and dull
___ Highly organized	___ Obsequious
___ Immersed in details	___ Sanctimonious
___ High integrity level	___ Ponderous
___ Blandly debonair	___ A grind
___ Fondness for filing	___ Icy demeanor
___ **TOTAL**	___ **TOTAL**

Powerful Personality

Strengths

___ Formidable attack dog
___ Good on the offensive
___ Slashing debater
___ Born leader
___ Fired with ambition
___ Driven
___ Workhorse
___ Implacable career focus
___ **TOTAL**

Weaknesses

___ Headline hog
___ Too ambitious
___ Aura of callowness
___ Two-faced
___ Needs to be in control

___ **TOTAL**

Total of your presidential profile of Perfect-Powerful strengths and weaknesses: _____

Are You a Leader Like Gore?

Sometimes a person who has the nature of a perfectionist with the drive and ambition of the Powerful personality can become so serious about life and so determined to win that he or she causes other people to back away. Although those with Perfect personalities can become great leaders, even statesmen, many don't reach their obvious potential because of their lack of people skills. They are much more interested in getting the job done perfectly than in humoring people along the way.

As we have learned, you can't be a leader if no one is inspired enough to follow you. You can have the right answers and be smarter than all the rest, but if people don't like you, your talent alone won't cause them to fall in line.

Richard Nixon, Hillary Clinton, and Albert Gore all have this combination of personality traits. There is no light touch, no ready smile, or automatic pat on the back. If you are of similar nature, realize that you need to relax in your relationships. Life won't come to an end if you waste a few minutes here and there in idle chatter. People will be flattered if you ask for their opinion or check on their families.

One major weakness of Perfect-Powerful personalities is the intensity with which they approach life. That deep, serious look that penetrates into the hearts of others scares off the followers and puts fear in the place of admiration. Look in the mirror and stare intently. Now *smile!* Is there a difference? A smile costs nothing to produce, but for those with Perfect personalities it may take a few practice sessions to be able to turn it on quickly and sincerely.

Try to accept the people around you as fallible human beings who deserve to be treated with grace and compassion. Don't try to put people in alphabetized manila folders; they won't fit, and you'll hurt them when you try to shut the drawer.

Another lesson to be learned from the actions of Gore is never to correct your boss in front of other people. If there is an issue you feel strongly about that is in contrast to the stated opinion, make an appointment and discuss this privately. If the other person is a Powerful personality, preface your comments with affirmations such as, "I know you work harder than all of us and have excellent ideas so I hesitate to mention a new thought; however. . . ." Remember, people with this personality see things as black or white; there is no gray in the middle. Their desire for loyalty in the ranks causes them to see you as either with them or against them, and if they sense you are undermining their authority you too could be sent off to summer camp!

24

TAKE YOUR BEST SHOT AT THE BRASS RING

RUSH LIMBAUGH

Well-known broadcast personality: 19??–?
Personality: Powerful-Popular
Principle to Learn: Always aim to be number one.

In a book on presidential personalities, is there any reason to bring in an outsider who isn't even a politician? Can a conservative radio personality make enough noise and catch enough attention to become a threat to a liberal president? Can political satire from a brilliant, retentive mind coupled with a mouth that never stops scare the government to the point where it hunts for legal ways to turn him off?

In any other time the answer would be no, but with the rise of sunny, moonfaced Rush Limbaugh the challenge is a phenomenon of fear-filled reality. He has become the mouse that roared, a conservative voice that has captured the hearts and minds of enough people to give the Clinton camp some sleepless nights. While the religious right have been floundering around in search of a captivating message, Rush has captured their crowd and is busy being right without being religious. He's preaching their gospel with an E-mail altar call.

Reason and Humor

Why has a conservative commentator in a liberal media become so popular? In his own words, "Because I say what they are thinking. People respond to what I say because it is right; my wit and wisdom are like a lifeline of reason tossed to a culture nearly drowning in confusion and murkiness. No wonder more people are clinging to my hopeful and incisive words every day!"[1]

While his words may seem arrogant on paper, his delivery of them has enough humor to lessen the bite and make the whole dish tasty, especially to those seated on the right side of the table.

For years, Americans have defined rush hour as that time at the end of the working day when traffic is lined up bumper to bumper and when normally balanced people start to lose their cool. Today, however, "Rush hour" is when Rush Limbaugh comes on the radio with his sharp-edged political humor. Restaurants set aside Rush Rooms for diners who like to get a rush while eating a Reuben sandwich, and businesses have Rush breaks where employees can tune in for a quick fix of conservative values before going back to work.

Steven Roberts, a reporter for *U.S. News and World Report,* wrote, "Rush Limbaugh has evolved into a true American original, fusing the worlds of entertainment and information into a new form of communication: Part carnival, part classroom, part church service . . . even his critics conceded that he is funny."[2]

Where many radio personalities enjoy poking fun at politicians, few dare to take a stand so strong that they might alienate listeners and lose their audience. Part of the Rush success is that he lets everyone know right from the start that he doesn't care if you agree with him. His lay-it-on-the-line approach is refreshing, and one liberal activist was heard to say, "I have to fight the temptation to like his show."

Rush is obviously a born leader who relishes every ounce of control he is able to grasp. As a Powerful personality he finds it natural to be in charge of all his surveys. He doesn't have to mull it over or make a chart on it; he just opens his mouth and says it—in all due confidence that he is right! His success has been surprising to his critics, who predicted his demise when a Democrat moved into the White House. Instead of dying with the Democrats he has been in high gear ever since Clinton and his good ol' boys arrived from Arkansas and brought Hillary with them.

As Clinton has gone through his early mistakes, he has provided Rush with hilarious material comedians would die for. And Rush, who is also part Popular personality, needs fresh material every day to maintain a high level of humor and to inform his people on what is really going on in the world. No news is dull news when Rush is reporting it and filling fifteen fast-paced hours a week on radio plus two and a half hours on TV, often defeating competition like David Letterman and Jay Leno and roundly whipping Whoopi and Arsenio right off the air.

The Original American Epic

How does he do it? How has Rush moved from fifty-six stations to six hundred in less than five years? How has he produced a book that sat on the top of the *New York Times* best-seller list and sold two and a half million copies in less than a year? Is he an overnight success?

His own answer to these questions is the best. "My story is nothing more than an example of the Original American Ethic: hard work, overcoming obstacles, triumphing over enormous odds, the pioneer spirit. I've been fired six times. I've been broke twice. I've been hopelessly in debt. I've gone through periods in which I made very little money. I've also been near the top. I've seen life from all sides."

Rush didn't fall into success or wake up one morning rich and famous. He has spent years of preparation, filling the file drawers of his brilliant mind with endless material ready to be brought to his lips with no hesitation. Not only has Rush done his homework and filled his reservoir, but he has never let down his pursuit of excellence long enough to let sloppy thinking get in the door. He maintains an intellectual high that has not been equalled in talk radio in anyone's memory. Who else could talk steadily for three hours, with no music to give him a breather or no guests to play with? Who else could keep this pace up extemporaneously, live, with no cue cards or TelePrompTers? Only a person with a high IQ and a passionate desire to succeed would even attempt what appears to be so effortless. Only a Powerful personality would take the risks Rush has dared to attempt, bounce back so quickly from defeat, and thrive in the throes of criticism and attack. Only a Popular personality could be so consistently entertaining while basking in the spotlight of national attention.

Imagine how thrilled Rush must have been when he found he was the subject of a three-credit course at Bellevue College in Nebraska entitled "Is Rush Right?" The eight-week course aims to promote critical thinking and guide the students into making informed decisions about current issues.

Each day Rush has to prove himself all over again to his audience, showing them one more time that he is on top of the news. His faithfuls know that whatever cabinet members have been subpoenaed overnight will be given full and fun funerals at the first of his program. Listeners can count on Rush to keep them up to date on each moment's happenings and to make reports of the news into fascinating features.

On his television show, he mixes truth with creative conjecture by showing actual film clips of Clintonians that, taken out of context and laced with his commentary, become skits of comic proportions. One night he played a few lines from a presidential spokeswoman trying to cover up the Paula Jones accusations of sexual harassment by Clinton, making her pitiful prerecorded attempts hilarious once Rush introduced her as the chairman of "bimbo control" for the president.

The night after Hillary made her articulate explanation of why she had collected a huge profit from cattle futures, Rush played portions of the tape, pointing out humorous details most of us had missed on the first showing. I hadn't thought much about how her handlers had strategically placed her in front of a portrait of Abraham Lincoln, denoting honesty, or how her hot-pink jacket was selected to soften her cool, calculating image. Rush sees all there is to see—and then some!

This well of insight and information doesn't come without effort. He reads nine newspapers a day as well as countless magazines and books. He is alert to everything around him and around the world and can make fun out of the most trivial of events. Something that slipped by the average viewer of the nightly news can be retrieved by Rush and dressed up to fill three hours the next morning.

Throwing the Gauntlet

As Rush continues to ridicule the Clintons, the president gets more and more upset over the talk-show host and his political satire. In June 1994 Clinton's temper flared when he was doing an interview from Air Force

One with radio station KMOX in Saint Louis. He lashed out at the religious right and at talk-show hosts and the news media in general for "fueling cynicism and twisting the facts and making scurrilous and false charges."

"Remember," he stated loudly in a dubious reference to Scripture, "Jesus threw the moneychangers out of the temple. He didn't try to take over the job of the moneychangers."

He went on to criticize Jerry Falwell and people who "put on the mantle of religion and then use it to justify anything they say or do." Clinton saved his best indignant tone for Rush Limbaugh. "After I get off the radio today with you, Rush Limbaugh will have three hours to say whatever he wants. And I won't have any opportunity to respond. And there's no truth detector."

Always looking for a lead-in to his spontaneous satire, Rush was thrilled with the president's reference to him by name. Nothing feeds ratings like high-level controversy, and Rush could hardly wait. "The gauntlet has been thrown," he responded with a twinkle in his eye and a sardonic smile on his chubby face. As he played back the president's words he kept stopping the tape to laugh, ridicule, or just shrug in such an expressive way that his eyes said, *Can you believe that?*

In a combination reference to Clinton's indecision on what to do in foreign policy and the Limbaugh acceptance of the gauntlet throwing, cartoonist Mike Ramirez depicted soldiers in the war room facing tactical maps. The man at the switchboard says, "The president has had it. He's finally committing troops . . ." The soldier holding the pointer on the map asks, "Haiti? Bosnia? North Korea?" The third one answers, "No. The Rush Limbaugh Show."[3]

Can't you imagine how Rush chortled at seeing himself portrayed as a foe worthy of invasion?

When Clinton announced it was legal for him to accept donations to a defense fund for responding to the Whitewater accusations and for what Rush calls "bimbo control," Rush jumped in with a suggestion: If you're going to solicit money to defend the president, shouldn't you set up a separate fund for the other side? Isn't that only fair? An independent auditor could keep count and we could gauge the mood of the people by how much money came in.

Rush especially enjoyed Clinton's anger at the accusation that White House staff members had stolen towels during a visit to an aircraft carrier in Europe. Rush loves the Clintons because, as he says, "They never let me down. There's some new faux pas every day!"

Always a feast; never a famine for the Rush hour!

Time magazine said about Limbaugh, "He meets his own challenge—to inform and entertain—and those who don't get it are always free to tune out. But even some righteous liberals are closet Rushophiles, because the man is so good at what he does. And knows it. And tells you, in a voice whose every syllable bespeaks a 25-year apprenticeship in radio oratory, without fear of repetition or contradiction."[4]

Rush sums up his Powerful-Popular personality by saying, "I knew my career would be important and fun."

Rush walks in where angels fear to tread and makes the whole trip an adventure. It was his sense of humor while ripping apart serious subjects that first attracted Ed McLaughlin, a former president of the ABC Radio Network. "He had all the elements: innate intelligence, a high curiosity and the desire to be a star," McLaughlin said.[5] McLaughlin brought Rush to New York's ABC studios and created the so-called Excellence in Broadcasting Network—an impressive name for a company that does not, in fact, exist.

When people ask Rush, "Did you ever expect to rise to the top the way you have?" he answers, "Yes of course. I was striving for it. I didn't move to New York just to be in the top five. My eye was always on Number One. Ever since I was a little kid, I was never intimidated by the prospect of failure. I knew that if I missed the mark, I could live with myself. What I couldn't live with, however, was the prospect of not having taken my best shot at the brass ring."[6]

How many of us, wanting to be successful, are willing to do what it takes to grab for the brass ring? How many of us are disciplined enough to read voraciously, keep alert to every nuance in the world, and practice twenty-five years in order to become an overnight success?

During the 1994 campaign Rush ridiculed the Democrats and stirred the conservative voters to action. The fear Clinton had carried for two years came true as the Republicans took over the majority leadership in each house providing Rush with days of fresh "I told you so" material.

Time featured the familiar face on its January 23, 1995, cover and asked, "Is Rush Limbaugh Good for America?" They reported the surge of interest and influence in talk shows and credited the Rush Republicans with bringing in the votes.

Not only did *Time* give Rush credit but the incoming freshman Republicans orientation banquet became a love feast to Limbaugh where they made him an honorary member of the House of Republicans and named themselves the Limbaugh Congress saying he had given them "the courage to take back our country." Conservative Vin Weber extolled Rush and gave him credit for the victory: "Talk radio, with you in the lead, is what turned the tide." Yes, a conservative talk show host can make a major difference in an election—if he happens to be Rush Limbaugh.

Rush Limbaugh
Powerful-Popular Personality

The following lists of strengths and weaknesses include words and phrases used in newspaper articles, magazines, books, television, and radio to describe Rush Limbaugh's personality, a combination of Popular and Powerful traits. Check the characteristics that also apply to you.

Powerful Personality

Strengths
___ Incomparable level of
    performance
___ Goes all out—all of the time
___ Confident in his success
___ Wants to be the best
___ Competitive
___ Never intimidated
___ Pursues excellence
___ Intense concentration
___ Peak performer
___ Motivated
___ Passionate believer
___ Incomparable conqueror
___ Presents logical analysis
___ Challenging
___ Risk-taking
___ Enjoys debating
___ **TOTAL**

Weaknesses
___ Workaholic
___ Blowhard
___ Egotistical
___ Maniacal determination
___ Bombastic
___ One-sided
___ Totally self-centered

___ **TOTAL**

Popular Personality

Strengths

___ Full of good cheer
___ Wry wit
___ Offers hope
___ Very funny
___ Convulsively entertaining
___ Loud and colorful
___ Multimedia motor mouth
___ Impish and rowdy
___ Class clown
___ Friendly full-moon face
___ Twinkling eyes
___ Mischievous look
___ **TOTAL**

Weaknesses

___ Too sarcastic
___ No sensitivity
___ Needs the spotlight
___ Too loose with the truth

___ **TOTAL**

Total of your leadership profile of Powerful-Popular strengths and weaknesses: _____

Are You a Leader Like Limbaugh?

Even though Rush Limbaugh has not become the president of the United States, he does have unique leadership qualities we can compare to ourselves. He shows us that you can get away with strong and vocal opinions if you can add enough humor. A spoonful of sugar *does* make the medicine go down! What would be offensive if it were presented as straight arrogance can become entertaining when delivered with an impish look and twinkling eyes.

If you checked off many of the Limbaugh traits, you are Powerful with an engaging touch of the Popular; you could be an even more successful leader than you are now. You were born with the ideal personality for political and performance-related achievement. For this you need the willingness to spend dedicated years in preparation for each step up the ladder of progress.

You need to seek truth and not settle for shallow substitutes. You need to study, stay tuned to each nuance in your area, and keep up with world and local events and opinions. You must have a high level of physical stamina in order to keep going and a passionate desire to make it to the top. You need to cultivate your sense of humor and never appear to be so impressed with yourself that you turn people off.

The weakness in this strong personality is the tendency to carry your strengths to such an extreme that they become offensive. Your ability to do everything faster and better than everyone else is apt to intimidate others. When they are afraid of you they won't look to you for leadership.

You need to ask yourself whether you handle conflict thrust upon you or whether you cause some of it yourself. Limbaugh creates controversy to maintain his ratings, but in the real world a leader who is constantly embroiled in problems loses his or her appeal. Can't we have a week without crisis?

One of Clinton's weaknesses is his apparent attraction for potentially disastrous situations. Don't keep your followers hanging over a cliff, afraid to take a deep breath. You can be the dynamic leader you desire to be as long as you don't become so bossy or arrogant that people leave your fold or business, as long as you don't try to impress others with your brilliance or intimidate others with your power, and as long as you don't continue to light little fires so you can get credit for putting them out.

Take your best shot at the brass ring, but don't hurt others while you're reaching.

25

THE POLITICAL UPSET
OF 1994

Principle to Learn: When voters are angry, a pretty face is not
enough.

The euphoria the Democrats felt in the 1992 victory and the installation
of a new, young, exciting president had dissipated decidedly by the
midterm election of 1994. The "President of Charm" had lost some of his
Kennedyesque glamour.

Gore Vidal had extolled Clinton because he was a man without values and would therefore not try to push preconceived notions. He would
be more open-minded than a rigid moralist would be, Vidal said.

This blank-page presumption of free thinking was to match the liberal
morals of the electorate, but in two years of increased crime and general
fear for survival, Clinton learned that charm without conscience can't last.
As Democratic incumbents faced possible defeat and even Ted Kennedy
had to mortgage his estate to finance his campaign, Clinton geared himself up to head for the hustings and magnetize the electorate with his winning personality.

It didn't work!

As Bill Kristol, former Quayle chief of staff, wrote following the Republican landslide, "The nation just cast a massive vote against anything that even looks like the Clinton agenda."[1]

The Bounce-Back Kid

Clinton, the first Democratic president since Harry Truman to face a solidly Republican Congress, was optimistic right up until the end, believing he could charm the public into voting his way. He may have gotten some levers pulled for Ted Kennedy, but he couldn't save House Speaker Thomas Foley (D-Washington), the first sitting Speaker to be ousted since 1860.

Ever the Bounce-back Kid, Clinton tried to smile and be Sanguine about the future of his political career. "We can work together," he declared at the postelection press conference, but those who knew the confusion and chaos of his own White House staff and his dealings with a friendly Congress wondered how he could begin to work with a gleefully obstreperous opposition.

After the election of 1994 Clinton needed every ounce of his bounce-back bravado. As White House aides scurried to reinvent the president, one suggested he become national Comforter-in-Chief as Roosevelt had done so effectively and let us know that we've overplayed our hand. All we have to fear is fear itself. Then again he could let us know how angry he is with us, have a national temper-tantrum, and "give us hell" like Harry. Or better yet, as some defeated congressmen brought forth, the president could create some original ideas or programs that would excite the public as did Lyndon Johnson's Great Society. Political advisor Paul Begala began research on old nemesis Ronald Reagan to find out what the "irrelevant Neanderthal" did right that kept him so popular. Begrudgingly he admitted that "The American people knew what Reagan stood for."

David Gergen added that after the squandering of two good years "the public still isn't sure where Clinton stands."

Clinton took the blame for defeat in part but suggested the people weren't aware of how much he had accomplished in his two years. The problem was in faulty communication, he felt, more than in rejection of his programs.

The Popular personality is one master excuse-maker, and Clinton is convincing when he puts on his hurt-little-boy look and begs us to love him.

The Odd Troika

The new Republican Congress may not love him though. Euphoric in victory, its Republican members can hardly wait to take control. Bob Dole, now Senate majority leader, and Newt Gingrich, now the Speaker of the House, are both Powerful personalities, and they will have little time or desire to spread love around the White House.

USA Today reporter Richard Wolf wrote, "It won't always be amiable. How these three very different men mesh in the months to come will tell a lot about whether voters see cooperation or confrontation from the nation's capital in 1995–96."[2]

"This is not the odd couple. It's the odd troika," wrote Norman Ornstein of the American Enterprise Institute. "It would be hard to find, in many ways, three more different personalities."[3] Popular Clinton, forty-eight, is the "populist from Arkansas"; Powerful Dole, seventy-one, is the "pragmatist from Kansas"; and Powerful Gingrich, fifty-one, is the "pugilist from Georgia." They may be different in some ways but they all have Power personalities that are bound to clash in the years ahead.

Gingrich, nicknamed Godzilla, loves a good fight, and Dole is noted for his confrontational behavior. Before the '94 election, Gingrich called Clinton "the most destructive president in modern times" who "shrinks beneath the aura" of his office. Does this sound like a verse from a valentine?

The *New York Times* headlined, "One hand tied, Clinton offers the other." Beneath the headline the morning-after summary stated, "The White House was grim today as Mr. Clinton's advisers tried to grapple with the magnitude of the defeat."[4]

In an editorial column, the *Times* said that one-third of the voters personally disapproved of the president. "The polls were not specific," the editorial noted, "but something about Mr. Clinton—Whitewater, the early foul-ups over important appointments, a White House staff that uniquely combined hubris and incompetence, perhaps even his wife—has clearly nettled many voters to the point of distraction."

Clinton has learned that charm without conscience won't last. As Lucy says in a *Peanuts* cartoon, "A pretty face is not enough." At least not in 1995!

Part IV

APPLYING WHAT WE'VE LEARNED

26

WHAT MAKES
A GREAT LEADER?

As we have reviewed the personalities of American leaders from 1933 to the present, we have seen that each person is born with a basic personality pattern. In this book I've tried to break those personalities down into four major categories. Then I've sorted those four primary personalities into bite-size pieces—strengths and weaknesses—so you have a concise version of the personality-analyzing device Fred and I have taught for more than twenty-five years. This explanation of how each of us differs changed our marriage, helped us raise our children as individuals, gave us insight into the behavior of coworkers, and provided us with a basic understanding of each person's leadership potential. I hope this knowledge can have an equally positive impact on your life as it has on ours.

Once we comprehend the personality pattern that predetermines a person's reactions, we are able to add on his or her childhood experiences, which have either increased the strengths by parental affirmation or have decreased his or her feeling of worth by repeated putdowns and rejections.

As we have looked at the personalities of our leaders and seen their strengths and weaknesses, I hope this information has added a new dimension to your own sense of worth and challenged you to become a leader. No matter what your personality pattern is, when you understand it, you can develop your abilities, talents, and gifts to achieve your leadership potential.

If you are a Popular personality like Ronald Reagan, rejoice in your communication skills; use your sense of humor to lighten serious situations and warm up the crowds with your engaging smile and infectious laugh. But be sure to do your homework! Base your grand statements on fact, and don't be caught using creative statistics.

If you are a Popular-Powerful combination, you are like so many successful leaders. You have the power to influence other people and the charm to make them want to do it. Roosevelt, Kennedy, Johnson, Clinton, and Limbaugh, although different in looks, background, and moral values, all had the charisma and drive to mount a campaign, inspire people to work for them, keep smiling in adverse circumstances, and create lasting leadership legends. If you have a similar personality pattern, be grateful for your inborn motivational skills, but be careful to temper your eagerness with a loving concern for those around you. Put the interests of the group over your own personal pleasure, and appreciate and compliment the devoted workers who helped you reach the top because you may meet them face to face on the way back down!

If you are the Powerful personality like Truman, Dole, and Perot, you have a single-minded purpose to succeed and you don't care what anyone thinks about it. Control, direction, and correction come as naturally to you as breathing. You don't stand at the door of opportunity and wonder if you should turn the knob. You push the door open wide and stride into the control position. With you, the impossible just takes a little longer and tragedies cause you to say, "I'll show them."

All of these leadership skills will move you up the ladder quickly, but remember that no one likes a person perceived as bossy, manipulative, angry, and impatient. Remember those pawns on your chessboard of life are real people with real feelings, and they really count. Don't let your direction and correction lead them to insurrection!

If you are a combination Powerful-Perfect like Nixon, Gore, and Hillary Clinton, you have the best attributes for leadership because you easily take control of each situation and you want to do everything correctly. You can make quick decisions without being impulsive, lead strongly without being insensitive to the needs of the people, have a quick grasp of the facts without getting bogged down in details. The caution is to guard against letting the end justify the means and compromising your standards in order to win the game.

If you are a Perfect person—deep, thoughtful, analytical, remote, and mystical like Jimmy Carter and Gary Hart—you can be an inspirational leader. You can make the ordinary things of life seem beautiful, poetic, and majestic. You can raise people's expectations of themselves to new heights and articulate people's inner needs in spiritual terms, but you must not set the standards for yourself and others so high that you can't hope to meet them or rise to such an intellectual level that your feet don't reach the ground, you're out of touch with reality, and you reside in the remote reaches of your ivory tower. Dare to dream, but don't get depressed when your hopes get dashed against the big rock of reality.

If you are a combination Perfect-Peaceful like presidential candidate Michael Dukakis, you are a cool and detached leader whose skills are in management rather than inspiration. Your Perfect side gives you the ability to plan, chart, and add up columns but allows you to become discouraged and disheartened when life doesn't balance out perfectly. Your Peaceful part provides impartial judgment and an ability to mediate in sticky situations but keeps you indecisive and unenthusiastic. As a leader you will be faithful and loyal to your troops and expect the same from them. You will keep your head while those all about you are losing theirs, but you may appear to be cold and unemotional.

If you are a Peaceful personality—inoffensive and noncontroversial like Eisenhower, Ford, and Bush—your greatest leadership skills will be keeping people happy and producing few enemies. You can bring the Popular people into serious thinking, the Powerfuls into a sense of humility, and the Perfects into an attitude of joy. You are the great balancer of life, the one person we can count on to keep us out of trouble. You may not come up with grand plans or innovative legislation, but you will hold true to your quiet beliefs, and no one will have a bad word to say about you. You won't jump into impulsive decisions but will weigh the possible consequences of each action before taking the first step. You may be considered bland or even boring, but we can count on you to keep the peace.

If you are a Peaceful-Popular, like former Vice President Dan Quayle, you have a cool allure and a low-key sense of humor that attracts people to your side. You don't turn others off with an intense drive for either achievement or perfection, you're content to be relaxed and happy and you take the easy road if at all possible. You're not as loud or desperate for attention as the Popular, but you have their wit and charm blended with the Peaceful, easygoing nature. As a leader you will draw people's support and admiration for your pleasing personality, but you will need to discipline yourself to do the dull work and to keep going until the goal has been reached.

As you have analyzed your own abilities and learned to keep yourself and others functioning in their strengths instead of plodding through their weaknesses, you have come to see your potentials as a leader and have found new ways to get along with others. You don't need to hurry to catch up with the rest; you are already out in front.

The following chart summarizes the personalities of the leaders we have studied in this book. Where would *your* name appear on this personality profile chart?

Personality Profile Overview

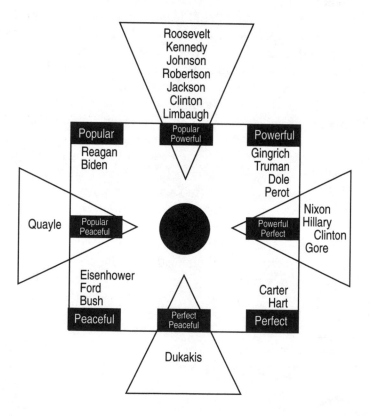

27

HOW TO
CHOOSE LEADERS

Personality Principle: With every set of strengths comes a corresponding set of weaknesses.

In the beginning of this book, we looked at the four personality types and used them to analyze our own basic strengths and weaknesses. Next we read about the presidents and others who thrive in the public eye. We saw that what the public wants is an impossible dream—the strengths of all and the weaknesses of none—but we must remember that with each set of strengths come corresponding weaknesses.

To apply what we've learned in analyzing any kind of leader, let's look at some simple steps.

1. Realize that politics is a game of personalities. As soon as we can establish the strengths of a candidate for office or employment, we can project his or her probable weaknesses. To get acquainted with the person in question, read as many articles, books, resumes, or references on the person as possible and look for descriptive words that give you some insight into his or her emotions and gut-level reactions. But remember, after determining a candidate's personality, you must look at his or her voting record. Where does the person stand on the issues that are impor-

tant to you? The candidate's past record is a clear indication of what he or she will do in the future. Don't read too much into speeches as these are prepared to suit the needs of the people, and since they frequently are written by somebody else, these messages may give no clue as to the person's real feelings.

2. Watch the candidates on television to assess their reactions to circumstances. Observe their glances, movements, and responses when they aren't "up front." When they're being interviewed, watch their body language for clues to their personality types.

3. Check off their strengths on the Candidate Chart on pages 278–80. Remember that each set of strengths is quietly accompanied by weaknesses that will emerge later. Check off any weaknesses that are apparent.

By following these steps you can predict where political candidates will shine and what problems may arise with them in the future so that you will not be caught unaware. (To learn how to use the personality types to analyze prospective employees in business situations, see *Personality Puzzle* by Florence Littauer and Marita Littauer. To analyze the personalities of your family members, see *Personality Tree* by Florence Littauer.)

We all love to be amateur psychologists and analyze other people. Once we understand the personalities we can easily see how Mrs. Popular would be more so if she just knew when to stop talking. Mr. Powerful could be more effective if he weren't obsessed with controlling every person he met. Mr. Perfect would be easier to get along with if he'd just realize that nobody's perfect. Ms. Peaceful is so pleasant and inoffensive, but if she could only make up her mind once in a while and act as if she cared she would be a much stronger leader.

How easy it is for you and me to see the faults in others and know how they could improve. When properly channeled, this talent for objective analysis is a strength in our human makeup. This instinct for quick evaluation and intuition about the nature of others can be put to powerful use in our human relationships if we first recognize we have this ability, and second, know how to harness it to lead our analysis in the right direction.

We are not to become junior psychiatrists or set out to be spies and sleuths but to use our new understanding to give us a productive edge over those people who blunder through life wondering why the Populars are always turned on and excited, why the Powerfuls grab control even of the seating arrangements at someone else's dinner party, why the

Perfects can never give a compliment without tagging on, ". . . but the next time you do this . . . ," and why the Peacefuls always manage to escape the blame and come out clean.

Now that we understand the basic differences in human nature and realize that just because someone is different doesn't make him or her wrong, we can quietly practice our skills and become the kind of person who seems to get along with everyone. By using political personalities for our examples, we are not taking sides but are practicing analytical skills on public people who will never know or care. By watching people we can view frequently on television and read about in the newspapers, we can find new enjoyment in observing public personalities with whom we might have nothing in common. This parade of political people across our television screens takes on new meaning when we look at it as a practice time in developing our relationship skills.

Dr. Eli S. Chesen, in his book *President Nixon's Psychiatric Profile,* bases his analysis on the public view of Nixon. "The profiles in this book are not secret, and for the most part were compiled in my own living room as I watched my own television set, using methods that are completely open to question and scrutiny. . . . My television set served me well as a surrogate for opportunities not otherwise available to me or anyone else. . . . I have taken great pains to listen carefully to the words of all these men, to watch for displays of emotion—or lack of emotion. Patterns of dress, use of humor, candor and general attitude were scrutinized most carefully."

Although Dr. Chesen based his analysis on the performance of participants in the Watergate scandal as they passed across the screen, we can do the same with each season's parade of public personalities whether it be the local mayor, the potential president, or the characters in situation comedies.

How quickly we all did amateur analyses of Oliver North based on nothing but his televised performance in congressional hearings! At the beginning of the "Ollie Show," few of us knew anything about him and expected to see some schizophrenic spy who would wilt under the scrutiny of the sophisticated senators. Surely, his advance press was far from positive, yet when he looked straight into the camera and began to speak, friends and foes were fascinated with what he had to say and how he said it. He combined the Powerful military presence with the innocent humor and quavering voice of a beguiling little Popular boy. Sud-

Applying What We've Learned

denly, senators seemed insensitive, and the hard-nosed lawyers were picking on Tom Sawyer. The press did an about-face and began to march to the tune of a new drummer: "Ollie Captures the Hill," they headlined. But when he ran for the U.S. Senate from Virginia in the 1994 election he lost to Lyndon Johnson's son-in-law, Charles Robb.

As Dr. Chesen said in his book, we "can make valid judgments by analyzing the facial expressions and words of a man being televised. In other words, not only can a psychiatrist glean insights by observing someone on television, but so can the layman."

We can use TV, newspapers, and magazines to train ourselves in analyzing others, not to be their critics, but to benefit our relationship skills with our mates, our children, our friends, and our coworkers. We can use the simple principles described in this book to help us practice on the public figures ever before us, remembering that with every set of strengths there will be corresponding weaknesses. We can analyze our own leadership skills while watching others rise and fall, and we can do as that old popular song suggested, "Accentuate your positives, eliminate your negatives."

Candidate Chart

To use this chart, be aware of descriptive phrases and accounts in news reports about the candidates, then check the items in the following lists of personality traits that seem to apply to the specific candidate you're analyzing. By noting which chart has the most checks, you should be able to determine the candidate's personality type.

Strengths

Popular
Talker
____ Magnetic personality
____ Storyteller
____ Sense of humor
____ Entertaining
____ Charming
____ Inspiring
____ Talkative
____ Friendly

Powerful
Worker
____ Commanding personality
____ Controlling leader
____ Straight talker
____ Goal-oriented
____ Business minded
____ Motivational
____ Logical
____ Persistent

___ Creative and colorful   ___ Risk-taker
___ Dramatic   ___ Practical
___ Optimistic   ___ Quick organizer
___ Enthusiastic   ___ Authoritarian and efficient

Perfect
Thinker
___ Analytical personality
___ Detail-conscious
___ Serious and thoughtful
___ Deep and intellectual
___ Likes charts and graphs
___ Sees problems
___ Schedule-oriented
___ Holds high standards
___ Organized on paper
___ Artistic, musical
___ Philosophical and mystical
___ Sensitive to others
___ Long-range goals

Peaceful
Mediator (with listening skills)
___ Low-key personality
___ Well-behaved
___ Patient
___ Conservative
___ Agreeable and adaptable
___ Competent and steady
___ Team-oriented
___ Administrating
___ Moderate
___ Maintaining status quo
___ Cooperative
___ Diplomatic
___ Easygoing

Totals of Strengths

Popular	Powerful	Perfect	Peaceful
_____	_____	_____	_____

Weaknesses

Popular
Controls by charm
___ Compulsive talker
___ Exaggerates
___ Rather talk than work
___ Can't remember details
___ Surface and no depth
___ Poor follow-through
___ Undisciplined
___ Loses things

Powerful
Controls by anger
___ Angers easily
___ Impatient
___ Bossy and pushy
___ Intolerant
___ Workaholic
___ Rude and tactless
___ Manipulating
___ Demanding

280

___ Needs rewards
___ Messy surroundings
___ Distracting
___ Interrupts
___ Irresponsible

___ Makes rash decisions
___ No time for research
___ Not a team player
___ End justifies the means
___ Blames others

Perfect
Controls by moods
___ Easily depressed
___ Bogged down in details
___ Too much preparation
___ Too slow to action
___ Too perfectionistic
___ Emphasis on negatives
___ Inflexible
___ Pessimistic
___ Suspicious
___ Moody
___ Standards too high
___ Critical
___ Too mysterious

Peaceful
Controls by procrastination
___ Indecisive
___ Not self-motivating
___ Procrastinates
___ Compromises standards
___ Underlying will of iron
___ Stubborn
___ Lazy and laid back
___ Dull and bland
___ Resists change
___ Passive
___ Low self-worth
___ Shy
___ Unenthusiastic

Totals of Weaknesses

Popular   **Powerful**   **Perfect**   **Peaceful**
_____   _____   _____   _____

Combined Totals of Strengths and Weaknesses

Popular   **Powerful**   **Perfect**   **Peaceful**
_____   _____   _____   _____

NOTES

Chapter 1: The Presidential Handshake: A Full-Body Experience

1. Bob Woodward, *The Agenda* (New York: Simon and Schuster, 1994), 324.

Chapter 8: The Fireside Chat—Franklin Delano Roosevelt

1. Franklin Roosevelt's September 23, 1944, speech during a Teamsters dinner, quoted in Grace Tully, *F.D.R. My Boss* (New York: Scribner, 1949).
2. Ibid.

Chapter 9: "Give 'em Hell!"—Harry S. Truman

1. Lyndon Johnson, quoted in Robert Donovan, *Tumultuous Years* (New York: Norton, 1982).
2. Benedict K. Zobrist, quoted in the *Los Angeles Times,* 13 September 1992.
3. General George C. Marshall, quoted in David McCullough, *Truman* (New York: Simon and Schuster).

Chapter 10: "We Like Ike!"—Dwight Eisenhower

1. Merle Miller, *Ike the Soldier,* quoted by Russell F. Weigley, *New York Times Book Review,* 20 December 1987.
2. Charles R. Morris, *A Time of Passion—America 1960–1980* (New York: Harper and Row, 1984).
3. Sherman Adams, quoted in Theodore H. White, *The Making of a President* (New York: Atheneum, 1961).
4. White, *The Making of a President.*
5. Ibid.

6. Harry Truman, quoted in Tip O'Neill with William Novak, *Man of the House* (New York: Random House, 1987).

7. Ibid.

Chapter 11: Camelot—John F. Kennedy

1. Clarence B. Carsen, *The Welfare State 1929–1985* (American Textbook Committee, 1986).

2. Cyrus Sulzberger, quoted in George Brown Tindall, *America, A Narrative History,* vol. 2 (New York: Norton, 1984).

3. Richard Reeves, *President Kennedy: Profile of Power,* quoted in *Time* magazine, 22 November 1993.

4. George Brown Tindall, *America, A Narrative History.*

5. *Time,* 30 May 1994, 26.

6. *USA Today,* 20 May 1994, 2A.

7. *New York Times,* 22 May 1994, 4-E.

8. *Newsweek,* 30 May 1994, 38.

9. *Time,* 30 May 1994, 24.

Chapter 12: "All the Way with LBJ"—Lyndon Johnson

1. Diana Dixon Healy, *America's Vice Presidents* (Baltimore: McClelland and Steward, 1984).

2. Bob Pierpoint, *Parade* magazine, 27 November 1977.

3. Oswald Chambers, *My Utmost for His Highest* (Grand Rapids: Discovery House, reprint 1935, 1963), April 18.

Chapter 13: Knowledge Is Power—Richard Nixon

1. Eli S. Chesen, M.D., *President Nixon's Psychiatric Profile* (New York: Wyden, 1973).

2. Donald Nixon, quoted in Ralph P. Detoledano, *One Man Alone* (New York: Funk and Wagnalls, 1969).

3. *Time,* 4 May 1987.

4. Ibid.

5. Stephen Ambrose, *The Education of a Politician* (New York: Simon and Schuster, 1987).

6. Ibid.

7. Ibid.

8. Richard Nixon, quoted in *Newsweek,* 19 May 1986.

9. Doris Kearns Goodwin, "Ford and Carter," *Ladies Home Journal,* November 1976.

Chapter 14: A Time for War and a Time for Peace—Gerald Ford

1. Doris Kearns Goodwin, "Ford and Carter," *Ladies Home Journal,* November 1976.
2. Ibid.
3. Ibid.
4. Gerald Ford, quoted by Ross Baker, *Los Angeles Times,* 7 May 1983.

Chapter 15: Jimmy Who?—James Earl Carter

1. Goodwin, "Ford and Carter."
2. Ibid.
3. *Newsweek,* 27 September 1982.
4. *Newsweek,* 23 July 1979.
5. "Text of President Carter's Address to the Nation on Energy Problems," 20 July 1979, *Facts on File* (New York: Facts on File, Inc., 1979), 533–34.
6. *Newsweek,* 23 July 1979.
7. Ibid.
8. *Newsweek,* 16 November 1987.
9. *Washington Post,* 19 September 1994.

Chapter 16: The Great Communicator—Ronald Reagan

1. Francis X. Clives, *New York Times,* 20 August 1984.
2. William A. Rusher, *The Rise of the Right* (New York: William Morrow, n.d.).
3. *Newsweek,* 6 February 1984.
4. Lance Morrow, *Time,* 7 July 1986.
5. Ibid.
6. Huge Sidey, *Time,* 24 August 1984.
7. Madhuri Talibuddin, letter to the editor, *Time,* 30 March 1987.
8. *Newsweek,* 27 August 1984.
9. Ibid.
10. Tom Morganthau, *Newsweek,* 27 August 1984.
11. Richard Moose, *New York Times,* 22 August 1984.
12. Sam Donaldson, *Hold On, Mr. President* (New York: Random House, 1987).
13. James Reston, *San Bernardino Sun,* 16 March 1984.
14. Ronald Reagan, quoted in the *New York Times,* 21 August 1987.
15. *Time,* 24 November 1986.
16. *Time,* 30 December 1986.
17. *Time,* 6 April 1987.
18. *Time,* 24 August 1987.
19. *The People, Press and Politics,* a Times-Mirror report, September 1987.

20. *Newsweek,* 8 June 1984.

21. Charles Colson, quoted in *Newsweek,* 19 October 1987.

Chapter 17: The Comical Campaign of 1988

1. *Newsweek,* 31 October 1988.

2. Goodwin, "Ford and Carter," *Ladies Home Journal,* November 1976.

3. *Newsweek,* 4 January 1988.

4. *Time,* 18 May 1987.

5. *New York Times,* 31 August 1987.

6. *Time,* 22 June 1987.

7. *The Honolulu Advertiser,* 22 September 1987.

8. Ibid.

9. *U.S. News and World Report,* 16 November 1987.

10. *Newsweek,* 16 November 1987.

11. *Insight* magazine, 9 May 1988.

12. *U.S. News and World Report,* 18 April 1988.

13. *Dallas Morning News,* 17 July 1988.

14. *USA Weekend,* 15 July 1988.

15. Walter Shapiro, *Time,* 27 April 1987.

16. *Time,* 18 May 1987.

17. Ibid.

18. *Time,* 11 January 1988.

19. Gail Sheehy, *Vanity Fair,* January 1988.

20. Kevin Menida, *Dallas Morning News,* 8 November 1987.

21. Ibid.

Chapter 18: A Kinder and Gentler Nation—George Bush

1. *New York Times,* 30 October 1988.

2. James David Barber, *Presidential Character,* cited in *New Orleans Times-Picayune,* 18 August 1988.

3. *Los Angeles Times,* 22 November 1987.

4. Ibid.

5. Gail Sheehy, quoted in *Los Angeles Times,* 22 November 1987.

6. *Time,* 29 August 1988.

7. *USA Today,* 21 October 1988.

8. George W. Bush, quoted in *Vanity Fair,* February 1987.

9. Nicholas Brady, quoted in *Time,* 21 March 1988.

10. Dan Quayle, quoted in *Time,* 19 August 1988.

11. Tom Kean, quoted in *USA Today,* 17 August 1988.

12. *Wall Street Journal,* 18 October 1988.

Chapter 19: Personalities at Work: The Amazing 1992 Campaign

1. *New York Times Magazine,* 8 March 1992, 63.
2. Ibid.
3. *New Yorker,* 5 April 1993, 46.
4. *Newsweek,* 16 May 1994, 19.
5. James Carville, quoted in *New York Times,* 22 March 1992.
6. Karen Hosler, quoted in the *New Yorker,* 5 April 1993, 43.

Chapter 20: Ross for Boss—Ross Perot

1. *Newsweek,* 27 April 1992, 21.
2. *USA Today,* 15 May 1992.
3. *New Yorker,* 14 May 1992.
4. *Time,* 25 May 1992.
5. *Newsweek,* 15 June 1992.
6. *Time,* 19 June 1992.
7. Eleanor Clift, *Newsweek,* 27 July 1992, 30.
8. *Newsweek,* 9 November 1992.
9. Jonathan Alter, *Newsweek,* 27 July 1992, 35.

Chapter 21: All Things for All People—William Jefferson Clinton

1. Lee Iacocca, quoted in *Fortune,* 30 May 1994, 70.
2. *Newsweek,* 19 September 1994.
3. Ibid.
4. *USA Today,* 10 March 1994.
5. *Time,* 3 January 1994.
6. *Newsweek,* 4 April 1994.
7. *USA Today,* 15 July 1992.
8. *Newsweek,* 27 July 1992, 33.
9. Ibid., 32.
10. Suzanne Garment, *Los Angeles Times,* 23 May 1993.
11. *Time,* 21 June 1993, 78.
12. Barbara Ehrenreich, *Time,* 21 June 1993, 78.
13. Lou Klein, *Newsweek,* 27 July 1992, 34.
14. Lou Klein, *Newsweek,* 4 April 1994.
15. Howard Fineman, *Newsweek,* 7 February 1994, 16.
16. *New York Times,* 25 October 1992, 1.
17. Auckland, New Zealand, *Sunday Star,* 16 January 1994.
18. George Church, *Time,* 30 May 1994, 40.
19. Ibid.
20. Michael Kramer, *Time,* 30 May 1994, 48.

21. Walter Isaacson, *Time,* 16 November 1992, 16.
22. Ibid.
23. Ibid.
24. William Schneider, *Los Angeles Times,* 24 January 1993, M-1.
25. *Newsweek,* 18 July 1994.

Chapter 22: Two for the Price of One—Hillary Rodham Clinton

1. *Newsweek,* 18 September 1994.

Chapter 23: Play Second Fiddle Softly—Albert Gore

1. *Newsweek,* 20 July 1992, 30.
2. *USA Today,* 27 July 1992, 32.
3. *Fortune,* 23 August 1993, 59.
4. *Newsweek,* 13 September 1993, 39.

Chapter 24: Take Your Best Shot at the Brass Ring—Rush Limbaugh

1. Rush Limbaugh, *See, I Told You So* (New York: Pocket Books, 1993), xiv.
2. Steven Roberts, *U.S. News and World Report,* cited in *Dallas Morning News,* 19 December 1993.
3. Mike Ramirez cartoon, *USA Today,* 27 June 1994, 12A.
4. Richard Corliss, *Time,* 26 October 1992.
5. Ibid.
6. Limbaugh, *See, I Told You So,* 12.

Chapter 25: The Political Upset of 1994

1. *USA Today,* 10 November 1994.
2. Ibid.
3. Ibid.
4. *New York Times,* 10 November 1994.